ALESSANDRO FARNESE

PRINCE OF PARMA

GOVERNOR-GENERAL OF THE NETHERLANDS

(1545-1592)

ALESSANDRO FARNESE

Engraving by R. de Hooghe
(Collection of Engravings concerning the Revolution of the Netherlands, located at the Library of the University of Leuven, № B 6544).

ANDRÉ MAREK Y VILLARINO DE BRUGGE

ALESSANDRO FARNESE

PRINCE OF PARMA
GOVERNOR-GENERAL OF THE NETHERLANDS
(1545-1592)

VOLUME IV
THE SIEGE OF ANTWERP
(1584-1585)

MJV ENTERPRISES LTD., INC.
2020

For further information, please address:

MJV Enterprises ltd., Inc.
14011 Clarkdale Avenue #2188
Norwalk, CA 90651

The paper used in this publication meets the minimum standard requirements of American National Standard for Information Sciences — Permanence of Paper for Printed Library Materials, ANSI Z39.48-1984.

Printed in the United States of America by KindleDirect, an http://Amazon.com company.

ISBN: 979-8-4837-7752-6

Bibliographic cataloging information:

Author	Don André Marek y Villarino de Brugge.
Main title	Alessandro Farnese, Prince of Parma, Governor-General of the Netherlands (1545-1592) The Siege of Antwerp...
Published/created	MJV Enterprises ltd., Inc.
Description	5 v. fronts., plates, ports., plans. 29 cm.
Classification	DH194 .E7
Contents	v. 1. 1545-1578.–v. 2. 1578-1582.–v. 3. 1582-1584.–v. 4. 1584-1585.–v. 5. 1585-1592.
Notes	Vol. 1 without series title. Bibliography: v. 1, p. 302-315; v. 2, p. 349-356; v. 3, p. 249-254; v. 4, p. 149-153; v. 5, p. 422-428.
Series	Library of the Sixteenth Century
Subjects	Alessandro Farnese, Duke of Parma, 1545-1592. Netherlands–History–Eighty Years' War, 1568-1648.

«Y este fue el más memorable sitio del mundo, y adonde se mostro de veras la perseverancia, y valor y fortaleça del capitán y de los soldados, especialmente de la naçion española».
("And this was the most memorable place in the world, and where the perseverance and courage and strength of the captain and the soldiers, especially of the Spanish nation, were truly shown.")

ANTONIO CARNERO. *Historia de las guerras civiles que ha havido en los Estados de Flandes*, p. 201 (Brussels 1625).

TABLE OF CONTENTS

CHAPTER III

THE OFFENSIVE BY THE BESIEGED AND GIAMBELLI'S "INFERNAL MACHINES"

CHAPTER IV

THE BATTLE OF KOUWENSTEIN

CHAPTER V

MARNIX ENTERS INTO NEGOTIATIONS

CHAPTER VI

THE ANTWERPIAN NEGOTIATORS IN THE PRINCE OF PARMA'S CAMP

LIST OF ILLUSTRATION PLATES

SKETCHES

TO THE READER

It would appear that if van der Essen had taken Chapter XII from Volume III and made it the first chapter in this Volume, the latter could virtually be a stand-alone book about the siege of Antwerp. Mind you that presenting a comprehensive history of the Spanish Netherlands / Dutch Revolt during the time of Alessandro Farnese's rule is very difficult. As you have already seen, there were lots of events occurring concurrently and many of them affected each other, so writing about any of them as "stand-alone" events is not wholly feasible.

An interesting tidbit to note is that some of the small towns mentioned within the text such as Wilmarsdonk and Oorderen no longer exist due to the Antwerp port expansion of 1965.

So far, this volume had, by far, the most errata. For instance the footnote numbering in the first and second chapters is continuous followed with the numbers resetting for each chapter thereafter. It remains unknown if this was the author's error or the publisher's. I also found numerous typo and punctuation errors in this volume. There may be errata in the context which I questioned on page 146, note 42.

With van der Essen, this volume saw a change in publisher and a change in how the larger illustration plates were presented; they were fold-outs. Herein, due to printing constraints, they are presented as centerfolds.

André Marek y Villarino de Brugge
September 18, 2020

FOREWORD

In this volume, we present the account of the siege of Antwerp, which, in Alessandro Farnese's career, constitutes his culmination and which brilliantly concludes all the military operations and political maneuvers which he had conceived since 1581.

The siege of Antwerp has been described often [1], not only by the military writers of the time, such as Antonio Carnero, Alonzo Vasquez, and César Campana, but also by historians just after the events, such as Strada, who used, as always, the papers of the Farnese family.

Cardinal Bentivoglio, inspired by the memories of his nephew, who took part in this siege, in fact recounts it in his *Guerra di Fiandra* and, on behalf of the States-General, the historians J. F. Le Petit, P. Bor, and E. van Meteren have left us precious information about these events.

Among the modern historians, it is enough to cite especially Motley, Barado, and P. Fea, without mentioning the many articles among which the ones by our colleague Ch. Terlinden are particularly suggestive.

However, the existence of so many accounts has not prevented us from redoing the work of our predecessors. In fact, most of the latter were content to draw on the books of the military historians of the time or, more simply, to subserviently follow Strada, by combining the data from his rendition with the information provided by Bor and van Meteren. There are only three authors, Motley, Fea, and

[1] See the bibliographic list we give at the end of this volume.

Kervyn de Lettenhove, who have drawn from the original sources, including the correspondence of Farnese with Philip II or with his parents.

But they only used a fairly small portion of it and they were not familiar with the assemblage of documentation the likes of which we gathered; many first-rate documents have eluded them. Not only was there now means, but there was still a necessity to resume the study of the siege of Antwerp relying on broader information and by drawing more inspiration, for establishing the facts, from the original documents, emanating from the participants and the direct witnesses of the events. Above all, it was important to make a serious comparison and a preliminary critique of these testimonies.

Without having done so, all the accounts devoted to the siege of Antwerp contain a more or less considerable share of fantasy and imagination, and many inaccuracies. For the most part, that's the biggest fault with Motley [2]. Fea distinguished himself in his care of military descriptions, but, as in all of his works, he did not concern himself much with the political side of the issues or he did not study it in enough depth.

The entire history of the negotiations for the surrender of Antwerp had to be redone. The historians who preceded us, and who devoted their attention thereto, muddled the chronological order of the facts and distorted the real perspective of the events. This was the case with Motley; this was especially the case with Kervyn de Lettenhove, in volume VI of his work *Les Huguenots et les Gueux.* Moreover, in explaining the role of Marnix of Saint-Aldegonde during the capitulation of Antwerp, both authors allowed themselves to be guided by prejudices. Though Motley made a laudable effort to judge with fairness, Kervyn de Lettenhove showed a thoughtlessness and partiality that are unforgivable. By neglecting the scrupulous reconstruction of chronological elements, he has made the history of the capitulation of Antwerp a trial by media, which deprives his work of any empirical value.

Therefore, we devoted ourselves particularly to the study of the political side of the events and if we have exonerated Marnix of Saint-Aldegonde, it is because the careful study of the events, the

---

[2] See for example R. FRUIN, *Motley's geschiedenis der Vereenigde Nederlanden* in *De Tachtigjarige oorlog. Verzamelde opstellen*, v. V, pp. 103-106.

ANTWERP IN THE SIXTEENTH CENTURY
(According to a contemporary German engraving.)

critique of the testimonies — which most of the authors and especially Kervyn de Lettenhove totally neglected — and the psychological analysis of the characters led us to the conviction that this rehabilitation was necessary [3].

Our account of the siege of Antwerp will appear to many as less romantic than those of our predecessors; that is because we mercilessly banished any assertions and any descriptions which were not firmly supported by the original sources which, alone, served as the foundation for our work.

* * *

After the capture of Antwerp, the Prince of Parma had intended to actively push his military operations against the north: if he had, for a moment, allowed himself to imagine that the advantageous conditions accorded to the Antwerpians would facilitate the reconciliation of Holland and Zealand, he was quickly brought back to reality. For Philip II thwarted his designs, first by sending him to succor the Prince-Elector of Cologne in the latter's struggle against the reformers in his electorate; then, by subordinating the campaign against the United Provinces to the needs of his international policy.

The adventure of the *Invincible Armada* was, for Alessandro Farnese, the beginning of his misfortunes. The Spaniards did not forgive him for the failure of that enterprise, to which he had been forced to collaborate, and made him largely responsible for it. On the other hand, by twice sending him to help the League in France, the King forced him to exhaust himself in unprolific combat and to minimize the fight against the rebels of Holland and Zealand, which Farnese regarded as the main goal of the efforts that he still had to try.

After having followed, in the first four volumes of our work, the Prince of Parma's rapid ascent to glory, after having seen him successively overcome all obstacles, in the second part of volume IV, which will conclude our study, we will examine the successive stages of his decline [4], ending with his death in Arras on December 2nd, 1592.

---

[3] It had, moreover, already been successfully tried by M. H. VAN DER LINDEN, in the *Bibliographie nationale*, v. XIII, col. 800-844, although with incomplete documentation, and without taking into account all the elements of the problem.

[4] « Si le prince de Parme après telle victoire [Antwerp] eut pendu son épée au croc et se fust retiré en son pays, il eut avec grande gloire estenduë la carrière de sa vie au dehors des grandes envies et calomnies, dont en fin les services signalez qu'il a faict... ont esté agitez et blasonnez » P. COLINS, *Histoire des choses les plus mémorables...*, p. 635.

* * *

In the preparation of this volume, we used, as with the previous volumes, the invaluable assistance of Mr. J. Cuvelier, Archivist-General of the Kingdom of Belgium, Mr. V. Turner, chief curator of the Royal Library of Belgium, and Professor E. Van Vakeel, librarian of the University of Leuven. We are happy to, here, pay them the tribute of gratitude which is due to them for so many titles.

LÉON VAN DER ESSEN.

Leuven, March 23, 1935.

Acronyms used in the notes:

A. F. N. = Farnesian archives of Naples.
A. F. P. = Farnesian archives of Parma.
A. G. R. = General State Archives in Brussels.
B. N. P. = National Library of Paris.

Liber relationum = *Liber relationum eorum quae gesta fuere in Belgio et alibi per serenissimum D. Ducem. Alexandrum Farnesium* (MS. II, 1155 of the Brussels Royal Library).

Libro de las cosas = *Libro de las cosas que succedieron en Flandes* (National Library of Paris, Spanish MS. № 182).

FIRST CHAPTER

PREPARATIONS FOR THE BLOCKADE OF THE SCHELDT

The preliminary operations of the siege of Antwerp began with an attack on the forts located to the north of the city, on both banks of the Scheldt. By giving the Marquis de Richebourg the order to capture the fort of Liefkenshoek, and by prescribing to Mondragón to make himself master of the one at Lillo, the Prince of Parma had envisioned a specific purpose. The occupation of these two redoubts would have allowed the Spaniards to command the passage of the river to the north of the city and to cannonade the Dutch and Zealand ships which would pass by those locations destined for the besieged place, laden with succor troops, food, and ammunition [1]. It was with that intention that Farnese had brought together, in Kallo, two culverins and six large-caliber cannons, so as to equip the enemy positions as soon as they had fallen into his power [2].

When Mondragón's failure at Lillo made it impossible to carry out the first plan [3], Farnese decided to close the river to the passage

[1] STRADA, *Histoire de la guerre des Païs-Bas*, v. IV, pp. 6 and 15; C. CAMPANA, *Assedio d'Anversa*, p. 17.

[2] *Liber relationum*, f° 148vo.

[3] The only proof we have of this is the following passage from a letter by Farnese, dated Beveren, July 26, 1584: «haviendo sido el intento principal de apoderarse de Liloo el pretender por ese medio y el del fuerte que se ha ganado al oposito [Liefkenshoek] procurar de cerrar la rivera». (B. N. P., Spanish MS. 182, f° 374vo). The *Libro de las cosas*, f°s 263ro-263vo, affirms the same thing: «Y si esto se huviera considerado antes, no se fuera sobre el forte de Lillo, par donde se pensava primera serrar la rivera».

of Dutch and Zealand ships by way of a bridge built from one bank to the other [4].

This was not a new plan. Farnese had already applied this stratagem at the siege of Maastricht, when he had barred the Meuse to the north and the south of the city with the aim of completely isolating the place.

The project to close the Scheldt was met with strong and tenacious opposition from the Council of War. The senior and experienced officers, and especially the Flemish officers, had advised against this attempt because of the river's configuration and the great danger presented by the tides. They had also called the Prince's attention to the enormous costs of transporting the timber necessary for the construction of the bridge and the recruitment of carpenters [*]. Enervated by this opposition, Farnese categorically declared that he was committed to the execution of his project. "People who claim to give advice", he said, "can be divided into three categories. In the first, I rank those who only follow the impulses of their passion. That is why courageous men are only thinking of performing acts of honor and exposing their lives without ulterior motives, whereas those who lack courage never dare to undertake anything important and everything always seems impossible to them. In the second category, I put those who only listen to their own interests and who want to continually impose their own will. The third category includes those who use, in their councils, the light of intelligence and the sum of their knowledge. Those alone give good advice; the others, on the contrary, formulate only false and erroneous opinions."

Speaking in this manner, the Prince of Parma took aim at those of his councilors who did not wish that Antwerp should be conquered by the King's troops and who most of all dreaded to see Farnese covered with the glory of this conquest [5]. To close the mouths of his malicious opponents, the Prince concluded by declaring: "Those who wish me well and who are interested in the service of the King are asked not to speak to me about this matter. May those who really want to help me carry out the orders that will be given to them. If not, let them rest at home all winter long. I will summon them come

---

[4] C. Campana, *Assedio d'Anversa*, p. 20.

[*] Bentivoglio, *The Compleat History...*, p. 219.

[5] Paolo Rinaldi strongly affirmed it in his *Liber relationum*, f° 158. He had attended the Council of War.

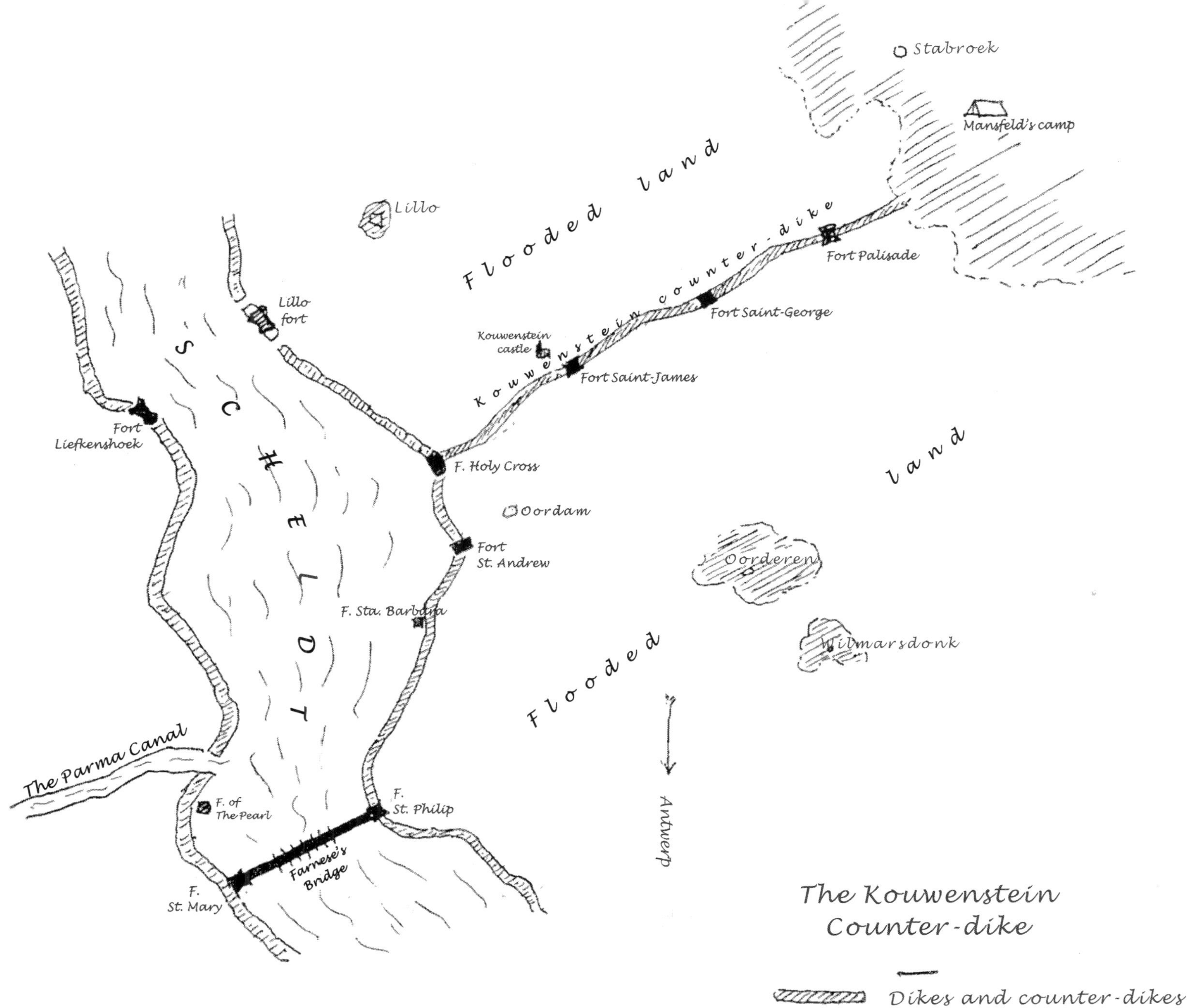
Stabroek
Mansfeld's camp
Flooded land
Lillo
Kouwenstein counter-dike
Fort Palisade
Fort Saint-George
Lillo fort
Kouwenstein castle
Fort Saint-James
Fort Liefkenshoek
S C H E L D T
F. Holy Cross
land
Oordam
Fort St. Andrew
Oorderen
F. Sta. Barbara
Wilmarsdonk
Flooded
The Parma Canal
F. St. Philip
F. of The Pearl
Antwerp
Farnese's Bridge
F. St. Mary
The Kouwenstein Counter-dike
Dikes and counter-dikes

next Spring and, by God! they will always arrive in time to render some further service to the King's cause." [6]

After consulting the engineers Barocci and Piatti as well as the old mariners he had in his army [7], the Prince resolved to have the Scheldt dam built south of Lillo, between Kallo (on the left [Flemish] bank) and Oordam (on the right [Brabantian] bank). In that location, the Scheldt had a narrower width and the depth was not as great as elsewhere, because a sandbank jutted out from the shore of Kallo and advanced towards the middle of the river. It would therefore be easier to drive piles therein upon which the bridge should be constructed. In addition, it had been observed that with the Scheldt bending to the north of that location, the enemy vessels needed to change direction for the wind and they could not pass straight through, nor in a single effort [8]. Farnese instructed the Marquis de Richebourg to build a new fort, which would be called Saint-Mary on the left bank, and ordered Mondragón to erect another on the right bank, which would receive the name Saint-Philip [9]. It was between these two redoubts that the military engineers had to start construction of the *estacade*. At the same time, the fort of Lillo located to the north of this barrier, on the master-dike of the Scheldt, and surrounded, on the land side, by the flood caused by its defenders at the time of the assault of Mondragón's soldiers, was cut off from Antwerp and completely isolated [10]. But, given the strong garrison that occupied it, it seemed necessary to reinforce the Liefkenshoek redoubt, however, and protect it from being flanked so as to guarantee it against any surprise. It was the Marquis de Richebourg who was in charge of that work; Farnese had raised a contribution of 50,000 florins in the bailiwick of Waas for the execution thereof.

* * *

---

[6] These words were noted by Rinaldi during the Council of War (*Liber relationum*, f°s 158ro-158vo).

[7] Farnese to his parents, Beveren, July 26, 1584, in A. F. N., *Carte farnesiane, Fiandra*, fasc. 1707.

[8] Farnese to the King, Beveren, July 26, 1584 (B. N. P., Spanish MS. 182, f° 374vo); *Libro de las cosas*, f°s 263ro-263vo; Strada, *o. c.*, v. IV, pp. 15-16; *Liber relationum*; f° 150; C. Campana, *Assedio d'Anversa*, p. 24 «Ma perche le navi nemiche al tempo della marea, andando a piene vele si giudicavano di eccessiva forza e atte a far gran rottura, fu il detto ponte fermato in una certa piegatura del fiume, ad effetto ch'essendo quivi le navi costrette di voltar vela rimettessero molto dell' impeto loro». Cf. Bentivoglio, *o. c.*, pp. 218 & 220; Moir, *The Siege of Antwerp*, p. 309.

[9] Farnese to the King, Beveren, July 26, 1584 (Loc. cit.); *Libro de las cosas*, f°s 263-264; *Liber relationum*, f° 150; Strada, *o. c.*, v. IV, p. 16; Motley, *History of the United Netherlands*, v. I, p. 164.

[10] *Liber relationum*, f° 150.

The discussion and execution of all these measures had taken place in the last half of the month of July, 1584. The construction of the new forts of Saint-Mary and Saint-Philip required a considerable amount of time, before the end of which one could not think of establishing the bridge to link them.

Meanwhile, Farnese conceived the project of going to besiege Dendermonde. The capture of that city was of considerable importance. As long as it was not in the power of the Spaniards, its garrison could harass the troops besieging Antwerp. Furthermore, as the Ghentians obstinately continued to resist and had no intention of resuming the interrupted negotiations with the Prince of Parma, the fall of Dendermonde, from which they were still trying to resupply themselves, could make their situation more critical than it already was, and bring them to capitulate more quickly. Once again, an opposition had manifested itself at the Council of War. Some members of the latter proposed to more actively push the blockade of Ghent; others claimed that all attention should be focused on the construction of the Scheldt dam; finally, others were frightened at the thought that Farnese would be absent from the camp before Antwerp and feared that, during his absence, there would be some dangerous loosening of order. It was especially Mondragón who, knowing the strength of the city of Antwerp, made these objections. But the Prince of Parma showed himself unshakable [(11)].

He had already ordered the available artillery as well as the necessary ammunition be brought from Oudenaarde, by way of the Scheldt, so as not to lose his positions before Antwerp [(12)]. On August 4th, he left with a detachment of his troops in the direction of Dendermonde: the bulk of the forces consisted of the Spaniards from the *tercio* of Pedro de Paz and Italian ensigns. The place was so rapidly surrounded that the inhabitants, who believed the Prince of Parma was completely absorbed with the siege of Antwerp, were unaware of the danger which threatened them. The Spanish Captain Juan de Gamboa was sent ahead with a considerable troop to capture the Dendre sluice gate, by which the enemy could have flooded the countryside around the city. The guard of the sluice gate was quickly put to flight. At the same time, Karl von Mansfeld appeared, coming

---

[11] *Liber relationum*, f°s 149ro-149vo.

[12] *Ibid.*; *Libro de las cosas*, f° 264ro.

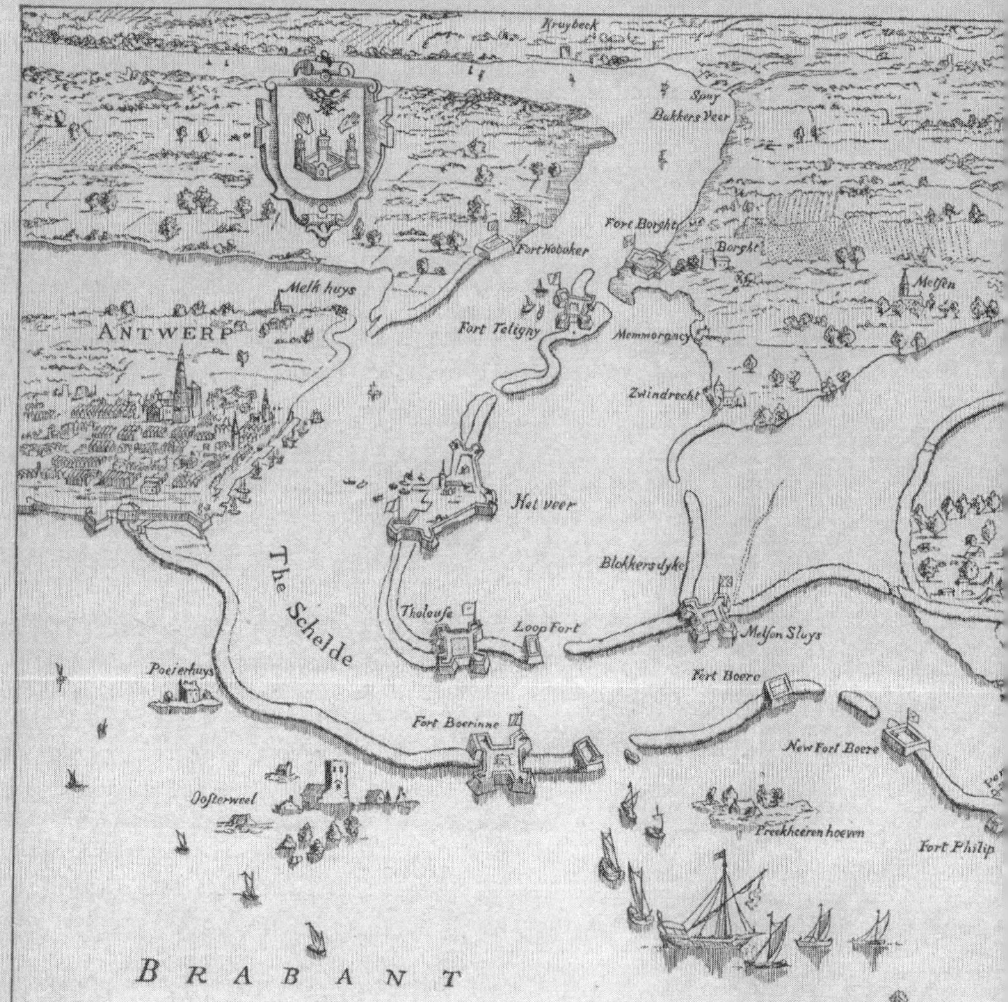

BIRD'S-EYE VIEW OF THE S

ANTWERP.—(*From an old Print.*)

BIRD'S-EYE VIEW OF THE SIEGE OF ANTWERP

Engraving by Jan Luyken

(We see the attack on the Kouwenstein dike.)

from the Brussels side, with five cornets of cavalry and some Walloon companies. At last Farnese himself advanced via Waasmunster with the Spanish troops [13]. As a precautionary measure, the fort and the bridge of Wetteren had been given an additional garrison, to prevent any possible attempt by the Ghentians to send succors.

Dendermonde was well fortified and surrounded by deep fosses filled with water: a strong redoubt protected the Brussels gate and forbade access to it. Ryhove, who had been Governor of the city since fleeing from Ghent, was not there. He had in his place Philippe vander Gracht, Seigneur de Mortagne [14], who had with him a garrison of 800 soldiers, not to mention the burgher militia companies. Without waiting long, the Prince of Parma put his cannons in battery on both sides of the ravelin of the Brussels gate and opened fire. The enemy replied with ardor: Mortagne had positioned his best marksmen in the ravelin and the latter inflicted cruel losses on the assailants. The *Maestre de campo* Pedro de Paz and the *proveedor* General Don Pedro de Tassis were killed. The death of their leader irritated the Spanish soldiers, who would have liked to launch an assault, but the breaches made by the besieging artillery were not wide enough yet to risk it. The high number of dead and wounded, whose bodies littered the paths from the besiegers' camp to the location of their artillery, gave evidence to the excellence of the defenders' fire. But soon an incident came to bring the wrath of the Spanish and Italian soldiers to a paroxysm. The besieged, having removed from one of the churches of the city a statue of a saint, mounted it on the rampart of the ravelin and there, before the eyes of Farnese's soldiers, slashed it with knife cuts. They eventually raised it on pikes and, amid mockery and sacrilegious blasphemy, hurled it into the fosse. The Spanish officers were struggling to restrain their soldiers, who immediately wanted to rush forward to punish the heretics. But the Prince of Parma postponed the assault until the next day, the eve of the Assumption of the Virgin Mary (August 15th) and the day in which he hoped — as he said to the captains — "that the Queen of Heaven would avenge the insult made to the Saints."

---

[13] *Libro de las cosas*, f° 264ro; STRADA, *o. c.*, v. IV, pp. 16-17.

[14] Arriving before Dendermonde, Farnese sent a letter to the Governor of the city urging him to surrender and return to his duty. (*Correspondance de Granvelle*, v. XI, pp. 662 & 668 note 2).

On August 14th, at five o'clock in the afternoon, the attack on the ravelin of the Brussels gate was unleashed. The Spaniards, who were joined by a number of Italian "adventurers" or volunteers, as well as the Walloons, began to attack the bulwark and made themselves masters of it. Quickly, fascine retrenchments were established along the walls of Dendermonde, so as to guard against a sortie by the defenders. The latter immediately opposed another retrenchment. Furthermore, in the case where the ramparts of the city would be taken, they had built, inside, a second line of defense, consisting of a demilune with a fosse and wooden bastions.

However, Farnese had sent pioneers to dig a flow channel, intended to cause the fosses of Dendermonde to be drained, and advanced his artillery to directly bombard the ramparts. At the sight of these preparations, the besieged, who had vainly awaited for succors from the Ghentians, felt their courage faltering. They sent a parliamentarian to Karl von Mansfeld, who commanded the besieging artillery, to beg him to intervene in their favor with Alessandro Farnese. The latter consented to enter into negotiations: on August 17th, the capitulation of Dendermonde was a fait accompli. The Prince of Parma, despite the losses which his troops had suffered and the provocative attitude of the heretics of the city, showed himself merciful. The Governor of the place, as well as his soldiers were at liberty to depart, with sword and dagger, but without baggage. The burghers received their pardon: on the condition that they accepted within their walls the presence of a garrison, which they would be obliged to maintain and pay. To redeem themselves from the sack, they had to pay 60,000 florins, a relatively small sum, the amount of which the Prince of Parma had not wanted to increase because of the poverty of the town, which had been pillaged by the French soldiers of the Duke of Anjou (15).

Coming out of the place, the garrison noticed, not without astonishment, the presence of a bridge of boats, furnished with artillery, which had been quickly built to stop any succors from Ghent, and

---

15 Farnese to his parents, Dendermonde, August 11, 16, and 17, 1584, in A. F. N., *Carte farnesiane, Fiandra*, fasc. 1707; Farnese to the King, camp before Dendermonde, August 13, 16, and 17, 1584 (B. N. P., Spanish MS. 182, fos 384 and 386); Letter by the same, in French, of August 18 (*Bulletin de la Commission royale d'histoire*, 3rd series, v. XIII, p. 100); C. CAMPANA, *Assedio d'Anversa*, pp. 20-23; *Liber relationum*, fos 150-152vo; *Libro de las cosas*, fos, 264-266; STRADA, *o. c.*, v. IV, pp. 16-20; Text of the capitulation of Dendermonde is in the *Bulletins de la Commission royale d'histoire*, 3rd series, v. XIII, pp. 99-100.

small forts erected on both banks of the Scheldt in the Direction of Antwerp, to render the arrival of troops advancing from that side impossible. On the Dendre, another bridge had allowed the Spanish artillery and cavalry to be brought unencumbered. The enterprise of Dendermonde had been conducted with consummate art and with astonishing rapidity, which struck the experienced warrior who was Colonel de Mondragón with surprise (16).

After replacing the magistrate and reestablishing order in the city, Farnese lodged therein three Spanish companies from the *tercio* of the late Pedro de Paz and two Italian companies, and entrusted the position of Governor to Juan de Rivas, a very courageous old captain, who had distinguished himself during the siege through conspicuous gallantry (17).

The capture of Dendermonde was to bring about the surrender of Ghent: the occupation of that place had removed any subsequent possibility of resupply and succor from the Ghentians (18).

* * *

After the capitulation of Dendermonde, the Prince of Parma returned to Beveren to actively push for the completion of the forts of Saint-Mary and Saint-Philip. He found that during his absence, the work had not been carried out with all necessary vigor. On the right bank of the river, where Mondragón was to take charge of the construction of fort Saint-Philip, the operations were delayed by an attack from the Antwerpians which had occurred on August 10th. Four hundred men had landed by surprise on the master-dike of the Scheldt, not far from Oorderen, had pierced that dike, and into the land thus flooded had launched a few galliots, which cannonaded Mondragón's workers. The latter, however, had managed to put the adversary on the run: it was not long before Téligny, who had commanded that expedition, was captured (19).

While Farnese himself had taken the lead and was trying to

---

16 *Liber relationum*, f° 152vo.

17 STRADA, *o. c.*, v. IV, p. 20.

18 « Le prince... se résoult de forcer premièrement ceux de Terremonde, jugeant que ceste ville réduicte en l'obéissance du roy, il serait plus aisé de venir à bout de ceux de Gand, qui, par ce moyen, demeureroient forclos de pouvoir espérer commerce ou secours de vivres d'Anvers, par la rivière de l'Escaut... » *Mémoires du marquis de Varembon*, p. 55.

19 *Libre de las cosas*, f° 264vo.

quickly put the two new forts into a state of defense, he had sent Karl von Mansfeld in the direction of Ostend. The inhabitants of Bruges had not ceased harassing the Prince, supplicating him to deliver them, without delay, from being pillaged by the garrison of Ostend [(20)]. Mansfeld went to Kortrijk with La Motte and with Don Juan del Águila, Governor of Nieuwpoort, to agree on the preparations to be made. But with the secret having been leaked, the people of Ostend fortified themselves in such manner, and accumulated so many defenses, that it seemed wise to postpone the attempt to make themselves master of that town [(21)]. Mansfeld was then sent to Vilvoorde, which the Prince of Parma wanted to capture as soon as possible in order to threaten both Mechelen and Brussels, and prevent the resupply of the latter city. While concentrating his attention mainly on Antwerp, he did not forget to make the defense of the few strongholds which had hitherto remained beyond his reach more aleatory and whose downfall could facilitate or hasten the definitive operations against the commercial metropolis. After having used canon fire to capture some castles situated along the Rupel, Mansfeld had sent forth the infantry and cavalry to take control of the canal sluice gates. Soon the artillery was in position before Vilvoorde. It took no more than two days of siege preparations to bring about the capitulation of the garrison without firing a single shot. On September 16th, the 500 defenders of the place departed with arms and baggage, and the burghers surrendered to the mercy of the victor. Mansfeld established in this location, so important from a strategic point of view, a Spanish garrison, whose mission would consist of disrupting communications, regularly ongoing until then, between Brussels and Mechelen [(22)].

* * *

The taking of Dendermonde had been a decisive blow for the Ghentian rebels. Since the day where they had broken off the negoti-

---

[20] These pillaging expedtions extended to Ypres and Saint-Omer: «Los de Ostende hazen gran daño par todo esso de Ypre y Santome que no dexan pasar hombre seguro», *Don Juan de Aguila, gouverneur de Nieuport, à Farnèse*, April 14, 1584 (A. F. N., *Carte farnesiane, Fiandra*, fasc. 1665).

[21] Farnese to the King, Beveren camp, September 14, 1584 (B. N. P., Spanish MS. 182, f° 378); *Libro de las casas*, f° 266vo.

[22] Farnese to the King, Beveren camp, September 14, 1584 (Loc. cit.); *Liber relationum*, f° 154; *Libro de las casas*, f°s 266ro-266vo.

ations begun with Farnese, they had been tightly blockaded by the Spaniards. The latter had systematically destroyed the crops around the city and had immediately assailed every convoy of food that tried to reach the great Flemish city [23]. All the rivers which led to Ghent had been severed by the establishment of bridges, guarded by soldiers and equipped with artillery, the main roads had been furrowed, and a very tight string of troops were strictly controlling all the entrances and exits [24]. Before long, famine was making its appearance.

On the other hand, the political situation was fraught with confusion. The trial of Jan van Hembyze had been heard. He was accused of treason because he had treated with the Prince of Parma; of murder, because he had engaged one of his followers to kill the bailiff of Axel; of theft, because he had sold offices; and of violence, because he had surrounded himself with bodyguards. The former dictator of Ghent defended himself not without dignity. He might have escaped his torment, because of the memories of his past popularity, but when the town learned of the assassination of William the Silent, his doom was decided. He was sentenced to death and executed. On August 4th, 1584, he ascended the scaffold, erected opposite the Castle of the Counts. Before he died, he protested the love he had always shown to his country: his bloody head, planted atop an iron stake, was paraded amidst the crowd who had gathered together to witness his execution.

The fury of the partisans of William the Silent did not stop there: magistrates were deposed and thrown in prison, wealthy burghers were subjected to torture, and priests and clerics were expelled [25].

However, on August 10th, three Calvinist pastors from Ghent sent a letter to the Calvinist church in Antwerp, which was nothing more than a long distress call. Having noted the lamentable situation to which the city had been reduced by a blockade of more than seven months, the complete absence of trade and traffic that plunged a large working-class population into dire poverty, the danger of contagious diseases which became more and more threatening, and the extraordinary contributions required by the presence of the garrison, they supplicated the Church of Antwerp to organize a collection in favor of those of Ghent, especially to support, in their deprivation, the old dig-

---

23 *Liber relationum*, f° 153vo.

24 *Ibid.*

25 KERVYN DE LETTENHOVE, *Les Huguenots et les Gueux*, v. VI, pp. 570-572; V. FRIS, *Histoire de Gand*, p. 236.

nitaries of this church. The letter ended with the solemn warning: "If succors do not come within a few weeks, the atrocious misery will lead us to commit acts that will not be profitable to us, to you, or to our neighbors. Take this advice to heart, while there is still time." [26]

It was at this moment that the town of Dendermonde was captured by Farnese. Terror seized the magistrate of Ghent. He wrote a letter to the Governor of Lécluse to lament about this misfortune and to point out that the surrender of Dendermonde removed the last means of being succored from Brabant and Antwerp. He supplicated the Governor not to neglect anything in order to provoke a succor expedition on behalf of the States-General. Why not abandon the siege of Zutphen, which they had undertaken, in order to devote themselves to the defense of the last cities of Flanders and Brabant which still resisted the Spanish? That letter also ended with a disguised threat: that they should not be paid any more false promises, for they will be settled according to the well understood interest of the city and commune of Ghent [27].

Since the hope for succor was not realized and the situation in the city became more and more intolerable, the people took up arms and threatened the leaders, in case they refused to re-open negotiations with Alessandro Farnese [28]. On September 1st, the magistrate took a decisive step: he sent to the camp of Beveren a trumpet from the city, as a parliamentarian [29], with a letter of which the content undoubtedly brought a smile to the lips of the Prince of Parma. In the name of the aldermen, elders, and deans of the city of Ghent, Roland de Hembyze, first secretary of the magistrate, began by recalling the "accident" which, on May 15th, had interrupted the negotiations with Farnese. He explained that, since that time, the task of the magistrate had consisted mainly of "gradually restoring the altered hearts and dissenting minds to good union and harmony", but that he had always remained desirous of resuming negotiations, at the first favorable opportunity. The letter also affirmed that the magistrate had realized that this internal war would only result in the

---

26 *Correspondance de Granvelle*, v. XI, pp. 666-668.

27 Roland de Hembyze to Seigneur de Groenvelt, Governor of Lécluse, Ghent, August 20, 1584 (*Correspondance de Granvelle*, v. XI, pp. 668-670).

28 *Liber relationum*, f° 154vo; *Libro de las cosas*, f° 267vo.

29 On the resumption of negotiations, we are informed by the letter from Farnese to the King, September 14, 1584, published in the *Bulletins de la Commission royale d'histoire*, 3rd series, v. XIII, p. 102.

great damage of His Majesty and a calamitous and deplorable devastation of the country. The example of tranquility and good treatment enjoyed by the people of Bruges since their reconciliation was also likely to engage the Ghentians in imitating them. After discussions with their fellow citizens, the members of the magistrate had found the latter quite inclined to reconciliation, as long as they could obtain reasonable conditions. Could His Highness send safe-conduct for the delegates which were ready to be sent him? [(30)]

What is interesting to note is that the Ghentians had already been in contact with the magistrate of Bruges and that, citing the solidarity which had united them in the first negotiations with Farnese, they had asked him to intercede with the Governor-General so that the latter would consent to receive their parliamentarians and grant favorable conditions of surrender.

The inhabitants of Bruges had acceded to this desire [(31)] "for the sake of our love for each other as members of one body and one province."

The Prince of Parma, deep down in his heart, must have exulted with jubilation at the thought that the great Flemish city would soon be in his hands and that he might find there the necessary aid to carry out his plans against Antwerp, but he did not show it. He granted the desired safe-conduct and sent the Ghentian parliamentarian back accompanied by a Spanish trumpet. Three days later, three aldermen and a Pensionary of the city of Ghent made their way to the camp of Beveren. Farnese postponed the hearing they sought to the next day, but in the meantime he managed to learn of the proposals they were to make to him: they offered to reconcile themselves under the same conditions as those which the city of Bruges had obtained.

The next day, the Prince of Parma pretended to be indignant and very disgusted: he reproached the Ghentians for the shameful conduct which they had adopted at the time of the dissolution of the previous negotiations. What could the delegates say, if not to blame it on "some malicious men?" [(32)] Meanwhile, Farnese had to deploy all his energy and implement all his finesse to stand up to the demands from the members of his Council of State and Council of War.

---

[30] *Correspondance de Granvelle*, v. XI, pp. 671-672.
[31] *Correspondance de Granvelle*, v. XI, pp. 673-675.
[32] *Libro de las cosas*, f° 267vo.

Most of these advisors were asking for exemplary punishments. Several went so far as to demand that they remit into their hands twelve Ghentians, chosen by lot, who would be crucified, or hanged, or even tied up in sacks to drown them in the Scheldt [33]. Farnese contented himself with rejecting the proposals of the Parliamentarians: he felt that, since the surrender of Bruges, the circumstances had changed. One can imagine the anguish of the Ghentian delegates who, on leaving for Beveren, had promised their people not to return without a good peace [34]. Farnese sent them back to Ghent without making his final intentions known, believing that they deserved a lesson. Concurrently, he sent with them, without their knowledge, the *audiencier* Louis Verreycken, who was instructed to notify the magistrate of the Prince of Parma's indignation and to make him understand that they would proceed against Ghent with much greater rigor than was the case with other cities that had reconciled [35]. The Ghentian delegates, during their stay in Beveren, had furthermore learned of these intentions straight from Richardot's own mouth, and the latter had confided in them that he had seen with his eyes a secret letter from Philip II to the Prince of Parma, prescribing that the latter not impose on the Ghentians more favorable conditions than those which the Emperor Charles V once granted to that rebellious city [36].

On hearing this ominous news, the magistrate of Ghent hastened to send to Farnese two gentlemen, Pierre de Vos and Pierre Corvilain, and three captains from the garrison with their councilor Stuperaert, who, all together would present to the Governor-General a project for reconciliation, dated September 9th [37]. What's more, Champagney accompanied them; his presence was obviously intended to help calm the wrath of the Prince of Parma [38].

Farnese first received Champagney alone. Then, it was the other delegate's turn. Admitted to the presence of the Prince on September 17th, they demanded a treaty similar to that of Bruges, but added some points concerning the exercise of the reformed religion. They wanted to obtain authorization to exercise it if not in a church, at

---

33 These details are provided by Paolo Rinaldi in his *Liber relationum*, fº 155.
34 *Liber relationum*, fº 155.
35 *Libro de las cosas*, fº 266vº; *Correspondance de Granvelle*, v. XI, p. 678.
36 STRADA, *o. c.*, v. IV, p. 27.
37 *Correspondance de Granvelle*, v. XI, p. XXXIV.
38 *Libro de las cosas*, fº 267rº.

least in a private house, either in the city or in the countryside, wherever the Prince would find it suitable. To this, for him, unacceptable pretense, Farnese replied curtly that they were very audacious in making similar proposals to him: they must have known that he was formally opposed to it, knowing the King's "holy inclination" on this point [(39)]. How, on the other hand, could they expect the same condition as Bruges, which had spontaneously reconciled with Philip II? Should he remind them of the stern letter he had sent them at the time when the negotiations broke down?

After much discussion [(40)], the articles of capitulation were definitively agreed upon at the camp of Beveren on September 17th, 1584. Alessandro Farnese granted the Ghentians, in the name of the King, a pardon for past offenses and restored to them their former privileges. He demanded that only six inhabitants be handed over to him, so that they would suffer the kind of punishment he would like to inflict, except capital punishment. The city was obliged to pay 200,000 florins. The citadel and the destroyed churches would be restored. The clergy would have restored to them the property they had possessed and of which they had been stripped during the last disturbances. Catholic worship would be fully restored and the heretics would have two years of time to put their affairs in order and, afterwards, would withdraw freely to a place of their choice. The soldiers of the garrison would depart with their weapons. The Prince could establish in Ghent a new garrison, composed of soldiers of such nations as he would like [(41)].

Such was the end of that famous Calvinist Republic of Ghent, whose leaders had committed abominable crimes, where much blood had been shed, who had mocked the States-General and had thwarted the policy of William the Silent, and who bore the primary responsibility for the separation of the Walloon provinces. For years, Catholics had been oppressed by a minority of rabid sectarians, and priests and clerics had been the principal victims of these demented individuals.

---

[39] Farnese to the King, letter published in the *Bulletins de la Commission royale d'histoire*, 3rd series, v. XIII, p. 102.

[40] See the documents in the *Bulletins de la Commission royale d'histoire*, 3rd series, v. XIII, pp. 102 sqq.

[41] Text of the capitulation in the *Bulletins de la Commission royale d'histoire*, 3rd series, v. XIII, pp. 104-109. Cf. GRIMESTON, *A Generall Historie of the Netherlands*, o. c., p. 862A.

In these circumstances, the Prince of Parma showed an astonishing clemency, which he incidentally believed it necessary in order to justify himself to the King, saying that he had been so magnanimous towards these heretics because the example of Bruges had shown him that in treating them thusly, many were coming back from their errors and were returning to the sincere exercise of the Catholic religion [(42)].

On September 19th, President Richardot, *audiencier* Verreycken, and Secretary Le Vasseur arrived in Ghent and were received there with signs of the most complete submission. Brought to the City Hall, they published the Treaty of Reconciliation, in the midst of a great contest of people, without any incident taking place [(43)]. On September 24th, the garrison, still counting 760 soldiers, departed, one portion heading towards Brussels, the other towards Lécluse. Immediately thereafter; the royal troops made their entrance, under the command of the Castellan Olivera, and Champagney took over the government of the city. The Archbishop of Mechelen, Joannes Hauchin, came to reorganize worship, reinstall the priests and the clerics, and reconcile with the church those who wanted to abandon Calvinism [(44)]. On November 15th, the magistrate was changed and only fervent Catholics were admitted thereto. All Calvinists were dismissed from their offices and jobs. Eventually, in March 1585, the Council of Flanders came back from Douai and resumed its meetings at the Castle of the Counts [(45)].

* * *

The capture of Ghent was very important for facilitating the construction of the bridge over the Scheldt at Antwerp [(46)]. In the great Flemish city, the Prince of Parma was able to procure boats, artillery, carpenters, sailors, wood, rope, and all sorts of instruments necessary

---

[42] Farnese to the King, Beveren camp, September 17, 1584 (B. N. P., Spanish MS. 182, f° 380ro); Farnese to his parents, Beveren, September 18, 1584, in A. F. N., *Carte farnesiane, Fiandra*, fasc. 1661.

[43] *Correspondance de Granvelle*, v. XI, pp. 681-682; STRADA, *o. c.*, v. IV, pp. 28-29.

[44] V. FRIS, *Histoire de Gand*, p. 237.

[45] Philip II particularly thanked Farnese « des peines, ennuys et incommeditez qu'avez eu avant conduire à si bonne fin le chief-d'œuvre de réconciliation d'une ville tant principalle et importante » (*Bulletins de la Commission royale d'histoire*, 3rd series, v. XIII, pp. 112-113).

[46] "The enemy, besides money, has found there [at Ghent] great store of artillery, munition and ships." Bizarri to Walsingham, Antwerp, October 16, 1584 (*Foreign Calendar, Elizabeth, August 1584-August 1585*, p. 92).

for the work of the estacade [47].Farnese also, in making the news of the capture of Ghent known in Spain, wrote to the King that "among the good successes he had won in the Netherlands, I had never experienced the goodness of God on a more favorable occasion than in the taking of Ghent, which is, of course, important in itself, but which is yet to be the cause of a much greater success." [48]

The Prince of Parma, from that moment on, personally directed the preparations for the construction of the bridge over the Scheldt, as well as supervising the bulwarks on both the Brabantian bank and on the Flemish bank, and continuously traveled from one place to the other [49]. He began by gathering a considerable supply of planks and fascines in the Waasland: more than 10,000 trees had been used for this purpose. He had also brought in from Denmark and other northern countries 1,500 ship masts, which he was going to use to drive, into the riverbed, the pilings needed for the construction of the bridge, and a large quantity of bituminized piles, as well as chains and anchors.

For that purpose he had secretly entered into a contract with a French merchant in whom he could trust. The latter had carried all this material up into the ports of Holland and Zealand, without anyone suspecting its destination. The vessels had even been detained at the port of Flushing for more than a month, as a result of headwinds, but given the nationality of the master of the flotilla, they had not been the subject of any visits or any harassments. Eventually, all the cargo had been unloaded at Dunkirk, from where it was conducted to the building sites at Kallo and Beveren. The Prince of Parma had strictly fulfilled the terms of the contract concluded with the Frenchman, and had presented him with a gold necklace valued at 500 ECU [50].

Meanwhile, craftsmen in Ghent and in the communities of the region had manufactured more than 200,000 nails, destined for the work of the bridge. The Prince then strengthened and raised the

---

47 Farnese to the King, Beveren camp, September 17, 1584: «para faciliar la maquina que se trae entre manos por las grandes comodidades que podemos tener de baxeles, artilleria, maderame, carpenteros, marineros, xarçias y otras cosas de que padesciamos extrema necessidad» (B. N. P., Spanish MS. 182, f° 380ro); *Libro de las cosas*, f° 267vo; STRADA, *o. c.*, v. IV, pp. 29-30; MOIR, *o. c.*, p. 313.

48 STRADA, *o. c.*, v. IV, p. 30.

49 Farnese to the King, Beveren camp, September 14, 1584 (B. N. P., Spanish MS. 182, f° 378).

50 *Liber relationum*, f° 158vo.

dikes and counter-dikes on both the Flemish and the Brabantian banks by means of fascines and planks, so that they could easily get around on them by foot, horseback, or with wagons and artillery.

In suitable locations, he built redoubts to control the dikes and waterways through which, across the flooded countryside, the enemy ships, which were resupplying Antwerp and returning to Holland, could slip through without much damage. Undoubtedly, the forts of Saint-Mary and Saint-Philip, by now completed, were guarding the Scheldt with their cannons pointed towards the river, but the distance separating them from one bank to the other was too great for their fire to gravely reach and sink the supply vessels.

The latter usually approached the fort of Lillo and anchored there while waiting for the high tide; then, thanks to the latter, passed easily in the direction of Antwerp. There they waited for the tide to ebb and went down the river to return as they had come [51].

The construction of the bridge on the Flemish side of the riverbank had already begun: about one hundred tree trunks, 30 to 70 feet long, and tapered on one of the ends, had been driven down into the river bed in rows of three. To prevent the Antwerpians from disrupting this work and to closely watch over the Scheldt, the Prince of Parma had hired a considerable number of sailors from everywhere: three hundred, in particular, had come from Genoa. He had armed some barks and, having loaded them with soldiers, had sent them onto the river, hunting enemy ships, especially during the night. These vedettes also scoured the flooded countryside north of Antwerp and captured several barks, loaded with victuals, which were trying to reach the city [52].

---

[51] *Liber relationum*, f° 259; J. F. Le Petit (*La grande chronique ancienne et moderne de Hollande...*, v. II, p. 500), claims that they occasionally had from 100 to 120 vessels at one time, but he adds, translated by Grimeston, *o. c.*, p. 863C: "True it is, that there arrived some daily, carrying men and women, where of some were slain, and others without arms and legs, but all this did not stop the passage."

[52] *Liber relationum*, loc. cit. — « Trois iours passez sont entrez icy environ 140 navires, chargées de diverses choses, le plus de vivres, lesquelles ont esté plus de vingt iours embas de Lilloo attendants le vent propice. Lesquelles, avecq demy vent et une nuict obscure se sont aventurées de passer pardessous le canon, duquel ont esté bien endommagées ». *Avvisi* from Antwerp, sent via Cologne, October 17, 1584 (A. F. N., *Carte farnesiane, Fiandra*, fasc. 1665). — « Icy arrivent iournellement navires chargées de vivres, desquels pour le présent avons en abondance, sy le proffict et gaignaige fuisse pour gaigner argent pour les pouvoir achepter. Lesdites navires viennent aulcunes fois bien mal tractées, des quelles vont aulcunes au fond comme ceste semaine at esté une... » *Avvisi* from Antwerp, November 10, 1584 (A. F. N., *Carte farnesiane, Fiandra*, fasc. 1670).

In this region north of the besieged place, the country offered a strange and desolate appearance. The sluice gates had been opened in the vicinity of Saftingen, on the Flemish side, so that, from Hulst, the waters from the Scheldt had spilled over the dikes and almost touched the *Tête de Flandres*, opposite of Antwerp. A very wide, albeit shallow, blanket of water covered the fertile plains, while the tops of lofty trees, and, here and there, church steeples and the turrets of a castle scarcely lifted themselves above the inky waters. Only the high grounds of Doel, Kallo, as well as Beveren, where the Spanish headquarters was located, remained above the reach of the waters. On the Brabantian bank, but further down, other sluice gates had been opened and given passage to the waters, which had rapidly inundated the plains, orchards, meadows, and villages. Wilmarsdonk, Oorderen, and Ekeren had become like islands in the middle of the ocean, while many hamlets were completely submerged [53]. Thus, the entire region north of Antwerp had the appearance of an immense lake or almost that of a sea, from which emerged the master-dikes of the Scheldt. In the midst of these desolate solitudes, the latter defined the course of the river, and on them stood, facing each other, the redoubts of the Spaniards, bearing the flag of the Cross of St. Andrew (the Cross of Burgundy), and the redoubts of the Antwerpians, whereon flew the orange, white, and blue banners of the supporters of William the Silent.

Extending perpendicular from the master-dike of the Scheldt, on the Brabantian side, up to the village of Stabroek, where Mondragón was quartered with his troops, was the Kouwenstein counter-dike, which exceeded the water level considerably. It constituted, on that side, a serious obstacle to the communications of Holland and Zealand, with the Antwerpians; a more fatal obstacle, perhaps, than could be offered by the bridge which Farnese was busy building. Understanding the importance of Kouwenstein, Farnese had the height of the dike raised and three forts built to defend its approaches [54]. On the master-dike of the Scheldt, a little north of the fort of Saint-

[53] MOTLEY, *o. c.*, v. I, p. 160.

[54] Farnese to the King, Beveren camp, September 14, 1584 (B. N. P., Spanish MS. 182, f° 378): «los reveldes que tenian intento, segun lo que se entendia por diferentes vías de ellos, que aeste effecto y con fin de navigar por alli maquinan que fuera y sara imposible una vez salido con ello, ora con tempestad, ora por fuerça estorbarselo ni remediarlo, le he commençado a poner tal qual conviene para que no nos puedan por alli impedir ni desturbar nuestro desiño ni salir elles con el suyo».

Philip, and, so to speak, on the river itself, he erected the fort of Saint-Barbara or Oordam, named after the village which, below the dike, was almost entirely covered by the waters. A second fort was built to complete the protective system, at the very head of the Kouwenstein counter-dike, where the latter joined the main-dike of the river: this redoubt was thus a sort of outpost facing toward the fort of Lillo, which was still occupied, further north, by a garrison of Antwerpians. It received the name of Fort Holy Cross (Saint-Croix). South of the latter, near the counter-dike and in the direction of the flooded countryside, the fort of Saint-Andrew was erected. In these three bulwarks, the Prince of Parma ordered the placement of large-caliber artillery and culverins, and entrusted their command to officers of Spanish nationality.

Finally, on the Kouwenstein dike itself, between the Scheldt and the inundated lands of the village of Stabroek, three strong redoubts were raised: that of Saint-James, near the manor-house of the Lord of Kouwenstein, that of Saint-George, in the middle, and that of the *Pilotis* (Palisades), not far from the agglomeration of Stabroek. In the Castle of Kouwenstein, Farnese installed Camillo del Monte with his *tercio* of Italian soldiers [(55)].

One can imagine the anger of Marnix of Saint-Aldegonde and the confusion of the Antwerpians when they found out that not only had Farnese made himself master of the Kouwenstein counter-dike, but he had rendered it, so to speak, impregnable. How long before they regreted not having listened to the advice of the Prince of Orange beforehand and not having pierced the Blauwgaren dike, which would have had the effect of completely submerging the Kouwenstein and facilitating, on that side, the navigation of flat-bottom boats from Zealand which were trying to resupply Antwerp?

No doubt, they had pierced the Saftingen dike, on the Flemish bank. But, as William the Silent had foreseen, it was a gross mistake. For the inundation on the left bank of the Scheldt would provide Alessandro Farnese with the means of transporting, across the flooded countryside, the materials he needed for the construction of the estacade.

Indeed, in October 1584, the Prince of Parma brought from Ghent, by way of the Scheldt, twenty-two ships loaded with equip-

[55] *Liber relationum*, f°s 259-260; C. Campana, *Assedio d'Anversa*, pp. 25-26; Motley, *o. c.*, v. I, pp. 206-207.

ment, under the protection of one galliot and 600 soldiers. At Dendermonde, the convoy was joined by three other ships and additional succor troops. After following the Scheldt to the confluence of the Rupel, where they were under the protection of the castle of Rupelmonde, in the hands of the Spaniards, the boats would normally have followed the course of the river and passed in front of Antwerp before reaching the forts of Saint-Philip and Saint-Mary. Yet, they would obviously be exposed to the danger of seeing the Antwerpian fleet attacking and destroying the convoy.

Now, upon arriving at Burcht (Borght), where the Spaniards had built a redoubt, the convoy left the Scheldt, and, through an opening cut into the master-dike, entered the flooded countryside. After waiting for the tide, the boats were able to easily navigate through the fields and meadows, that were under water, until Melsele. Here, an opening was cut into the counter-dike, and after crossing another flooded region, the convoy was finally able to get back onto the Scheldt not far from Kallo, near the place where Farnese was busy building the estacade [(56)].

Great was the surprise of the sailors who manned the Antwerpian fleet and who, near Burcht, had tried in vain to intercept the Spanish convoy. Thus, in order to, henceforth, render a second attempt of this type impossible, Téligny seized the breach of the Scheldt dike at Burcht with his vessels and built a redoubt to close and defend the passageway [(57)].

Due to the Prince of Parma's audacious spirit of invention, having greatly worried the defenders of Antwerp, a Council of War was held under the chairmanship of Marnix. Téligny offered to go to Holland and Zealand to, there, ask for the greatest possible amount of provisions, before the Scheldt was completely closed by Farnese. One night he took advantage of the ebb to leave Antwerp with six well-armed barks and sailed in the direction of Lillo.

He was surprised on the river by Robles de Billy, who, in the momentary absence of the Marquis de Richebourg, had guard and command of the work of the estacade: Téligny and his men were taken prisoner [(58)]. It was a painful loss for the defenders of Antwerp,

---

[56] *Libro de las cosas*, f° 268; STRADA, *o. c.*, v. IV, pp. 30-31; C. CAMPANA, *Assedio d'Anversa*, pp. 28-29.

[57] *Ibid. Liber relationum*, f° 262vo; MOIR, *o. c.*, p. 320; GRIMESTON, *o. c.*, pp. 863F-864B.

[58] *Liber relationum*, f° 160ro; STRADA, *o. c.*, v. IV, pp. 31-32, GRIMESTON, *o. c.*, p. 866B; Farnese to the King, Beveren, November 20, 1584 (B. N. P., Spanish MS. 182, f° 388vo).

who had found in the son of La Noue a courageous and inventive warrior, inheriting the fine qualities of his father.

* * *

Ghent continued to be a great arsenal from which the Prince of Parma sourced the necessary materials for the completion of the bridge. The time had come to transport the iron pieces, the wooden facings, and the deck planks for the estacade to fort Saint-Mary. The assemblage represented a load of 35 to 40 boats and the transport thereof seemed to last six months. How was this to be done, since the fort erected at Burcht by Téligny no longer allowed the resumption of navigation through the flooded lands of Melsele and Kallo? In vain, the Prince questioned his engineers and the men who possessed a great knowledge of the country: there was no acceptable solution. It was then that Farnese gave the full measure of his audacious activity and when he displayed all the strength of his inventive genius. He imagined creating a canal which, from the village of Stekene, would wind through the Waasland towards the castle of Beveren and thence toward the estacade to empty into the Scheldt near that great bulwark. Not far from Moerbeke, the small river of La Moere flowed into the Scheldt, and an arm of the Moere extended to the village of Stekene. It was in this latter place that the Prince of Parma began the construction of a canal, which then went in the direction of the village of Saint-Gilles (Waas), through open fields where the water table was very shallow; then, passing through Verrebroek and Beveren, the route went to the camp of Kallo. Not far from there, with the Scheldt dike having been pierced, the canal was flowing into the river, near the fort of Saint-Mary [59]. By this ingenious means, Farnese had therefore put his construction site in communication with the Scheldt, and therefore with Ghent; but, moreover, thanks to the fluvial network of Flanders, he could source, to the benefit of his army before Antwerp, products and materials from Hainaut, Artois, and French Flanders [60].

At the place where the canal emptied into the Scheldt, Farnese built a fort, known as The Pearl, to defend this strategic point

[59] STRADA, *o. c.*, v. IV, pp. 32-33; *Libro de las cosas*, f°s 268-269; *Liber relationum*, f° 162; BENTIVOGLIO, *o. c.*, p. 221.

[60] *Libro de las cosas*, f° 269; MOIR, *o. c.*, pp. 320-322.

against the enterprises of the enemy [61]. As the number of pioneers he had on hand was insufficient, the Prince had to appeal to the indigenous labor force, and especially to the peasants of the Waas region, to dig the canal. The soldiers of his army, who found work of this kind repugnant, had been brought to participate therein following the kind words, encouragement, and promises that their leader, faithful to his custom, had bestowed upon them [62]. The materials prepared at Dunkirk, Nieuwpoort, and Diksmuide were transported by water to Ypres; from there, they went by land, to Warneton, whence boats carried them to Ghent [63]. The ease of supply delivery which this transport system provided to the soldiers inspired them to name it, out of gratitude to Farnese, the *Parma Canal* [64]. As soon as it was finished, the Prince sent thereon 17 ships of every configuration, plus 32 taken from the enemy, among which were two galliots, to the estacade under construction on the Scheldt [65]. Some of these ships were used to strengthen the guarding of the river, the rest were used to defend the work of the bridge and were stationed in the proximity of the latter [66].

[61] Farnese to the King, Beveren, November 20, 1584 (B. N. P., Spanish MS. 182, f° 388vo). *Liber relationum*, f° 160vo; STRADA, *o. c.*, v. IV, p. 33.

[62] STRADA, *o. c.*, loc. cit.; *Libro de las cosas*, f°s 268-269.

[63] *Libro de las cosas*, f° 269.

[64] STRADA, *o. c.*, v. IV, pp. 33-34; BENTIVOGLIO, *o. c.*, p. 221.

[65] *Liber relationum*, f° 162vo.

[66] *Liber relationum*, loc. cit.

CHAPTER II

THE "FARNESE BRIDGE"

While the Prince of Parma was actively pushing the work of the siege of Antwerp, he hadn't stopped concerning himself with the consequences of the death of the Prince of Orange and the policy which the States-General would follow after the disparition of the leader of the revolt. He was regularly kept abreast of the overtures which had been made in Paris to the King of France, Henry III, to whom the Duke of Anjou had bequeathed, in death, all his rights to the Netherlands. He knew that a delegation from the States was currently in talks with the French monarch and Catherine de' Medici to urge them not to abandon the rebels of the Netherlands and that, following a memorandum written by Marnix, the question was raised as to whether the sovereignty of the country would be offered to Henry III, in the absence of effective succors from Elizabeth of England ([67]).

The danger of intervention by the French, whose specter still haunted him, prompted Farnese to try to make himself master of Antwerp through gentleness and persuasion, even if it meant resuming the path of arms if the besieged refused to enter into talks with him. He scarcely had enough troops to execute his grand design: what would happen if Henry III decided to intervene in the conflict with all his forces?

It was probably under the influence of these concerns ([68]) that, on

---

[67] On the subject of this issue, see STRADA, *o. c.*, v. III, pp. 416 sqq.; MOTLEY, *History of the United Netherlands...*, v. I, pp. 25 sqq.; KERVYN DE LETTENHOVE, *Les Huguenots et les Gueux*, v. VI, pp. 577-594. On this subject, see the observations of P. GEYL, *The revolt of the Netherlands*, pp. 194-196.

[68] This is the opinion of MOTLEY, *o. c.*, v. I, p. 166-168.

N
M
O
O
P
I
L
G
F
D
C
A
B
A Alexandro Farn
Maria . C . castillo .
E . S Phelipe . F . Bar
para defensa delpu
H . Navios de guard
gáleras y nabios de
L . Rio escalda . M .
P . dique . havierto . Q . quarte

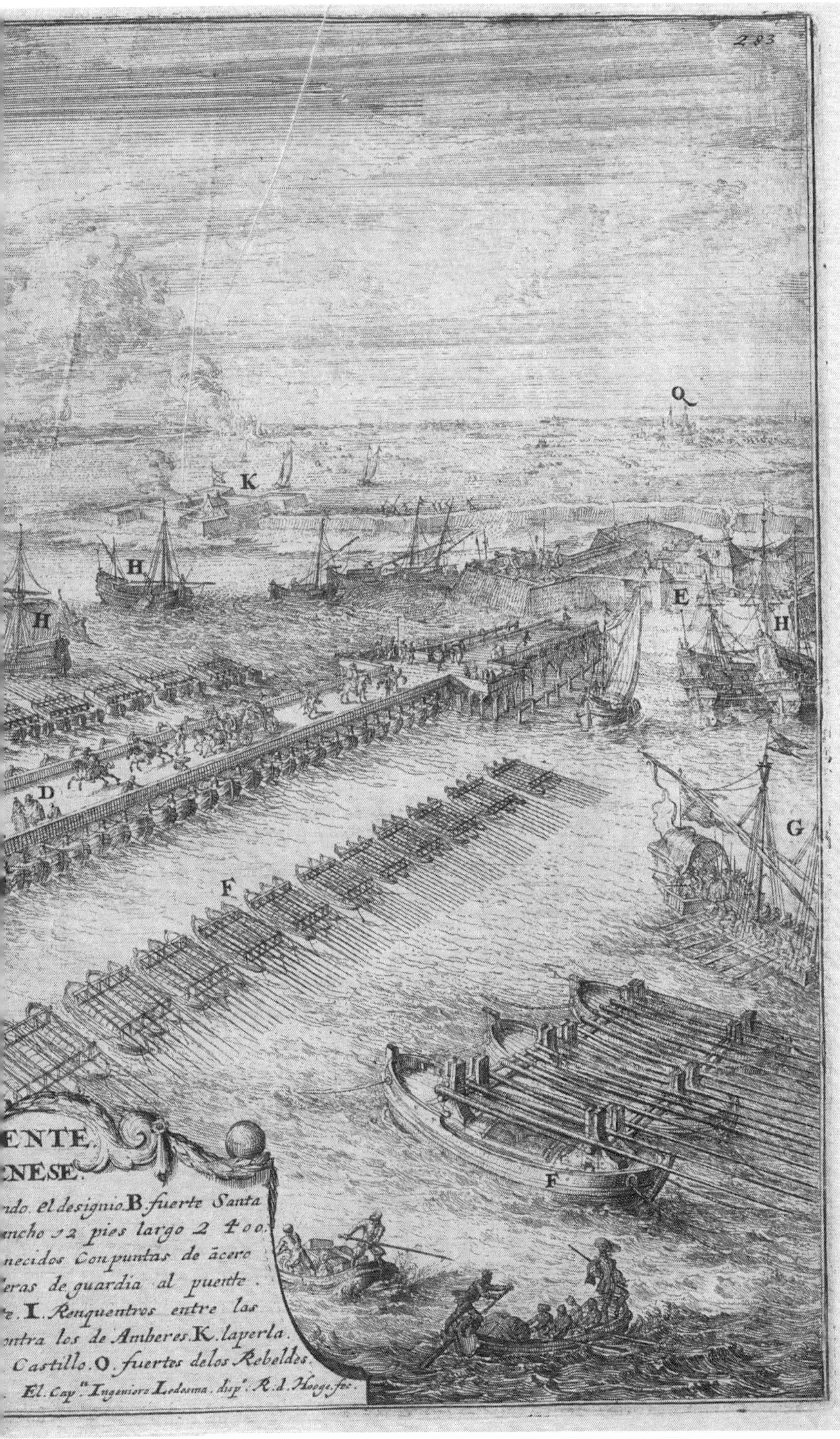

THE BRIDGE BUILT BY FARNESE

Engraving by R. de Hooghe
according to master engineer Ledesma

November 13th, he sent a letter to the magistrate of Antwerp, the contents of which is important to publicize [69]. The authors of the troubles from which the country suffers, wrote the Prince, have only had their own selfish goals in view. Thus the Prince of Orange never thought of raising the siege of a single city besieged by the King's troops. As for Anjou's Frenchmen, we know how they wanted to treat the women and children of the inhabitants of Antwerp, in recognition of the honor they had been given! Since it had pleased God to remove both Orange and Anjou from the Earth, and to see the growing success of the royal forces, it was time, for the Antwerpians, to think of the welfare of the people and their own safety. It was for the sake of the country where he had resided in his youth, that Farnese had decided to let them know how to achieve peace. With the previous letters written on this subject having been intercepted by William the Silent and his accomplices, the Prince wrote them one last time to ask them to remember their wives, their children, their abandoned fatherland, and to consider the happiness which they once enjoyed, when they were loyal subjects of the King.

"Knowing", wrote Farnese, "that more than half of the people of Antwerp desire peace, we will do everything to listen to you, if you decide to enter into negotiations with us, as long as your proposals are honest and reasonable: you will see that it is only our paternal affection that impels us, not personal interest. If you continue to persist in the revolt, you will unnecessarily aggravate the conditions of your reconciliation. Moreover, we are already protesting that we will not be responsible for the innocent blood that will be shed and the misfortunes that will befall you. So that no one is unaware of our good will, we also write to the *Breeden Raedt* (Broad Advise or Broad Council) and the guilds of the city, praying to God to move the hearts of those who have the most influence with you."

As soon as the magistrate of Antwerp had received this missive, he summoned the *Breeden Raedt* and gave a reading of the proposals

---

[69] The text is contained in a booklet entitled *Sendt-brief ghesonden door den Prince van Parma aen Borgemeesteren, Schepenen ende Magistraet der Stadt van Antwerpen*, which is located in the National Library of Paris, French MS. 9018, f°s 417 sqq. It was published by A. LACROIX, *Œuvres de Philippe de Marnix de Sainte-Aldegonde. Écrits politiques et historiques*, pp. 315 sqq., and GACHARD, *Documents concernant le siège d'Anvers par le prince de Parme et la réconciliation de cette ville avec Philippe II*, in the *Bulletins de la Commission royale d'histoire*, 3rd series, v. XII, pp. 189-192.

from the Prince. After discussion [70], it was decided to respond in the following terms. After thanking Farnese for his advice, the Antwerpians pointed out to him that he was misinformed about the origin of the disturbances. Who, indeed, could not know that they had been led there, in spite of themselves, by the ruse of those who, under color of religion, had excited the King to organize the most cruel persecutions against all the inhabitants of the country, putting to death people who had only gathered to pray to God and evoke him through Jesus Christ? Contrary to the agreements concluded with Margaret of Parma, the mother of the Prince, there came the executions ordered by the Duke of Alba and the Spaniards, of which not only were the common people victims, but also the greatest leaders of the country, who had rendered to the King such great services.

Had they not then seen the suppression of ordinary justice, the erection of the citadel, the imposition of illegal taxes, and the attack on all public liberties? Farnese could not have imagined that the rebels had engaged in this war with a joyful heart and because they wanted it, and certainly not because they would have been pressured by the Prince of Orange. It was an ineluctable necessity that forced them to do so and they desired nothing more than to put an end to it by way of a happy and general peace.

The authors of the letter then extolled the Prince of Parma, saying that they could not sufficiently praise his magnanimity, which placed him above any of the governors, his predecessors, while at the same time they admired his skill in the profession of arms. "If we had been able to understand", they said, "that Your Highness was completely authorized to grant us what, according to his wise opinion, would have been necessary to surely arrive at a good peace, we would not have waited so long to throw ourselves into his arms." What they were asking for was freedom of religion. However, much evidence has been provided that the granting of such a concession was not within the power of the Prince. The King of Spain himself could not grant it, submissive as he was to the inquisition and to the Pope. There was therefore no hope of obtaining the only concession likely to bring about peace. After having sent petitions to Spain for twenty years in vain, the rebels had been forced to approach foreign princes.

---

[70] See the text of the deliberation in GACHARD, *Documents concernant le siège d'Anvers...*, loc. cit., pp. 192-193.

They could not conceal from Farnese that they had already approached the King of France and that they had begged him to receive them as his subjects. Since a general and solemn agreement had been concluded with Henry III, it was no longer possible for the Antwerpians to undertake further negotiations with the Spaniards, without being guilty of the basest inconstancy and ingratitude.

"Moreover," they continued, "we exist as but one member of the 'Generality' and we pledged ourselves not to conclude a peace without the concurrence of the other members of this Union. We do not have the power to negotiate with Your Highness without the authorization of the 'Generality' and that of the King of France, to whom we believe we can communicate your letter."

Since Farnese had declared himself, in advance, innocent of the blood that was yet to be shed, they too could speak likewise, since they were only engaged in a defensive war to protect their homes, the freedom of their conscience, and the invocation of God through Jesus Christ, their only Savior. What's more, in order to avoid even more bloodshed, it was enough that Farnese, as evidence of the sincerity of his feelings, order the cessation of hostilities himself [(71)].

The Prince of Parma did not want to leave this letter unanswered. On December 10th, he told the Antwerpians that Henry III was far too discreet, and too friendly with Philip II, to help them in their revolt. If, however, the King of France took their side in this quarrel, the King of Spain had every means at his disposal to thwart his efforts. For the rest, Farnese did not want to discuss the religious question in vain. Nevertheless, so far as he in his simplicity could understand the true nature of a Christian, he did not believe that it could be in agreement with the doctrines of Jesus Christ, nor with the dictates of conscience, to take up arms against the legitimate sovereign, nor to burn, to steal, to pillage, to pierce dikes, to overwhelm their fatherland, and to reduce all things into misery and chaos in the name of religion [(72)].

---

[71] This letter, dated November 23, is in the booklet cited in the previous note. The text is published by A. LACROIX, *o. c.*, pp. 320 sqq. and GACHARD, *o. c.*, loc. cit., pp. 193-198. An exact summary of this correspondence can be found in the *Libro de las cosas*, f[os] 269-271. See the letters from the magistrate of Antwerp to Henry IV and Catherine de' Medici, in the *Bulletins de la Commission royale d'histoire*, 3rd series, v. XII, pp. 202 sqq.

[72] A. F. N., *Carte farnesiane, Fiandra*, fasc. 1706: *Copye van eenen brief van mijn here den Prince van Parmen...*, Kallo, December 10, 1584. The text was published by GACHARD, *Documents concernant le siège d'Anvers...*, loc. cit., pp. 207-210, according to the minutes, preserved in the General Archives of the Kingdom, in Brussels.

CHAPTER II

There ended the correspondence between the besieger and the besieged. Force alone would decide the outcome of the conflict.

* * *

Since the beginning of December, the Prince of Parma did not allow one day to go by without personally taking care of the labors of Antwerp: every morning he went to the construction sites and spent hours overseeing everything. The laborers he had at his disposal, while working diligently, were, however, guided only by his interests, and the lack of sappers was sorely felt. Nevertheless, by the middle of the month, the dikes, the counter-dikes, and the forts were in a good state of defense, and the necessary artillery was about to be installed there (73). Although the days were short and the bad weather often forced interruptions of the work, the construction of the bridge had made great progress and little by little, the estacade had taken its final form.

This is the time to describe, with some detail, this bridge (74), which remained famous in military history for years. The two heads of the bridge, on the Brabantian (right) bank and on the Flemish (left) bank, consisted of the forts of Saint-Philip and Saint-Mary respectively, which were to be used to defend the labors. Starting from fort Saint-Mary, the estacade was formed by large, solid tree trunks, deeply driven into the riverbed or into the sandbar, spaced three feet apart from each other in width, and four feet in length. These tree trunks were planted as close to the middle of the Scheldt as possible, out to a distance of 450 feet, the point where the depth of the riverbed no longer allowed piles to be driven. This formidable matrix of piles was joined together by heavy wooden beams, well nailed and immobilized by chains, which gave the entire structure an unfailing rigidity and stability. On this foundation was laid a pathway, made of heavy wooden planks and beams, which formed the bridge itself, and which was protected, on both sides — on the Antwerpian (up river) side and on the Zealander side (down river) — by a musket ball proof parapet made of wood and packed with clay. Between the fort of Saint-Mary and the center of the bridge, but closer to the fort than to the middle

[73] Farnese to the King, Beveren, December 18, 1584 (B. N. P., Spanish MS. 182, f° 392).

[74] We follow the description by Paolo Rinaldi, who was present at the siege of Antwerp, and who closely followed the work (*Liber relationum*, f°s 162vo-164).

of the river, on each side, Farnese had twelve equally massive piles driven into the riverbed, securely chained and connected by heavy beams; these piles advanced a few meters into the Scheldt, beyond the main line of the estacade, so as to form a kind of ravelin with parapet. On this ravelin, which projected out from the estacade, the Prince installed a battery of three demi-cannons, for the defense of the bulwark against an attack by enemy ships, and stationed fifty soldiers there. A little bit beyond each side of the bridge along its length, between the fort of Saint-Mary and the end of the ravelin, were additional piles driven into the sandbar, slightly exceeding the water level of the river, and interconnected by heavy beams, which, in this way, constituted a sturdy stop barrier for enemy ships or machines which could come up against the estacade.

Starting at fort Saint-Philip, an estacade constructed exactly like the one which we just described, extended out from that side towards the middle of the river, for a distance of 950 feet. Between the two parts of the bridge which were thus advancing to meet one another, a large space of about 1,000 paces, had remained open, where the depth and flow of the Scheldt did not allow tree trunks or piles to be driven into the riverbed.

Alessandro Farnese had 32 large barks, which had been brought from Ghent by way of the Stekene Canal, placed side by side, one next to the other. At the bow and stern, these boats were each immobilized with two anchors and chained one to the other. Each boat was equipped with two pieces of artillery. There was a distance of about 10 feet between them, but they were held in place and in line by a solid chain which ran from one to the other and connected them all together, and by way of a deck that covered all of them.

In order to defend the approaches of the entire bridge, the Prince had put just beyond, approximately within reach of a line, both on the Antwerpian side and on the Zealander side, a row of 33 boats arranged in groups of three. The three boats of each group were joined together by strong pieces of wood, and upon the boats were lying, pointed in the direction of the enemy and securely fastened, the ship masts which had been fetched from Denmark and the Scandinavian countries. Each of these masts was fitted at the tip with a large iron point, in the form of a lance, and was to be used to keep at some distance the boats, the ships, and the machines that the enemy would probably not fail to send toward the estacade with the intention of destroying it. The soldiers called these two barriers, which resembled rafts, "the floaters."

To complete this defense system, twenty vessels were stationed near the Flemish riverbank and twenty near the Brabantian riverbank, ready to intervene at any moment.

The entire span of this gigantic structure was no less than 2,400 feet in length from one bank to the other [75].

However, in December 1584, the central part of the deck supported by the boats had not yet been made and there was still this large empty space between the two parts of the estacade. The winter squalls, the frost, and the impetuosity of the Scheldt's waters raised by tempestuous winds, had forced the workers to postpone the setting up of the boats. This explains why, from time to time, Hollander and Zealander ships were still able to pass through and bring food and ammunition to Antwerp. But the enterprise was becoming more and more hazardous, and it was necessary to have an unwavering courage to face the artillery, which was already installed on the completed parts of the bridge and which was often able to sink the boats and vessels passing within its firing range [76]. Aside from that, the Spanish ships or the armed vedettes stationed on the river succeeded more than once, after engaging in battle, in making themselves masters of the loads transported by the Hollanders [77].

* * *

The titanic effort required for the construction of the bridge had

[75] The description given by Paolo Rinaldi corresponds entirely to that given by STRADA (*o. c.*, v. IV, pp. 23-26 and 36-37), who, while in Rome, had the opportunity to see the model of the bridge and the two forts at its termini, made on the order of Farnese by a worker from Ghent, named Louis Gambian, and which the Prince of Parma had sent, accompanied by a sketch, to the Roman Court (*o. c.*, v. IV, p. 23). What Rinaldi says is also consistent with what Farnese himself relates in his reports to the King, and in particular in his letters of December 18, 1584, January 26, and March 10, 1585 (B. N. P., Spanish MS. 182, f[os] 392, 394, 397), and with the description by C. CAMPANA, *Assedio d'Anversa,* pp. 23 sqq., which was documented by Cosimo Masi, Farnese's secretary. Cf. MOIR, *o. c.*, pp. 328-330; MOTLEY, *o. c.*, v. I, pp. 181-182; BENTIVOGLIO, *o. c.*, pp. 225-226.

[76] Farnese to the King, Beveren, January 26, 1585 (B. N. P., Spanish MS. 182, f° 394); *Libro de las cosas*, f° 270vo. — « Une charue grande venant d'Angleterre en laquelle estoient plus de 300 tonneaux de cervoise et quelques draps d'Angleterre d'ung coup de canon at eu le mast rompu en pièce, laquelle l'eau a iecté vers Calloo, et est demeurée en mains des gens du Roy, et aultres deux enfondrées, lesquelles estoient chargées de tourbes. En les dites navires estoient beaulcops des gens, mais la plupart femmes, toutes se retirants pour la maladie qu'est en Zeelande ». *Avvisi* from Antwerp, 1584 (A. F. N., *Carte farnesiane*, *Fiandra*, fasc. 1665).

[77] *Libro de las cosas*, f° 271ro.

been conceived, undertaken, and pushed under conditions that had to render its execution difficult and very painful [78].

Already by September 1584, the Prince of Parma had written to the King that, as a result of the absence of drinking water in the forts and camps established in a region that is sandy and largely inundated by salt water, the number of soldiers and officers that were sick was considerable. More than 900 Spaniards had been brought to the hospital at Beveren, and the number of infirmed belonging to the regiments of other nationalities was almost as high [79]. At the beginning of January, 1585, Farnese reported, in shocking terms, the dreadful conditions in which his men had to live and fight: "They suffered", he said, "as much as is humanly possible." [80] This was because, as always, the money sent from Spain was insufficient. Undoubtedly, during the year 1585, Philip II had 150,000 ducats per month sent to the army of Flanders [81], but the arrears of pay which the Prince of Parma owed to his men were such that, as soon as it arrived, the money was consumed and there was not one maravedis left with which to face the future. "The million you promised me", he wrote, "arrived piecemeal, and with so much ceremony, that I haven't ten crowns at my disposal. I myself cannot understand how I managed to keep even this handful of soldiers — yea, the army is reduced to such miserable proportions that your Majesty would be astounded." [82]

The provisioning conditions were, on the other hand, miserable: the soldiers were often forced to fetch their food ten or twelve leagues from the camp. How could they have done otherwise in a region where most of the villages, abandoned by their inhabitants, were half submerged or completely isolated in the middle of the flood? [83] Also, as a result of the illnesses, the ensigns had been reduced to a small number of men, but those whose robust constitution made it

---

78 Farnese to his father, Beveren, December 18, 1584 (A. F. N., *Carte farnesiane, Fiandra*, fasc. 1626).

79 Farnese to the King, Beveren, September 14, 1584 (*Loc. cit.*); Farnese to his parents, Beveren, November 17, 1584, in A. F. N., *Carte farnesiane, Fiandra*, fasc. 1661.

80 MOTLEY, *o. c.*, v. I, p. 173. On the conditions in which the Spanish soldiers fought in Flanders, one can consult the interesting introduction of the book by J. BROUWER, *Kronijken van Spaansche soldaten*, cited in our bibliography.

81 GACHARD, *Les bibliothèques de Madrid et de l'Escurial*, p. 135.

82 *Ibid.* Farnese to the King, Beveren, December 18, 1584 (B. N. P., Spanish MS. 182, f° 392).

83 Farnese to the King, Beveren, December 18, 1584 (*Loc. cit.*); C. CAMPANA; *Assedio d'Anversa*, p. 38.

possible for them to resist disease were fiercely determined to do their duty to the end. The Prince of Parma did not tire of recommending his men to the King's thoughtfulness and praising their courage, "which was almost superhuman." What he did not say was this — that desertions had not failed to occur. Driven by misery and despair, many soldiers abandoned their units to seek refuge in France, where the English agent Stafford counted them, with satisfaction, and hastened to notify Queen Elizabeth: "There past [sic] this way many Spanish soldiers", he wrote from Paris to Walsingham, at the end of December 1584 and early January 1585, "come from the camp so poor and naked as I ever saw any. There have been within this fortnight two hundred at a time in this town, who report the extremity of want of victuals in their camp, and that they have been four and twenty months without pay, and exclaim greatly upon the Prince of Parma, which soldiers Mendoza seeks to convey away in giving them money by all means he can." (84)

Farnese, however, made every effort to put an end to a situation for which he was not responsible (85). Certainly, the King was not indifferent to the enterprise of Antwerp, and he was aware of its extreme importance. He had already, on several occasions, expressed his lively satisfaction on this subject. But he could not imagine the multiple burdens which the Prince of Parma had to face in this campaign. Thus, the latter constantly put before the monarch a picture of the situation: at the moment when, at the beginning of January 1585, 250,000 ECU reached him, in small sums, from Madrid, 60,000 were already destined in advance to support Verdugo's troops in Friesland; another 25,000 were to be paid to Don Juan Manrique, to allow him to settle the back pay of his German soldiers billeted in Luxembourg, completely ravaged and pillaged for several months; another 20,000 ECU would serve the remainder of the troops commanded by Montigny and by the Marquis de Richebourg.

On January 15th, the Prince calculated that he had resources for no longer than one month, and he anxiously wondered if he would not be obliged to abandon the enterprise of Antwerp. Where to find the money for the daily wages of the sailors, the carpenters, the gun-

---

84 MOTLEY, *o. c.*, v. I, p. 173; MURDIN, *A Collection of State Papers...*, p. 433.

85 He had sent Count Pomponio Torelli to Spain to explain to the King the danger of the situation. (C. CAMPANA, *Assedio d'Anversa*, pp. 40-41).

ners, the pioneers, and other mechanics he had with him? The Waasland, formerly so rich, and which had served for some time to support the army, was completely emptied [86].

However, there was still a way to be provisioned from 's-Hertogenbosch, one of the four main cities of Brabant, which remained loyal to the King. Unfortunately, that city was attacked by surprise, at this grave time, by the troops of the States-General.

* * *

For about a month, no enemy ship had managed to reach Antwerp in order to bring provisions to that city. The States-General then decided to attempt one, then another, diversion which were to oblige Farnese to intervene with a detachment of his troops and thus lose his position on the Scheldt [87]. The first attempt was aimed at Brussels. The provisioning of that city had become, at that moment, very difficult for the rebels, because some Spanish cavalry companies had established themselves between Vilvoorde and Leuven, and with the aid of the garrisons occupying those two places, attacked all the convoys of food which the inhabitants of Mechelen directed towards the capital of Brabant. A hundred wagons had already been captured. At the beginning of January, the rebels gathered some 200 vehicles laden with food at Bergen op Zoom and arranged to convey them in the direction of Brussels, under the protection of an escort of 200 cavalry and 1,000 infantry.

As soon as Farnese got wind of this project, he ordered Giorgio Basta, Commissioner General of the light-cavalry, to assemble all the available companies in Brabant and The Campine, and prescribed him to prepare an ambush at the village of Ranst, through which it seemed that the enemy convoy would have to pass. A serious battle erupted in that location. The *Reiters* who made up the escort of the supply wagons were surprised in the middle of the night, and had 200 men killed, not to mention the prisoners from Lier and Herentals who the Spanish soldiers quickly came to rescue [88].

---

[86] Farnese to the King, Beveren, January 15, 1585 (A. G. R., *Copies de Simancas*, v. 16, non-foliated).

[87] *Libre de las cosas*, f° 272.

[88] Letter from Capt. Henry Ricardes to Walsingham, Antwerp, January 3, 1584 o.s. (*Foreign Calendar, Elizabeth, August 1584-August 1585*, pp. 203-204); *Libro de las cosas*, f°s 271vo-272ro; Farnese to the King, Beveren, January 15, 1585. (*Loc. cit.*).

Disappointed on that side, the States-General tried to surprise 's-Hertogenbosch [89]. It was the Count of Hohenlohe who was in charge of the enterprise. He brought together, for this purpose, a body of 4,000 infantrymen and 200 lancers. This most delicate operation was entrusted to Captain Juliaan Kleerhagen, originally from Brussels, whose wife was born in 's-Hertogenbosch. On the night of January 19th to 20th, Kleerhagen, with 40 or 50 elite soldiers, managed to approach the Antwerp gate [90] and occupy two small guard houses located between the drawbridge and the portcullis. This operation was done in such great silence that it did not arouse the attention of the burghers who were posted as sentinels on the walls. When, on the morning of the 20th, the Antwerp gate was opened and the drawbridge was lowered, Kleerhagen's men sallied forth from their hiding-places and rushed inside. A few harquebus shots quickly silenced those in the guardhouse forever. Immediately, 500 infantrymen and 200 cavalrymen of Hohenlohe, hidden not far from the walls, came running and rushed through the Antwerp gate following Kleerhagen's men. Completely surprised, the burghers were unable to react. The invaders quickly reached the main square, which they occupied, and seized the artillery and the ammunition magazine. 's-Hertogenbosch did not have a royal garrison, but as chance would have it, at the time of the attack of Hohenlohe's men, there was a small band of Burgundian and Italian lancers in the city, who had arrived the day before with a convoy of goods for which they were the escort. The Baron de Hautepenne was with them. At the sound of the skirmish, the latter came running with his men, while Helmont, the Governor of the place, gathered a number of armed burghers by his side. Rushing upon the enemy, who, already believing themselves to be the master of 's-Hertogenbosch, had begun pillaging, Hautepenne and his men pushed them back towards the Antwerp gate. Hohenlohe's soldiers fiercely defended themselves at that place, as they waited for the rest of the troops encamped in a nearby village. But then there was a dramatic episode. During the surprise of the Antwerp gate, an old gatekeeper had been seriously wounded

[89] See the letter from the magistrate of 's-Hertogenbosch to Farnese, February 6, 1585 and the *Bref discours d'une mémorable entreprinse*, in the *Bulletins de la Commission royale d'histoire*, 3rd series, v. XIII, pp. 117-126; Letter from Davidson to Walsingham, The Hague, January 20, 1584 o.s. (*Foreign Calendar, Elizabeth, August 1584-August 1585*, pp. 250-251). Cf. MOTLEY, *o. c.*, v. I, pp. 175-178.

[90] That is to say, the gate at 's-Hertogenbosch which was so named.

and had collapsed in a corner. At one point, the enemy soldiers who were guarding the gate, hearing the cries of victory in the city and supposing that their companions were already indulging in remunerative plunder, no longer held firm and abandoned their post. Immediately, the old gatekeeper, gathering all his strength, cut the ropes which held up the portcullis, making it fall, and thus preventing Hohenlohe's soldiers who entered 's-Hertogenbosch from going out, and the troops who were coming to their rescue, from entering.

At once, Hautepenne and his men, aided by the burghers, advanced upon the enemy, who thus became entrapped, and carried out a terrible carnage. Some of Hohenlohe's soldiers managed to get to the walls and jumped into the fosse, but most of them drowned. However, Kleerhagen and Justinus van Nassau managed to escape. Among the dead was Ferdinand Truchsess, the younger brother of the apostate Archbishop Truchsess and a bastard of the Palatine Casimir.

Hohenlohe, hastening with reinforcements, but restrained in front of the closed portcullis, could but helplessly watch the massacre of his best soldiers [91]. He withdrew, with his remaining troops, to Geertruidenberg, and, in a letter to the States-General, blamed the failure on a panic which had seized his men.

The misfortune of 's-Hertogenbosch spared Farnese a great concern, for it is certain that the occupation of that city would have had immediate repercussions on the siege of Antwerp [92]. In any case, in the mind of the enemy, this should have attracted a considerable number of troops hither which Prince of Parma needed to man his positions on the Scheldt.

* * *

Though Farnese's attention was not distracted from that side, he was however tormented at the thought that a French intervention could occur at any moment [93]. Letters intercepted by his spies had

---

[91] *Libro de las cosas*, f°s 272-273; *Liber relationum*, f° 261; STRADA, *o. c.*, v. IV, pp. 40-42; Farnese to the King, Beveren, February 12, 1585 (A. G. R., *Copies de Simancas*, v. 16, non-foliated); J. F. LE PETIT, *o. c.*, v. II, pp. 505-506; GRIMESTON, *o. c.*, pp. 869C-870A; Granvelle to Margaret of Parma, Zaragoza, March 6, 1585 (*Correspondance de Granvelle*, v. XII, pp. 21-22).

[92] On January 30, Hohenlohe wrote from Geertruidenberg: „In somma, God heeft het niet willen hebben, want so verre ick dese stadt hadde bekomen, soude des vijands leger niet lange voor Antwerpen gebleven hebben" (P. BOR, *Oorsprongk, begin en vervolgh der Nederlandsche Oorlogen*, 2nd part, f°s 558-559).

[93] He speaks of it in expressed terms in the letter he sent to Philip II on January 15, 1585 (A. G. R., *Copies de Simancas*, v. 16, non-foliated).

informed him that the negotiations of the States-General with Catherine de' Medici and Henry III continued to develop normally and that the States' delegates were, at this moment, making every effort to reach an agreement with the French. On January 3rd, a delegation from the States had embarked at Brielle and, after arriving in Boulogne-sur-Mer, had continued on its way to Senlis, where Henry III was waiting for it. The Spanish ambassador to Paris, Bernardino de Mendoza, had immediately made the necessary demarches to the Court, in order to obtain from the King of France that the delegation from the "rebels" was not to be received and that an order would be communicated to it to leave French territory without delay. Henry III made a reply to Mendoza that he was seeing them not as rebels, but as subjects of the King of Spain who were oppressed and that it was the tradition of the Kings of France to always lend an attentive ear to the supplications of the subjects abused by their Prince [94].

Did the attitude of the King of France not allow us to foresee a fervent desire to meddle in the affairs of the Netherlands? Farnese feared this and never ceased to communicate his trepidations to Philip II.

However, as the very rigorous winter did not allow the work for the completion of the bridge over the Scheldt to be pushed with all the desired energy, and with the arrival of ice sheets carried by the waters of the river preventing the complete closure the estacade [95], the Prince of Parma turned his attention towards Brussels, which seemed, by the end of January 1584, to begin to experience the first anxieties of hunger. He sent for artillery pieces from Mons and, after gathering together 1,000 infantrymen and 1,500 cavalrymen at Halle, sent these forces in the direction of the castle of Watermael-Boitsfort. The latter had been occupied a short time before by the States' soldiers coming from Mechelen and burned down so that it could not serve the Spaniards as a point of support in the operations they planned against Brussels. Farnese's soldiers installed themselves in the ruins of the burned castle and guarded it well, thus definitively cutting off all the relationships which the inhabitants of the blockaded city had maintained, until then, with the country of Liege, from whence had come many amenities to them [96]. In early February, the

---

[94] Documents in P. BOR, *o. c.*, f°s 524 sqq.; *Libro de las cosas*, f° 273; J. F. LE PETIT, *o. c.*, v. II, p. 507; GRIMESTON, *o. c.*, pp. 870E-871B.

[95] Farnese to the King, February 12, 1585 (A. G. R., *Copies de Simancas*, v. 16, non-foliated).

[96] Farnese to the King, February 12, 1585 (A. G. R., *Copies de Simancas*, v. 16); *Libro de las cosas*, f° 272.

Prince of Parma was convinced that the people of Brussels would soon begin negotiations with him for the surrender of the city and he implemented every measure to ensure that these negotiations could be carried out very quickly [97].

Meanwhile, winter's grip had gradually loosened, the work of the bridge had been pushed more actively and the boats that were to close the opening between the two parts of the estacade had been put in place. On Sunday, February 25th, the grandiose work was completely finished. It was the feast of Saint-Matthew, the day when Charles V. had always used to record successes or victories, as Farnese pointed out to Philip II [98]. "The boats are now in place," he wrote, "anchored on both ends, joined to each other side-by-side with chains and large planks, and across the top, we have cast the bridge, which will make it possible to travel from Flanders to Brabant." [99] One hundred fifty artillery pieces, including those placed in the forts, were to contribute in the defense or protection of the bulwark.

This was the moment when the King had to furnish maximum effort to support the colossal work his Governor-General had just completed. "Money!" repeated the Prince incessantly, "money, otherwise everything will have been done in vain. If the succors from Spain does not arrive within a very short time, my soldiers will have to abandon their posts and quarters, for if I do not dismiss them myself, they will go away without my being able to retain them. I have done all my duty and I decline any responsibility in advance. The cavalry is almost destroyed and starved, the garrisons can no longer be fed by the burghers, and the countryside is ruined. How then to feed my men in this hellacious region, where there are only dikes and saltwater? I earnestly supplicate Your Majesty to give me the help I seek without delay!" [100]

Great would have been, no doubt, the joy of the defenders of Antwerp if they could have guessed that their adversary, having succeeded, with makeshift means, and in the midst of a harsh winter, to finish the considerable undertaking which his genius had invented and that his tenacity and his military science had guided to comple-

---

[97] Letter cited from Farnese.

[98] STRADA, *o. c.*, v. IV, p. 37; Farnese to the King, Beveren, March 10, 1585 (B. N. P., Spanish MS. 182, f° 397ro). St. Mattthew's feast day is Sep. 21. In 1585, 9 saints had Feb. 25 as their feast day. Could it have a been different saint? Errata?

[99] Farnese to the King, February 27, 1585,(A. G. R., *Copies de Simancas*, v. 16).

[100] Farnese to the King, February 27, 1585 (*Loc. cit.*).

tion, saw in his eyes the peril of not being able to withdraw from his efforts the decisive result he had expected.

But they had only one preoccupation at the moment: the bridge was there, despite all their sarcasm and all their skepticism (101), and any succors coming down the Scheldt from Holland and Zealand was henceforth forbidden to them.

It was probably at that time that the Flemish complaint was composed, which reads as follows:

Geluckig zijn de steden, daer de Heer wort ghevreest
Ende oock aengebeden ootmoedich in den geest;
Die, met een hart verslagen, oock altoos sorge dragon,
Ja hebben een mishaghen der sonden minst en meest.
O Heer! aanhooret karmen des volcx t' Antwerp' in stat,
Wiltse doch nu ontfarmen, thoent haer doch eens den schat
Uwer grooter ghenaden, zij die nu zijn beladen,
Wiltse met troost versaden, opent haer doch den padt.
Zij zijn zeer starck beleghen, te water en te landt.
Heer! laat U eens beweghen en doetse doch bijstandt;
Want al de Spaensche fielen die soecken te vernielen
De welvaert onzer zielen, hier in dit Nedcrlandt..
....
Men liet hem daer volbringhen de brugh — wast niet een schandt? —
Daarmet hij nu can dwinghen Antwerpen, schier Brabant.
Maar Godt laat sulcks gheschieden omdat wij van hem vlieden,
En oock geen eer en bieden zijn heilich woord playsant.
Wij willen ons begheven tot U, o Heere goet!
Terwijl dat wij noch leven verwachten ghenade soet;
Wij hadden ons verlaten op ruyters en soldaten,
Doe wij noch liber saten; nu straft ghij den hooghmoet.
Prins, Heer en Godt almachtich! Sietse barmhertich aen,
Die tot U roepen klachtich. Wiltse ter noot bijstaen
't Antwerpen binnen der mueren, dat zijt moghen vordueren
Teghen die, 't allen uren, strengh nae hun leven gaen (102).

Marnix of Saint-Aldegonde had the promise of Henry III, in the eyes of his fellow citizens, not to let them perish, and to tell them that the people of Brussels, through the mouth of Van den Tympel, urged them to trust in the Count of Hohenlohe, he could not prevent

---

101 J. F. LE PETIT, *La grande chronique ancienne et moderne de Hollande...*, v. II, p. 498, "And although at the first it seemed a ridiculous thing to stoppe vp so large and deepe a riuer, where the tydes ebbing and flowing are so strong... This opinion of men, that hee should not preuaile anything, was the cause of their slackenesse and negligence to hinder him in the beginning, when as they had good meanes to doe it", as translated in GRIMESTON, *o. c.*, p. 860A. — "The people are all amazed, thinking no more relief will come by water..." Captain William Marten to Walsingham, Antwerp, February 25, 1585 (*Calendar, Elizabeth, August 1584-August 1585*, p. 284.); C. CAMPANA, *Assedio d'Anversa*, p. 27.

102 VAN VLOTEN, *Nederlandsche geschiedzangen*, II, pp. 295-296.

them from seeing the adversary's success and from shuddering at the thought of the fate that awaited them [(103)]. Also, the partisans of peace, who formed an important group in Antwerp, which only terror reduced to silence [(104)], began to stir and hold conventicles [(105)]. The Burgomaster, Marnix, with the intention of stopping the panic which could suddenly burst forth, resolved to send a spy to closely examine this bridge of Farnese, which so impressed his fellow citizens. The spy was surprised in the Spanish lines and he expected to be hanged. But, to his astonishment, he was taken before the Prince of Parma, who treated him with a great deal of humanity. He ordered him to visit the Spanish camp in Beveren, to closely examine the structure of the bridge, to count the forts, the vessels, and the cannons that defended it, then afterwards to come find him without any fear.

When he had Marnix's secret envoy before him again, he said to him: "Go now and return to those who have sent you here and say to them all, on my behalf, that their conscience and their sense of honor should make them abandon their obstinacy and their injustice. Tell them that I exhort them with benevolence to reconcile with their King and that thereafter they will find me at their full disposal. If they do not do this, let them know that the bridge over the Scheldt will either be my glorious sepulture or the pathway by which I shall enter victorious into Antwerp." [(106)]

He then sent the Antwerpian spy back, accompanied by his favorite trumpet. The arrival of the latter in Antwerp and the return of the spy provoked within the city an understandable emotion. The crowd followed the Spanish parliamentarian's every step, as though he had been the harbinger of salvation, and the supporters of peace publicly celebrated him. But Marnix put an end to these demonstrations, reading to the *Breeden Raedt* the text of a letter from Henry III, dated February 13th, and where the King of France made them

---

[103] *Libro de las cosas*, f° 273.

[104] VAN METEREN, *o. c.*, f° 233vo. The Zealanders indicted Admiral Treslong, accusing him of having done nothing to prevent the construction of the bridge. The Antwerpians went so far as to accuse the Hollanders, saying that "the prince of Parma could not have finished this worke without them: and it was generally spoken, that they had delivered him cables and ankers, wherewith he had made his worke firme." (GRIMESTON, *o. c.*, p. 873E-F); J. F. LE PETIT, *o. c.*, v. II, p. 510.

[105] *Libro de las cosas*, f° 274; *Liber relationum*, f° 166.

[106] *Liber relationum*, f° 166; STRADA, *o. c.*, v. IV, pp. 39-40. This incident is also told by J. F. LE PETIT, *La grande chronique ancienne et moderne de Hollande...*, v. II, p. 502, GRIMESTON, *o. c.*, p. 865E, and by C. CAMPANA, *Assedio d'Anversa*, p. 36.

the promise to succor them shortly. He then made all the assistants take an oath to no longer speak of an agreement with Farnese or of peace with the Spaniards, and threatened them, if they were not faithful, with capital punishment [107]. These precautions were probably not superfluous, as the government of the city of Antwerp was in reality an undisciplined democracy, where it was very difficult to maintain the principle of authority. The influence of the mayor and the magistrate was fought by a certain number of colleges and chambers, including the College of Colonels, which Orange had created in 1577-1578 to support his policy, and which, far from simply replacing the *Wijkmeesters* (district supervisors) at the head of the military organization, had become more and more influential, and were trying to diminish the power of the *Breeden Raedt.* The Colonels had sixteen captains on their side, who wanted to give their opinions in all things and would enter the Council whenever they wished. They often had quarrels with the College of *Hooftmannen* and the *Wijkmeesters*, the old leaders of the urban militia, who professed they would not let themselves be deprived. The deans of the guilds, on the other hand, were trying to maintain their position and also had a say in the assemblies of the *Breeden Raedt.* It was still necessary to take into account the deans of the trades and the chambers who occupied themselves with the ammunition, fortifications, and the fitting-out of the ships. How did Marnix, especially since the death of William the Silent, without being heavy handed, maintain any semblance of order in this complicated organization? [108]

Especially since the government of Antwerp, as of 1581, could only be maintained through threat and terror [109]. In that year, a predominantly Calvinist regime had been introduced, where the property of Catholics was used to organize Calvinist teaching and worship, and where only two small chapels had been left for the Catholics, however, they expelled the ecclesiastics from the city.

---

107 *Liber relationum*, f° 166. This fact is confirmed by J. F. LE PETIT, *La grande chronique ancienne et moderne de Hollande...*, v. II, p. 502; GRIMESTON, *o. c.*, p. 870B; C. CAMPANA, *Assedio d'Anversa*, pp. 44-45.

108 VAN METEREN, *o. c.*, f°s 233ro-233vo; F. PRIMS, *Oranje en de Antwerpsche colonellen,* in *Antverpiensia 1933*, pp. 150 sqq. — On the *Breetien Raedt*, see F. PRIMS, *De Antwerpsche Breede Raad en zijn Archief*, in the *Antwerpsch Archievenblad*, 2nd series, v. III, 1933, p. 32.

109 The sentiment of the Catholics is expressed in a memorandum intended to be put before the magistrate's eyes, and which has been published by A. ERENS, *Een „Apologie van den Vrede" te Antwerpen in 1584*, in the *Bijdragen tot de geschiedenis*, v. XXIV, 1933, pp. 145-182.

The military organization created by the Prince of Orange at the time of his arrival in Antwerp had armed only the "right-thinking" people, removing weapons from all those who were not partisans of his policy. Each month, a sum of 50,000 florins had been levied on wealthy citizens and any attempts to evade it resulted in the confiscation of the property of the recalcitrants "in the name of the Fatherland."

Also, as soon as Farnese had captured the Antwerpian forts of the left bank in July 1584, a considerable number of wealthy citizens had left the city, carrying away their wealth [(110)]. The magistrate's stern orders completely failed to stop this exodus. In the meantime, the Catholics had regained courage and organized secret meetings, wherein was discussed peace with Farnese. In September, the magistrate had summoned the fugitives to return within eight days, under penalty of proceeding against them with rigor. The registered lists of these fugitives included some 70 people of high quality. All these measures had not discouraged those who desired peace with Farnese, the "peiswillers" (peace lovers). One day, in full council, someone, after having shown that Farnese's bridge had cut Antwerp off from the rest of the world, dared to say: "Wherefore all these difficulties being well weighed and considered, in my opinion we should seek in time to reconcile ourselves to the King, else this siege will prove but so unfortunate for us." [(111)] The "peiswillers" acted skillfully. Knowing that the magistrate was steadfast in its opposition, they addressed the Chancellor of Brabant, Dirk van Liesvelt, who had taken refuge in Antwerp since Brussels was about to capitulate. Among those who went to find Liesvelt were former aldermen, merchants, and all kinds of people. On October 14th, the magistrate arrested a number of them [(112)] and had them examined by the *schultheiß* of Antwerp and two aldermen; after this investigation, the *schultheiß* indicted ex officio against eleven of the prisoners, among whom were the alderman de Pape and Jacques della Faille, who were charged with being "seditious and disturbers of the common peace." However, Chancellor Liesvelt did not consider it as such, he had listened to

[110] They were about a hundred, to believe the well informed author who was JEAN-FRANÇOIS LE PETIT, *La grande chronique ancienne et moderne de Hollande*, v. II, p. 491; GRIMESTON, *o. c.*, p. 851F.

[111] J. F. LE PETIT, *o. c.*, v. II, p. 502; GRIMESTON, *o. c.*, p. 864D-E.

[112] F. PRIMS, *De peiswillers* and PRIMS, *De bestraffing der peiswillers*, in *Antverpiensia 1933*, pp. 227-242; Bizarri to Walsingham, Antwerp October 27, 1584 (*Foreign Calendar, Elizabeth, August 1584-August 1585*, pp. 109-110).

their grievances, their desire for peace, and thanked them for their communication. Notwithstanding, the Calvinist magistrate sentenced them to severe fines, ranging from 100 to 6,000 florins [113].

It is therefore not surprising that the Spanish trumpet sent by Farnese to Antwerp reported, on the part of the magistrate, a polite but firm refusal to enter into negotiations with him. They had committed themselves, Marnix had said, to a mighty Prince, the King of France, who had promised to liberate them; that oath could not be broken [114].

The Prince of Parma drew the necessary conclusion: all he had to do was to rigorously strengthen the blockade and wait for the inevitable: Antwerp could not, save foreign intervention, escape its fate. She would have to give up like Ghent had given up. One day, Marnix and his colleagues would take the path to the camp of Beveren to humbly solicit the most advantageous conditions of surrender. In fact, Brussels itself was going to almost instantly give them an example.

* * *

A short while ago, as we have seen [115], in 1578, Brussels had almost been occupied by the Spaniards, following the victory won by Don Juan and Alessandro Farnese at Gembloux. However, the absence of artillery and the state of his army had not allowed the victor of Lepanto to seize the capital of Brabant and install himself there as Governor-General. Later on, in June 1579, the attempt by Count Philip of Egmont to surprise the city and occupy it on behalf of the *Malcontents* had failed miserably [116]. It was in the wake of this *coup de main* by Egmont that succor troops were sent from Antwerp to protect the city, which included five very anti-Catholic Scottish companies. The latter, aided by the populace, unleashed a violent iconoclastic movement, during which most of the churches were attacked, pillaged, and stripped of their sacred ornaments. In addition, the houses of the Counts of Mansfeld and Aarschot, and the palace of Granvelle were ransacked. These excesses resulted in, despite the protests from the nations, though very anti-Spanish, the *Religions-*

---

[113] Letters from Captains Lucar and Gachili to Walsingham, October 24, 1584 (*Foreign Calendar, Elizabeth, August 1584-August 1585*, pp. 101-102).

[114] *Liber relationum*, f° 166.

[115] See the first volume of our work, pp. 219-221.

[116] See v. II of our work, pp. 224-225.

vrede proclamation as well as participation in the Union of Utrecht. In July 1579, Olivier van den Tympel, Lord of Korbeek-Dijle, a supporter of Orange and a Calvinist, was installed as Governor of the city. It cannot be denied that this officer of great merit showed himself, on more than one occasion, tolerant and imbued with a remarkable mind for justice. It was with him, however, that the political supremacy of Calvinism began in Brussels. A War Committee was immediately formed, which had to take care of earnestly putting the city in a state of defense.

After the opposition from the nations had been shattered — an opposition which was manifested, above all, over the excesses of the garrison — van den Tympel and the War Committee were able to begin vigorous actions against all those who did not make a pact with the revolution and Reformation. The garrison soldiers recommenced attacking and pillaging the churches and convents on several occasions. This was the time when the Prince of Parma was already maneuvering to isolate Brussels as much as possible. But it was also the moment when the Calvinists, convinced that the city was impregnable, began to definitively organize themselves as the victorious party. They were, of course, no more than a restless minority, but, thanks to the protection of van den Tympel and a magistrate which was imposed by them, they were able to quickly establish their domination over the Catholics. As of 1580, Calvinist preachers, servants, and teachers were paid by way of property sequestered from convents. The Sectarians took over charitable organizations [(117)]. Finally, we come to the prohibition of Catholic worship: on May 1st, 1581, a proclamation from the magistrate made known that only churches in the possession of Calvinists could remain open, all the others had to be permanently closed [(*)]. The teaching of the Heidelberg catechism was no longer tolerated. Religious associations were dissolved or banned and their property confiscated. Meanwhile, van den Tympel acted valiantly to prevent Farnese from over-tightening the ring which gradually threatened, albeit still at great distance, to cut Brussels off from all communications with the outside. But in the autumn of 1584, as we have seen, Aalst, Willebroek, and Vilvoorde had fallen into Farnese's hands. Soon, after the capture of Ghent, the

---

[117] P. BONENFANT. *Un aspect du régime calviniste à Bruxelles*, in the *Bulletins de la Commission royale d'histoire*, loc. cit.

* See the proclamation in P. BOR, *o. c.*, fos 260-261.

capital of Brabant was in fact besieged, although no Spanish soldier was before its walls. The threat of starvation was emerging and an inventory of grain reserves was beginning to be drawn up. Pressing calls for succor were sent to Mechelen and Antwerp, but by the end of 1584, supply convoys were ruthlessly intercepted by Spanish troops at Vilvoorde and Willebroek [(118)].

From then on appeared, as in Ghent, the specter of discord. The Catholics began to raise their heads and on December 2nd, a mutiny of the garrison soldiers erupted, which van den Tympel managed to quell with great difficulty. Soon, it was realized that neither the supplications sent by the States-General to Henry III nor the promises of succors from Hohenlohe would be able to save the city [(119)]. As early as November 1584, the Secretary of the Governor, Jean Boghe (or Bochius), had become an active instrument for the movement favoring reconciliation with the King. He addressed memorandums to the colonels and captains of the garrison, and to the delegates of the three superintendents of the city to demonstrate that "no one is obliged to do the impossible." [(120)] In January 1585, requests were addressed to the magistrate by groups of important burghers. The end approaches. On January 24th, van den Tympel, sensing everything crumbling around him, warned the States-General that, if he did not receive succor before February 4th, he was determined to capitulate.

Undoubtedly, Brussels still counted at that moment, as defense forces, 16,000 burghers and able-bodied soldiers, but what could they do against an invisible enemy, who tightened the blockade every day? Hunger drove men and women to venture out of the walls to search the fields for some food, but the men were repressed with pistols by the Spanish cavalry, and as for the women, they took them, cut their skirts up above the knees, and were thus sent back to the city, to serve as an example [(121)].

It is therefore not surprising that, by January 1585, van den Tympel had finally listened to the solicitations of a Brussels officer in the service of Farnese, Captain Johann Tserclaes, Count of Tilly,

---

118 We traced this sketch of the events of Brussels from 1578 to 1585, based on the handwritten work of M. BOUSSE, *De Calvinisten te Brussel*, a work that was done under our direction and which earned the author the degree of Doctor of Philosophy and letters.

119 See the letter from van den Tympel to Marnix, Brussels, September 27, 1584, published in the *Bulletins de la Commission royale d'histoire*, 3rd series, v. VIII, p. 335.

120 *Bulletins de la Commission royale d'histoire*, loc, cit.

121 STRADA, *o. c.*, v. IV, p. 44; MOTLEY, *o. c.*, v. I, p. 186.

garrisoned in Leuven. A follow-up correspondence was established between them, in order to clarify the conditions of surrender which Farnese would be willing to offer or accept [(122)]. Finally, van den Tympel secretly sent his secretary Boghe to Vilvoorde, where the latter met officers in the service of the Prince of Parma, Ambrosio Landriano, Fabio Mattaloni, Francesco Corradino, as well as Tserclaes himself, and the dean of Sainte-Gudule, formerly expelled from Brussels. They had demonstrated to Boghe the futility of resistance and made it clear that if the people of Brussels wanted to obtain favorable conditions, they had to refrain from submitting their own proposals and rely entirely on the discretion of the Prince [(123)]. Following this interview, van den Tympel declared himself ready, on February 11th, to send a few delegates to Farnese "to hear his goodwill and thus proceed with a treaty." [(124)]

Soon, the delegates Jean van Malcote, councilor and chancellor of Brabant, Daniel van Bombergen, Colonel of the City of Brussels, and secretary Boghe arrived at the camp of Beveren with a letter of credence. They were responsible for listening to Farnese's proposals and for obtaining the ability of presenting a reconciliation project [(125)].

The Prince of Parma, desiring to show that he was the master of the situation, did not wish to negotiate with these delegates, who had no power to treat, and demanded the dispatch of genuine plenipotentiaries [(126)]. The magistrate informed the colonels, the captains, and the members of the Council of War of the garrison, and the three superintendents of the city of the negotiations which had just opened, who then appointed their delegates with full powers. Farnese had, in the meantime, made known to them that he authorized them to present their own project of capitulation, which he reserved to discuss with them. The three superintendents of the city sent nineteen delegates to the Beveren camp, including the burgomaster Henri de Bloeyere, secretary Boghe, representatives of the Reformed Church and the Augsburg Confession [(127)]. On February 28th, the negotiations began at the

122 Letters from van den Tympel to Tserclaes, January 27 and February 1, 1585 (*Bulletins de la Commission royale d'histoire*, 3rd series, v. VIII, pp. 354-356).

123 Report from Secretary Boghe on his mission to Vilvoorde, in the *Bulletins* cited, loc. cit.

124 Letter in the *Bulletins* cited, p. 362.

125 Letter from the Governor and the magistrate of Brussels to Farnese, February 12, 1585, in the *Bulletins* cited, p. 362.

126 *Liber relationum*, f° 166 sqq.; *Libro de las cosas*, f° 374.

127 See the documents in the *Bulletins de la Commission royale d'histoire*, 3rd series, v. VIII, pp. 362-373.

headquarters of the Prince of Parma. One of the delegates spoke on behalf of all of them in French: he recalled the memory of Margaret of Parma and expressed the confidence that the inhabitants of Brussels have in the benevolence and clemency of the King and Farnese. He affirmed that they did not want to blame the Prince of Orange for their long revolt and declared that they had sinned out of simple human weakness, but that they knew that they had made themselves guilty of the crime of lèse-majesté. "We rely on your Highness," this delegate eventually says, "vanquished through your valor, which equals that of the great Alexander whose name you bear." [(128)]

Without letting himself be moved by this flattery for even a moment, Farnese addressed the delegates, among whom were found several who bore a great responsibility in the troubles which had torn Brussels apart. He insisted on clearly reminding them of this responsibility, and then, dropping his reproachful tone, he announced to them that, as they loyally recognized their fault, His Majesty the King of Spain, and he himself, accepted their return to obedience. Then he sent them back to President Richardot and secretary Garnier, with whom they had to discuss the conditions of surrender.

The discussions were extended until March 10th; the counter-propositions from the Prince of Parma seemed to be too severe or too difficult to be rigorously applied [(129)]. Eventually, they reached an agreement. The capitulation of Brussels was signed in Beveren on March 10th, 1585 [(130)].

The Prince of Parma granted the city of Brussels pardon and forgetfulness of all the crimes, wrongdoings, and excesses which had been committed there. The burghers would retake possession of all their property. The "disinheritances", done out of religious hatred, from both sides, would be broken and voided. The privileges and customs of the city would be examined by the Council of Brabant, which would give its opinion to "cut off that what would be corrupt" and to add that what would be favorable for the tranquility of the people. The burghers of the city could live there for two whole years without being wanted or troubled, and in the meantime consider

---

[128] *Liber relationum*, f° 166.

[129] See the documents in the *Bulletins de la Commission royale d'histoire*, 3rd series, v. VIII, pp. 373-405.

[130] STRADA, *o. c.*, v. IV, p. 45; *Liber relationum*, f° 167; Farnese to his father, Beveren, March 10, 1585, in A. F. N., *Carte farnesiane, Fiandra*, fasc. 1723; MOTLEY, *o. c.*, v. I, p. 186; GRIMESTON, *o. c.*, p. 875B seq.

whether they were ready to live as good Catholics. Otherwise, within this two-year term, if they wanted to remain Calvinists, they could withdraw freely, keeping the full disposition of their property. The city would not have to harbor a garrison, if political circumstances permitted it. The ruined and demolished churches would be restored, in full agreement with the magistrate. The King would retake possession of his estates, as well as the prelates, colleges, chapters, monasteries, and hospitals which had been stripped of theirs. The precious furniture and jewels of the King, formerly seized from the chapel of the palace, would be restored or the value would be paid. Reasonable satisfaction would be given to Cardinal Granvelle, the Count of Mansfeld, and other lords whose homes had been pillaged during the excesses of 1578-1579. Given the poverty of the city, Farnese renounced the payment of a ransom, contrary to what had been demanded from Ghent and other rebel cities which had surrendered (131). A special capitulation was made with the garrison, to which, although Farnese may have had "infinite opportunities for resentment" against it, very favorable conditions were granted. The soldiers were able to depart freely with their guidons and their cornets, ensigns deployed, with horses, weapons, trumpets, and drums. All the leaders, officers, captains, and soldiers would enjoy their possessions in complete freedom, provided they withdrew to neutral countries and did not bear arms against the King of Spain. Governor van den Tympel was to swear, not to fight the King for a span of six months; three other senior officers would do the same for four months, and the rest of the garrison would refrain from serving for the same period of time in Brabant or Mechelen.

Once again, it will be agreed, and perhaps more than ever, Farnese had been lenient against the rebels who came to resipiscence. It is evident that the Prince, on the one hand, had wanted to acknowledge the spontaneity with which the city had reconciled itself, without going through the contradictions and cunning which had been shown by the Ghentians, and that, on the other hand, by showing so little vindictiveness, he wanted to impress the Antwerpians and urge them not to prolong their resistance. Finally, he undoubtedly tempered his demands, because it was the capital of Bra-

---

131 We only give the main clauses. See the full text of the capitulation treaty in the *Bulletins de la Commission royale d'histoire*, 3rd series, v. VIII, pp. 405-414.

bant and the city where he could soon establish himself as Governor-General, with his Court, after the fall of Antwerp.

As soon as the Brussels garrison had left, Farnese brought into the city 1,000 Walloon and Spanish infantrymen, of which he gave command to the Seigneur de Gougnies [132]. While President Richardot and Secretary Garnier presided over the renewal of the magistrate and took steps to reorganize the judicial government, and Farnese gave orders to the State, Privy, and Finance Councils to leave Tournai and to reestablish themselves in Brussels, their former residence, Olivier van den Tympel went away, not without having sent to the delegates of the States of Brabant a long justificatory memorandum, explaining why he had returned the city to the Prince of Parma [133]. He blamed it on those who had made great promises, but who had never sent any effective succor: the States-General, the States of Brabant, and Hohenlohe and Marnix. "There were fixed limits to the defense and maintenance of oneself and those who are under his jurisdiction. We have to save life, property, and reputation against those who want to dispel or remove them by force. This effect cannot be obtained when you want to keep the cities or places hungry, for in this case, continuing the defense would bring more harm and cruelty than the enemy's offensive. Do the authors disagree that famine is one of the most unbearable torments in the world? If, to the contrary, we surrender to the enemy, life can be preserved, albeit with some inconveniences. Divine and human right has always found it more reasonable and better suited to stubbornly oppose to the bitter end. Is there not the example of the people of Israel besieged at Bethulia by Holofernes, that of the same people, surrounded by the army from Jabesh-Gilead, and shouting to King Ogbonna that it was better to remain alive and praise God, even in captivity than, languishing from famine and suffering from thirst, perish in obstinacy?"

Thus spoke, in abandoning Brussels, a former companion of the Prince of Orange, one of the last, after the defection of Chimay, Marquette, and Hembyze, to hold the flag of revolt high and firm. In turn he had gone, bowing his head under the destiny and before the military genius of the Prince of Parma.

The surrender of Brussels put an end to the military expeditions

---

[132] Farnese to the King, Beveren, March 13, 1585 (*Bulletins de la Commission royale d'histoire*, 3rd series, v. VIII, p. 419-420); STRADA, *o. c.*, v. IV, p. 116.

[133] Text published in the aforementioned *Bulletins*, pp. 420-430.

which the garrison of that city had undertaken more than once towards Dendermonde, Oudenaarde, Leuven, Diest, and Tienen, with the aim of luring Farnese's troops and thwarting the operations of the siege of Antwerp.

* * *

Another important success came to comfort Farnese, a few days after the capitulation of Brussels. The city of Nijmegen, the capital of Gelderland, was occupied on March 16th by the Spaniards under the following circumstances. The city included a States garrison, consisting of 400 infantrymen and 200 cavalrymen. Adolf van Nieuwenaar, Count of Moers, Governor of Gelderland, had resolved to increase these forces, because he was wary of the city's Catholics. Not without reason, for the latter, disgusted with the Calvinist regime, were in contact with the Baron de Hautepenne, whom Farnese had sent to this region with a good number of soldiers [134]. The primary Catholics were ready to surrender Nijmegen to the King's soldiers, but they were afraid of the Calvinists, who had the government of the place in their control. They had, however, already managed to secure the sympathies of six infantry companies and a cavalry company. Hautepenne promised to help them. He managed to bring into the city a number local gentlemen, who served in his regiment, and whose presence in Nijmegen would not arouse any suspicion: he succeeded in thus introducing, in small groups, 220 in one month. On March 16th, twenty-five of these King's soldiers, aided by the Catholic conspirators, managed to capture the Grave gate. Then, arriving with a company of harquebusiers and two companies of lancers, Hautepenne entered the city through that gate and, despite the resistance of the Calvinists and that part of the garrison which were devoted to them, completely became the master of it. Soldiers loyal to the States were sent back to their homes, but they had to abandon their weapons, horses, and baggage. A tallage was placed on the heretics and the burghers were obliged to pay double wages to the royal garrison [*].

This capture of Nijmegen was of importance for future operations in the north: it further isolated Holland and Zealand, which, from this moment on, made communications with Cologne and with

---

[134] Farnese to the magistrate of Nijmegen, Beveren, January 3, 1585 (*Correspondance de Granvelle*, v. XII, pp. 191-192).

* Compare with GRIMESTON, *o. c.*, p. 874A-D, which is somewhat different.

Germany very precarious and difficult, since the city, located on the Waal, commanded passage to the Rhine [135].

It did not take long for Farnese's soldiers to concurrently make themselves masters of Ostend. As we have said, the Prince never forgot his plan to conquer Ostend, because of the danger posed from the audacious expeditions of the Ostender garrison to the Flemish ports in his possession, as well as to the cities of Bruges and Ghent [136]. The people of Bruges had not stopped demanding protection against this peril.

Farnese put La Motte in charge of the enterprise. The latter had already been prepared by way of the erection of a fort near Ostend, where Captain Ottavio Naldini, a native of Florence, was stationed with a company of soldiers, to fend off pillagers. With the aim being an attack on Ostend, La Motte gathered into the vicinity soldiers from the garrison of Ghent, the environs of Brussels, and from the Westkwartier, in all 2,000 infantrymen and 12 cavalry companies, composed of Spaniards, Italians, and Walloons. The assault began on Friday, March 29th, at three o'clock in the morning, on the sea side, in the old town district, which appeared to be the most propitious location. Captain Naldini, who had come by sea, had disembarked his men before the town garrison had been able to intervene and had quickly taken the estacade, massacring the sentinels and the foot guards. A group of 1,200 soldiers entered into Ostend, whose garrison immediately took refuge in the fortress. La Motte had the latter under observation by 300 men under the command of the Walloon Captain Jean de Namur, and went with the Seigneur de Werp to Bruges, to search for the artillery necessary for the bombardment of the castle, located in the new town. Meanwhile, the rest of La Motte's soldiers were busy pillaging the old town. The garrison, which had taken refuge in the citadel, opened a violent fire upon them and killed a rather large number of them. Jean de Namur immediately withdrew with his men. On seeing that, the Governor of Ostend, in turn, sallied forth from the Citadel with 350 men and fell upon the Spaniards, the Italians, and

---

135 *Liber relationum*, f° 168vo; Farnese to the King, April 13, 1585 (B. N. P., Spanish MS. 182, f° 399vo); Strada, *o. c.*, v. IV, pp. 47-48; Farnese to the King, April 10, 1585 (A. G. R., *Copies de Simancas*, v. 16, non-foliated).

136 The English captain Ricards wrote to Walsingham from Ostend, on September 9, 1584, that the flat-lands were destroyed, because the Ostend garrison goes as far as 15 to 20 leagues into the territory subjected to Farnese to pillage. They burn the houses to collect the iron from the frames, which is sold in Ostend for victuals (*Foreign Calendar, Elizabeth, August 1584-August 1585*, p. 56).

the Walloons, who were engaged in pillaging. Not one of the latter resisted: it was a lamentable stampede. Thus, when La Motte arrived with his artillery, irreparable damage had been done: his soldiers had fled in all directions, and the estacade on the sea side had been taken over by the Ostenders. Four or five Spanish captains had been killed and about 1,500 soldiers ended up dead.

La Motte, in the face of this collapse of his expectations, withdrew to Oudenburg and sent the rest of his troops to their quarters. The Walloon captain responsible for the defeat was imprisoned and severely punished. Two flags of Capizucchi's Italian regiment had remained in the hands of the enemy [(137)].

This failure of Ostend did not remain isolated, as it happens so often when fortune, blindly, turns its chances: the fort of Liefkenshoek was taken over by the Prince of Parma's troops.

---

[137] Gilpin to Walsingham, Middelburg, March 21, 1584 o.s. (*Foreign Calendar, Elizabeth, August 1584-August 1585*, pp. 367-368); Farnese to the King, Beveren, April 13, 1585 (B. N. P., Spanish MS. 182, f° 399vo); The same to the same, Beveren, April 10, 1585 (A. G. R., *Copies de Simancas*, v. 16, non-foliated); *Liber relationum*, f°s 169-170; STRADA, *o. c.*, v. IV, pp. 48-49; MOTLEY, *o. c.*, v. I, pp. 186-187; GRIMESTON, *o. c.*, p. 876C-D.

CHAPTER III

THE OFFENSIVE BY THE BESIEGED AND GIAMBELLI'S "INFERNAL MACHINES"

"The patriots", wrote Motley [1], "had been sleeping, as it were, all the winter, hugging the delusive dream of French sovereignty and French assistance. No language can exaggerate the deadly effects from the slow poison of that negotiation. At any rate, the negotiation was now concluded. The dream was dispelled." [2]

Indeed, the delegation from the States-General which had left Brielle for France had been received on February 13th, 1585, at the Louvre, where King Henry III had prepared a lavish reception for them. Long negotiations commenced between the Dutch delegates and the King and Catherine de' Medici. The Dutch had first offered the sovereignty of the Netherlands to Henry III, on condition that no religion but the reformed religion should be tolerated there, that the States would be consulted for all appointments to be made, and that the King of France demand no guarantees other than the oath and the loyalty of his future subjects. Then came the offer of unconditional sovereignty. But Henry III, after much tergiversation and ma-

[1] MOTLEY, *o. c.*, v. I, p. 187.

[2] „Maar overmidts den grooten noot ende benautheit waer inne wij ons vinden, deur dien dat zedert kersmisse hier niet een schip is commen, dunckt ons eenen dach een maent te wesen, dat wij de resolutie finale [van Frankrijk] niet en hebben, de welcke wij daegelijcx zijn verwachtende met grooter devotiën" *Lancelot Parisis à Ortel, agent des Etats Généraux à Londres*, Antwerp, May 14, 1585 (*Correspondance de Granvelle*, v. XII, p. 256). — "Everybody is awaiting the result of the negotiations in France." *Fremyn to Walsingham*, Antwerp, March 5, 1585 (*Foreign Calendar, Elizabeth, August 1584-August 1585*, p. 298).

neuvering, had ultimately rejected the gift which the delegates offered him. There remained only the souvenir of this visit to France, in the form of a weighty gold chain offered by Henry III to the negotiators, and the quip from Des Pruneaux, the former agent of the Duke of Anjou: "We are frequently called on to observe that things have a great variety of times and terms. Many a man is refused by a woman twice, who succeeds the third time." (3)

At the beginning of April, the delegation from the States-General had returned to The Hague, completely empty-handed. Henry III had not dared to defy the league, which would not tolerate the giving of succors to the enemies of Catholic Spain (4). The besieged of Antwerp stood alone before the enemy, in their flooded country, amid their dikes covered with forts and redoubts, threatened by Alessandro Farnese's "diabolical" bridge. From France, nothing more was to be expected. As for Elizabeth, she continued to cautiously tack, promising succor if Antwerp held and, at the same time, trying to convince Philip II of her ardent desire for peace.

For the time being, the only thing the Antwerpians could do was rely on themselves and call for help from Holland and Zealand. But what was Admiral Treslong's fleet doing? How to explain his inaction?

Alessandro Farnese had not neglected the danger which could threaten him from that side. Although he was ignorant of the secret resolution of the Assembly of Middelburg, which had decided to send that fleet to attack the Spaniards' positions, he knew the value of the old sea-beggar who commanded it. But he also knew that Treslong did not get along with the States of Zealand, as a result of the dispute he had with Adolf van Meetkercke, and he had not waited to secretly get in touch with the admiral, trying to attract him with the lure of an advantageous situation and by way of the prospect of be-

---

3 MOTLEY, *o. c.*, v. I, pp. 95-98. Cf. J. F. LE PETIT, *o. c.*, v. II, pp. 507-509; GRIMESTON, *o. c.*, pp. 871E-873A.

4 Cf. KERVYN DE LETTENHOVE, *Les Huguenots et les Gueux*, v. VI, pp. 595-596. — « Don Bernardino escript de la cour de France que les députés des rebelles qu'estoient là soient partiz, sans avoir peu riens accorder avec les François; ce qu'estoit apparent succéderoit ainsi, estans les affaires de France aux termes que l'on sceit, et puisque les villes qu'ils ouffroient pour la sheurté de la promesse qu'ils feisoient au Roy de France d'estre donnés à luy, ne vouloient recepvoir garnison de France et touteffoys vouloient que le Roy de France se desclara de guerre ouverte en leur faveur... » *Granvelle à Marguerite de Parme*, Saragosse, April 1, 1585 (*Correspondance de Granvelle*, v. XII, pp. 29-30). See also R. FRUIN, *Mottley's geschiedenis der Vereenigde Nederlanden*, loc. cit., pp. 114 sqq.

coming a Knight of the Order of the Golden Fleece. Did Treslong intend to betray the States? The fact remains that he took a long time to equip his vessels [5].

Suspicions arose; he was removed from office by order of the States of Zealand and thrown in prison. He explained his inaction by declaring that Farnese's positions were too strong to be attacked with any success, and he added that if it were not so, they could cut off his head [6]. In order to verify these statements, two Zealand ships were sent to the Farnese bridge in reconnaissance: two Antwerpian ships, from the other side, did likewise, but the latter were captured by the Spaniards.

In place of Treslong, Justinus van Nassau, bastard son of the Prince of Orange, was put in command of the fleet.

It was reinforced with a considerable number of ships which, from the sea, the Zealanders brought into the Scheldt [7]. It was this fleet which undertook the expedition against the Spanish positions, which had been decided on the news of the failure suffered by La Motte in Ostend [8].

On April 4th, nearly 200 ships loaded with ammunition and provisions, and, embarked thereon, a considerable number of sailors and soldiers, appeared in the Scheldt and, heading towards the coast of Flanders, attacked the fort of Liefkenshoek. An enemy vessel of large dimensions began to open fire on the fort, while, from the other bank, the States' garrison which still held the fort of Lillo supported the attack by means of its artillery [9]. In less than an hour, 500 cannon shots were fired against Liefkenshoek, so that it was impossible for the defenders to hold on for long. With the landing groups having reached the Flemish dike, the Walloons who occupied the redoubts retreated and evacuated this important position. When the troops alerted by Farnese arrived from Kallo to support the defenders of

---

5 STRADA, *o. c.*, v. IV, pp. 49-50; MOTLEY, *o. c.*, v. I, pp. 149-150. "If the admiral had done his duty, more than 300 ships would have come up to Antwerp, laden with all necessaries, before the river was shut up." Fremyn to Walsingham, Antwerp, March 5, 1585 (*Foreign Calendar, Elizabeth, August 1584-August 1585*, p. 298).

6 *Libro de las cosas*, f°s 273vo-274ro.

7 STRADA, *o. c.*, v. IV, p. 50; J. F. LE PETIT, *o. c.*, v. II, p. 509 and GRIMESTON, *o. c.*, p. 875D. Treslong, set at liberty at the request of Queen Elizabeth, succeeded in justifying himself, but he was not restored to his position as admiral.

8 *Liber relationum*, f° 170.

9 «Quei che battevano da Lillo facevono maraviglioso effetto perche la distantia non era tanta che punto se ne scemasse la forza dell' artiglieria» C. CAMPANA, *Assedio d'Anversa,* p. 45).

Liefkenshoek, they found that the fort was occupied by the enemy. The danger was great, especially since the commander of the fort of Saint-Anthony, located on the counter-dike which stretched along the Doel peninsula, evacuated towards solid ground with the numerous cattle and horses which he kept as spoils of his plunders, and basely abandoned the position, without waiting for the enemy. The loss of these two forts, followed by that of Ten Oort and Ter Venten, was a formidable blow for Farnese, because the enemy gained there, by the reoccupation of the Doel, an excellent point of support to attack the bridge which barred the Scheldt and could, by launching armed boats across the flooded countryside between Doel and Kallo, seriously distress the Spanish headquarters in Beveren [(10)].

In his *Liber relationum* [(11)], Paolo Rinaldi rejects the initial fault of this failure onto the Marquis de Richebourg. It was the latter who had received from Farnese the mission of supervising all the operations on the left bank of the Scheldt, and when in July, the fort of Saint-Anthony had been taken by the soldiers of the King's army, the Marquis had been instructed to put it in order, by equipping it with flankings and surrounding it with fosses, according to a plan drawn up by the engineer Piatti. He had a summons to procure the money needed for the work, but he had appropriated the sum and had done nothing. He was not, however, punished by Farnese. The wrath of the latter fell upon the two officers who had made the forts: that of Liefkenshoek was deprived of command of his company and banished from the army, that of Saint-Anthony suffered capital punishment [(12)].

The attack on Liefkenshoek had been carried out with a remarkable boldness and spirit: it was to be, however, only a prelude to a more important and more delicate operation which, if it had succeeded, would have put the Prince of Parma's entire enterprise against Antwerp in great danger. From Liefkenshoek, the master-dike of the Scheldt, emerging alone above the flood which had come to wet its base on the Waasland side, gave access, southward, to the Farnese bridge. It had been cut at a point located a little north of the fort of Saint-Mary. The plan was for Justinus van Nassau's soldiers to fol-

---

[10] Farnese to his father, Beveren, April 13, 1585, in A. F. N., *Carte farnesiane, Fiandra*, fasc. 1725; Farnese to the King, April 13, 1585 (B. N, P., Spanish MS. 182, f° 399vo); The same to the same, April 10, 1585 (A. G. R., *Copies de Simancas*, v. 16); *Liber relationum*, f°s 170vo-171ro.

[11] F° 171vo.

[12] *Liber relationum*, f° 171ro. Cf. MOTLEY, *o. c.*, v. I, p. 189.

low the dike to that place, to erect an entrenchment, and to install artillery there: thence, they could easily and relentlessly lay cannon fire on the part of the bridge which was connected to the Flemish bank and could perhaps end up tearing it to pieces [13].

But Farnese, through brilliant intuition, had foreseen the coup. In the night that followed the loss of Liefkenshoek, he sent all the soldiers he could spare at that moment [14], accompanied by pioneers and sappers, from Kallo towards the dangerous location. At daybreak, a fort had been raised at the end of the broken dike, at the exact spot where the enemy intended to install themselves with their cannons. The approach of the estacade was thus forbidden on that side [15].

* * *

The results of the attack which had just occurred were serious. It had revealed the numerical weakness of the besieging army. In fact, the Prince of Parma had to resort to using troops stationed near Brussels and the garrison of Ghent, and had ordered a detachment of Don Juan Manrique's German regiments, garrisoned in Luxembourg, to quickly come to the rescue [16]. Then the capture of Liefkenshoek and the forts of the Doel Peninsula had caused the Spaniards to lose all the advantages they had gained from the occupation of the Antwerpian positions on the left bank. From the mouth of the Scheldt to the bridge, navigation had once again become unobstructed and Liefkenshoek was an excellent base of operation for the fleet of Justinus van Nassau [17].

In the minds of the Antwerpians, the success of the Hollander-Zealander fleet was to set off the execution of an important enterprise which they had been secretly preparing for a long time.

Within Antwerp there had been residing an Italian named Federi-

---

[13] MOTLEY, *o. c.*, v. I, pp. 188-189. Marnix of Saint-Aldegonde had given express orders on this subject written from his hand and had sent an envoy to recall the importance of this enterprise (E. VAN METEREN, *o. c.*, f° 237vo; P. BOR, *o. c.*, 2nd part, f° 596).

[14] He notably returned the soldiers he had sent in the direction of Bruges to protect that city from the enterprises of the Ostender garrison. (Farnese to the King, Beveren, April 13, 1585, in B. N. P., Spanish MS. 182, f° 399vo).

[15] Farnese to the King, Beveren, April 13, 1585 (Loc. cit.), the same to the same, Beveren, April 10, 1585 (A. G. R., *Copies de Simancas*, v. 16, non-foliated); *Liber relationum*, f° 171; C. CAMPANA, *Assedio d'Anversa*, p. 46; STRADA, *o. c.*, v. IV, p. 51.

[16] Farnese to the King, Beveren, April 10, 1585. (Loc. cit.).

[17] STRADA, *o. c.*, v. IV, pp. 51-52.

go Giambelli (18), who was born in Mantua around 1530. After acquiring great experience as a military engineer at the school of Cesare da Napoli, he had gone to Spain to offer his services and his inventions to Philip II. But he could not gain an audience with the King: he wasted his time frequenting the palace's antechambers, where chamberlains and courtiers treated him with contempt or mocked him. Finally losing his patience and with his self-esteem deeply wounded, he left Spain aboard a Dutch ship, saying that "The Spaniards would one day speak of me in a way that would make them repent for having scorned my offers." He went to Antwerp, when Farnese was preparing to besiege it. There he married and put his talents at the disposal of Marnix and the magistrate (19). Soon he proposed a plan to destroy the bridge built by the Prince of Parma, a plan which relates to the inventions devised by several Italian engineers since the late fifteenth century (20). Giambelli requested that three ships from the Antwerpian fleet be put at his disposal, the *Orange*, a ship of 150 tons, the *Gouden Leeuw* (Golden Lion), of 500 tons and the *Gulden Post* (Gilded Post), of 350 tons, which he would have transformed into exploding fire-ships in order to destroy Farnese's bridge. He also requested that he be given 60 flat-bottom passage boats, of the kind that sailed on the Scheldt and which were called *pleyten*: these vessels would have been attached to each other by cables, chains, and beams, and, after having been loaded so as to be partially submerged, would have been sent in the direction of the bridge, arranged in the shape of a half-moon. Each boat thus submerged would have carried iron cleats and grapnels, thrusting out 10 feet above the water level, and whose role would have been to sweep away the beams from Farnese's structure and make the latter collapse. The magistrate was very skeptical about the effectiveness of such a project, which had been unheard of before, and felt that the costs would be too high. But he consented to give the Italian engineer two ships, smaller than those he had requested, the *Fortune* and the *Hope*, of 70 to 80 tons, and 10 flat-bottom vessels, which were esteemed to be sufficient for the experiment (21).

---

[18] Not Gianibelli or Genibelli as he is usually known by in studies that speak of the siege of Antwerp.

[19] *Liber relationum*, f° 174vo; E. SIMION. *La priorità degli Italiani nell' invenzione delle armi subaquee. Note di storia della tecnica navale*, in the *Rivista maritima* (Rome), v. LXIV, 1931, p. 19, note 1; STRADA, *o. c.*, v. IV, pp. 52-53, MOIR, *o. c.*, p. 333, claims he went to Elizabeth of England first, who dispatched him to Antwerp.

[20] On this subject, see E. SIMION, *o. c.*, loc. cit., pp. 16 sqq.

[21] E. VAN METEREN, *o. c.*, f° 237vo; P. BOR, *o. c.*, 2nd part, f° 596.

CHAPTER III

Giambelli was disappointed, but he took all possible advantage of the modest means which he was allowed to employ. In the hold or bottom deck of each ship, along its entire length, he erected a blast chamber out of brick and mortar. He filled that chamber with a very fine gunpowder, which he had made himself, probably composed of saltpeter, sulfur, and coal, with a certain amount of camphor and ammonium salt. He covered this blast chamber with old gravestones, pieces of marble, iron hooks, stone balls, nails, and scrap metal. To cover this cluster of projectiles, he built, with large stones, a roof which converged towards a point in the shape of pyramid, so that the chamber, at the moment of its detonation, not only had an effect from bottom to top, but from all sides. The free space left between the blast chamber and the hull of each ship was filled with paving stones and beams, held together by iron cleats. The whole fabric was then covered by a smooth light flooring of planks and brick-work. In the middle of that floor, he erected a pyre made of large pieces of wood coated with pitch, which, when lit, was to make the Spaniards believe that the ships that were heading towards the bridge were mere fire-ships [(*)].

To cause the explosion of the blast chamber, the *Fortune* was equipped with an ingenious piece of clock-work, built by the Antwerpian clockmaker Jean Bory. At the appropriate time, this machinery would produce a spark igniting the blast chamber. As for the vessel *Hope*, it was equipped with a slow-match cord coated with sulfur, which would burn in such a way so as to reach the powder charge at the precise moment when the infernal machine would touch the bridge.

Giambelli equipped, in addition, 32 *pleyten*, or small flat-bottom vessels [(†)], to be simple fire-ships without powerful explosives, and which were to serve only to distract the attention of the Spaniards at the moment when the *Fortune* and the *Hope* were at the point of reaching the estacade. Other flat-bottom vessels, laden with easily flammable powder, would accompany these fire-ships, in the hope of touching the "floaters" or rafts which obstructed the access of the bridge, to ignite them, and thus to more easily deliver to the two large Infernal Machines or "hell-burners" [(22)].

---

[*] MOTLEY, *o. c.*, v. I, pp. 191-192, gives a much more detailed description of the structure.

[†] They committed 10 but agreed to 32 (P. BOR, *o. c.*, 2nd part, f° 596)

[22] E. VAN METEREN, *o. c.*, fos 237vo-238ro; STADA, *o. c.*, v. IV, pp. 53-54; E, SIMION, *o. c.*, loc. cit., pp. 22 sqq.; G. HASSE, *Les brûlots de Gianibelli*, in the *Bulletins de l'Académie royale d'archéologie de Belgique*, 1911, loc. cit.

The Offensive of the Besieged and Giambelli's "Infernal Machines"

Sea Captain Lanckhaer and ship builder Pierre Timmermans had lent their services to Giambelli; everything was ready by the beginning of April 1585.

Marnix put himself in touch with Hohenlohe and Justinus van Nassau and informed them that, on the night of April 4th, the fire-ships would leave Antwerp; for that reason, the Hollander and Zealander ships had to stand ready to immediately pass, with a convoy of food and ammunition, through the breach which Giambelli's machines would not fail to make in Farnese's bridge (23).

Therefore, on April 4th, at nightfall, Giambelli's ships were introduced into the river through the cut made in the master-dike of the right bank of the Scheldt, where the Antwerpian fort of the Boerenschans (Boor's Sconce) was opposite the Spanish fort of Saint-Peter (24). Marnix of Saint-Aldegonde and Giambelli were near fort Boerenschans to witness the departure of the flotilla, and probably also to be the first to ascertain the effect that the exploding fire-ships would produce. Indeed, from the Boerenschans to Farnese's bridge, the distance was not great and one could see from afar the glare of the explosion and perhaps measure approximately the damage it would have caused.

The Antwerpian admiral Jacob Jacobsen had been instructed to direct the dispatch of the flotilla of fire-ships as well as the *Fortune* and the *Hope* towards the bridge. He did not carry out the orders as given. Instead of successively dispatching, at half-hour intervals, the four flotillas, each composed of eight fire-ships, he sent them off together, almost at the same time. Similarly, the two "hell-burners" the *Fortune* and the *Hope*, rather than being dispatched separately, the second some interval of time after the first, both left simultaneously. When this error was noticed, which could compromise the outcome of the operation, Giambelli's fury knew no bounds and Marnix threatened Admiral Jacobsen with the gallows (25).

Yet, the Prince of Parma had not remained ignorant of what the Antwerpians were preparing. The work carried out for the expedition of the fire-ships could not have been concealed from the spies he maintained in Antwerp. In fact, some clues had aroused his attention right away (26). With a view to preparing the way for the expedition,

---

[23] STRADA, *o. c.*, v. IV, p. 52.
[24] Farnese to the King, Beveren, April 13, 1585 (Loc. cit.).
[25] E. VAN METEREN, *o. c.*, f° 238.
[26] E. SIMION, *o. c.*, loc. cit., p. 21. — The Italian military engineers did not care much about

for several days already, Antwerpian sailors had approached the estacade at night, in small and nearly invisible boats, and had cut, without anyone seeing them, the cables of the anchors which held the rafts. The latter, thus liberated, had been swept away by the flow of the river. The engineer Barocci then had the cables replaced with chains, thus making a repeat of the enemy maneuver impossible, and had the approaches to the bridge illuminated by lighting large fires on both banks of the Scheldt [27].

As far as the shortage of available troops allowed it, Farnese reinforced the garrisons of the forts established along the river, between the estacade and Antwerp, as well as the defense of the bridge itself, and installed on the latter his army's best officers. Since the attack by Justinus van Nassau against Liefkenshoek, he no longer doubted an upcoming appearance of the enemy from Antwerp.

Therefore, on the night of April 4th, when Giambelli's ships appeared in fantastic clarity from the lights on their bridge, the Spaniards were not caught off guard. The alarm was immediately given, all the soldiers ran to their posts on the bridge, in the two forts of Saint-Mary and Saint-Philipp, and in the entrenchments high on both banks of the Scheldt. The fires maintained on the order of Barocci made their cuirasses and their morions shine, and revealed their presence to the bold Antwerpian sailors who were piloting the two large "hell-burners" *Fortune* and *Hope* towards the estacade [28]. Filled with anxiety, the Spaniards waited in silence. They saw the fire-ships advancing towards them, drifting at short distances from each other, and looming behind them, the two large ships laden with explosives. They did not suspect for a single moment the terrible danger that these two vessel concealed in their flanks.

Coming up to about two thousand feet from the bridge, the sailors who had hitherto guided the flotilla's course, descended into small boats, skiffs, which had accompanied them, and abandoned the fire-ships, as well as the *Fortune* and the *Hope*, to the action of the tide, ebbing towards the sea [29]. Most of the *pleyten* or flat-bottom boats,

---

the threat posed by the ships, on the pretext that the rafts placed in front of the bridge would stop their advance and, aside from that, fires and explosives had a lesser force in the water (C. CAMPANA, *Assedio d'Anversa,* p. 45).

[27] STRADA, *o. c.*, v. IV, p. 52.

[28] STRADA, *o. c.*, v. IV, p. 55.

[29] STRADA, *o. c.*, v. IV, p. 55; *Liber relationum*, f° 171.

which were used only to distract the attention of Farnese's soldiers, eventually drifted themselves against the rafts protecting the bridge and there slowly burned out: others had drifted towards the banks of the Scheldt and grounded in the reeds and the "schorren" or marshes. From the bridge and the forts, the Spaniards had considered this spectacle with a cautious curiosity, but little by little, confidence had taken over. Suddenly, two ships larger than the others emerged from the darkness. One, the *Fortune*, had its course embarrassed and was carried to the Flemish bank, where it stopped. After some time, the clock-movement set fire to the powder, there was a loud thunder, a flash that illuminated the two banks of the river for a moment, then a column of black smoke swirling up into the sky [30].

However, the bang of the explosion, which occurred at a relatively large distance from the bridge, was scarcely heard by the Spanish soldiers, because of the noise — cries, conversations, orders issued by the captains — which had followed the anguished silence from the beginning. All the attention of the Spaniards was now fixed on the second of the great ships, which, by chance avoided the rafts and, carried by the current towards the bridge, collided with the ravelin located on the Flemish side. The principal officers, *Maestres de campo*, and colonels, who had rushed up to that place to better see what was going on, identified, through the acrid smoke which emanated from it, a wood fire, whose flames were writhing in the wind. About twenty minutes went by, without anything happening: the fire continued to burn. In the midst of a group formed by military engineers, the Marquis del Vasto, Prince Caetani, Robles de Billy, among others, and the Marquis de Richebourg laughed out loud, saying that the enemy had probably wanted to warm them up free of charge. To extinguish this fire, soldiers in the nearby boats sprang onto the deck of the Antwerpian ship, and by means of lances and pikes, tried to

[30] *Liber relationum*, f° 171; Farnese to the King, Beveren, April 13, 1585 (Loc. cit.); The same to the same, April 10, 1585 (Loc. cit.). — Alessandro Farnese, in his letters to the King, spoke of *four* ships whereas Paolo Rinaldi, in his *Liber Relationum*, spoke of *three*. However, it appears, from the testimony of Bor and van Meteren, historians of the States-General, and therefore better able to know what the Antwerpians did, that there were only two ships; the *Hope* and the *Fortune*. Farnese's and Rinaldi's error can be explained by the fact that, among the flat-bottom boats used as fire-ships, there were several that also carried a light charge of powder, which was only to explode at the last minute. It was the explosion of some one, two, or three, of these *pleyten*, which would have made Farnese and Rinaldi believe that there were four "infernal machines" instead of two. Cf. SIMION, *o, c.*, loc. cit., p. 23 and the article by G. Hasse, already cited.

extinguish the pyre by causing it to collapse or dispersing the flaming pieces of wood. Those unfortunate men! They did not know that they were hastening the onset of the catastrophe; their actions, in fact, had the effect of hastening the transmission of fire to the blast chamber.

Alessandro Farnese, who had gone in the direction of the right bank of the Scheldt to examine whether everyone was at his post and ready for any eventuality, returned at that moment toward the left bank, and also stopped, out of curiosity, to look at, from the top of the parapets of the ravelin, the mysterious ship. He was busy exchanging his reflections with Richebourg and de Billy, when a Spanish *alférez* (standard-bearer) named Vega approached. The latter was well versed in mathematics and practiced engineering work during his leisure time. As he was an acquaintance of Farnese, he approached the latter and urged him not to stay in that location. The Prince refused to leave. Should he not, in these critical moments, remain amongst his men? Vega respectfully entreated him again to withdraw. Farnese, becoming impatient, dismissed him. But the *alférez* clung to his leader's heels, following him everywhere, ceaselessly preaching prudence to him. "Every bomb", he said, "is diabolical, their effects are never known in advance: do we know what the latter hides from us?" But the Prince mocked him. Then, abandoning all reserve and any mark of respect, the officer began to shout and protest loudly. This strange insistence eventually impressed the entire entourage of the Prince of Parma and most of the Lords present added their insistences with that of Vega. This time, as though moved by an inexplicable foreboding, Farnese yielded. He made his way towards the fort of Saint-Mary, followed by the Marquis del Vasto and some other officers. That was his salvation.

Indeed, scarcely had he moved away when the bomb, hidden in the flanks of the *Hope*, detonated amidst a horrible noise. Immense flames erupted forth, illuminating the area within a radius of several leagues. In a flash which had a supernatural appearance, one could see, for an instant, the forts, bridge, boats, riverbanks of the Scheldt, and even the fantastic silhouettes of distant half-flooded villages. The earth trembled, with a thud that seemed to propagate like thunder beneath the feet of the terrified soldiers. The waters of the river were cast into whirling columns and a kind of tidal wave swept over the

N
P
L
O
F
O
D
DERROTA DEL PUENTE FARNESE
A. Alexandro Farnese. àpartado del Riesgo porun alferez
èspañol. B. eldel Vasto. C. elalferez. D. St Maria. E. Caè
tano. F. navio defuego. que derroto. elpuente. G. Capitan
Tuci. H. navo defuego quesefue apique. I. dos navos. que
abortaron ala Orilla. K. naves conluminarias. L. el
Vizconde de Bruselas. M. vn soldado dela guardia.
de Alexandro. N. St Phelipe. O. destrozos del puente.
P. jente que entro desocorro alpuento para con
ponerlo accionque admiro atoda europa. R. d. Hooge: fec.

THE EXPLOSION PRODUCED BY GIAMBELLI'S "INFERNAL MACHINE"
Engraving by R. de Hooghe,
according to master engineer Ledesma.

forts of both banks, carrying away everything and flooding the Spanish positions. It seemed to the witnesses of the scene that for an instant they could see in the depths the very bed of the Scheldt. They claimed to have seen the water of the river, mixed with a flow of flaming fire, like molten lead, invade the riverbank and burn all those who were in its path. The gravestones, marble slabs, scrap metal, flagstones, and beams accumulated by Giambelli in his infernal machine were hurled in all directions and went to cause death among the garrison of the estacade and the forts. Cannon balls, chains, iron bars, and pikes were found buried in the countryside at a quarter of a league's distance from the point of the explosion [31].

The effect was disastrous with regard to the estacade. The wooden ravelin, where, a moment before, the Prince of Parma had found himself, was completely smashed: nails and chains, violently ripped off, flew into the air, the railing was pulverized, the deck planks sprang up, the large timbers supporting the latter, more than thirty in number, were knocked over or ripped from the bed of the Scheldt. Four pieces of heavy artillery were launched into the air and disappeared; four ships stationed near the bridge caught fire and sank with their crews, two others were destroyed. The swells of water capsized several boats and dropped the occupants and cannons that were thereon into the river.

Several officers had been thrown into the air by the tremendous concussion and fell back into the waters of the Scheldt or onto the riverbanks. Some, like the Viscount of Brussels, Jacques de Boussu, and Captain Tucci, miraculously escaped death. It was not the same with the Marquis de Richebourg and Robles de Billy, who both lost their lives in this catastrophe. Both had disappeared in the explosion: the corpse of Richebourg was not found until several days later, wrapped around an iron chain that hung from one of the boats of the bridge in the middle of the river; the remains of Robles de Billy were not identified until after the surrender of Antwerp, literally clinging to the timber-work of the estacade. They were recognized by the presence of a peculiar gold chain which Robles habitually wore.

---

[31] The *contador* Antonio Carnero, who was at the camp of Beveren, attests in his book *Historia de las guerras civiles...*, p. 191, the following: «No huvo naydie que no se aturdiese en espacio de dos millas. Y es cierto, porque yo lo vi que estava en Beveren que la casa en que alojava tiembló y las vedrieras de las ventanas se rompieron todas con tan gran estruendo que pensamos que toda la casa venta al suelo, al modo de quando en Granada tiembla la terra».

Between half-past one and two o'clock in the morning, one heard only the cries and lamentations of the wounded, crushed under the fallen material, mutilated by the explosion, or about to drown in the waters of the river [(32)].

In his letters to the King, the Prince of Parma shows as casualties only 300 dead and 150 wounded, but Alonso Vasquez and Captain Tucci, both present when the disaster occurred, claim that the number of dead reached 800, not counting the wounded and the maimed [(33)], which seems more likely.

The Prince of Parma himself did not come away from this adventure entirely unscathed. He had barely reached the front door of fort Saint-Mary when the "hell-burner" exploded. He was hit in the head and on various parts of his body by pieces of wood, stones, and other projectiles that fell down around him. The boiling water completely ruined the new clothes he had donned that day. "The gold of his uniform was like bronze: it looked like he had passed through fire", said Paolo Rinaldi, who was present at the scene [(34)]. The Marquis del Vasto, who accompanied Farnese, afraid of being swallowed up by the waves of the river that swept through the fort, firmly grabbed the Prince and clung to him until the moment when he felt safe [(35)].

After remaining stunned for few moments from the blows he received, Farnese regained his senses [(36)]. His first concern was to take a look at the bridge: he noticed with horror that the entire estacade from the Flemish bank had been destroyed, as well as the first three boats in the series that barred the middle of the river [(37)]. The dam-

[32] The description we have given of the effects of Giambelli's infernal machine is not from the imagination, but is based on the testimonies of eye-witnesses like Farnese, Paolo Rinaldi, etc. We used and closely followed the letters written by the Prince of Parma to the King, dated April 10 and 13, 1585 (Loc. cit.), the *Liber relationum* by Rinaldi (f[os] 171-174), verifying it against Strada (*o. c.*, v. IV, pp. 57-61), who used Farnese's letters and a report from Captain Tucci, C. CAMPANA, *Assedio d'Anversa* (pp. 47-51) and the story by Alonzo Vasquez in his *Sucesos...*, loc. cit., pp. 28 sqq. See also Davison's letter to Walsingham, The Hague, April 3, 1584 (sic) o.s., in *Foreign Calendar, Elizabeth, August 1584-August 1585*, p. 398. Cf. MOTLEY, *o. c.* v. I, pp. 192-197; MOIR, *o. c.*, pp. 335-342.

[33] STRADA, *o. c.*, v. IV, p. 59; ALONSO VASQUEZ, *Los sucesos*, loc. cit., p. 29.

[34] *Liber relationum*, f[o] 172[vo]. «Io posso dir per vederla...» said Rinaldi; C. CAMPANA, *Assedio d'Anversa,* p. 49.

[35] *Ibid.*

[36] Philip II reproached him, in a letter from May 28, for having again so boldly exposed his person, contrary to the repeated advice he had given him about it (*Correspondance de Granvelle*, v. XII, pp. 278 sqq.)

[37] Farnese to the King, April 10, 1585 (Loc. cit.).

age seemed irreparable, especially since the Hollander-Zealander fleet stationed in Lillo, which probably had to act in concert with the Antwerpians, could come at any moment and try to pass through the breach.

However, from the Boerenschans where they were, Marnix and Giambelli, their hearts full of anguish, had watched with their eyes the fire-ships which slowly descended the river and the two large ships loaded with explosives that followed them. They had seen them pass the fort of Saint-Peter and head straight for the bridge. Then they had glimpsed the fantastic flash of the explosion and they had felt, under their feet, the earth trembling. Was Farnese's bridge destroyed, as Giambelli had thought he could prophesize?...

They would soon find out. Indeed, it had been understood that the flagship of the Antwerpian Fleet would dispatch a fast boat to the site of the explosion to see the effect of the infernal machine. If they found the bridge opened by way of a breach, the men who manned the boat were to, on firing a rocket into the air, move at full speed through the opening thus made and quickly get to Lillo in order to notify Justinus van Nassau on the measures to be taken.

As soon as he saw the rocket announcing their success, the Antwerpian flagship would notify all the other ships by way of a cannon shot, which would be the signal of a general attack, on both the Antwerp side and the Lillo side. However, the sailors sent as scouts were so frightened by the noise of the explosion and the sight of the phenomena which accompanied it, that they did not dare to venture far enough: they returned in great haste without seeing anything and announced that no result had been obtained [(38)].

This explains the inaction of the Antwerpian ships and Lillo's fleet, at a time when victory had seemed to be near. Justinus van Nassau, having not seen any rockets and deprived of specific news, did not dare advance. It was the same with Admiral Jacobsen. That's what saved the Spaniards.

Farnese, quite astonished not to see the enemy fleet appear, immediately took measures in order to repair, in semblance at least, the damage caused. Deprived of the presence of Richebourg and that of Robles de Billy, he exerted himself more than ever in person. Without losing his head for even a moment, he had barracks prepared to hos-

---

[38] E. van Meteren, *o. c.*, f° 238; J. F. Le Petit, *o. c.*, pp. 511-512; Grimeston, *o. c.*, pp. 875E-876C.

pitalize the wounded, and he sent a number of boats onto the Scheldt to remove those who were about to drown from the water. He dispatched two galliots in the direction of Lillo and another two in the direction of Antwerp: through them he knew that no enemy ships from either side seemed to be preparing for an immediate attack. Temporarily reassured on this side, he summoned all the men he at his disposal, assigned them each a position on what remained of the bridge as well as in the forts, and had artillery put in position to counter the enemy if he presented himself. After having installed Karl von Mansfeld in place of the now deceased Richebourg, he ordered all the tradesmen to be at the bridge at daybreak and had the necessary materials brought in order to replace those which had been destroyed. By dawn, he had new piles driven into the riverbed, chained them together, nailed the beams, put the floorboards back, replaced the boats which had disappeared, and brought in large-caliber artillery. Under his energetic leadership, everyone put so much zeal and ardor thereto that, on April 5th, at noon, everything was again in order. The work ended with the replacement of the protective rafts which had been smashed: the Prince had, this time, added a second line in case the enemies were to risk another attack [(39)].

Of course, one should not imagine for a moment that Farnese succeeded in rehabilitating, in one night and one morning, a bulwark for which the construction had required months: the hasty repair which had just been done had, at least, the effect of rendering, more or less, a primitive silhouette of the bridge. That was what mattered most, to deceive the enemy, who, from a distance, could not ascertain that the reconstructed part did not have the same strength and perfection as the one which had been destroyed by Giambelli's machine [(40)].

It was not until three days afterward that a sailor, who was expressly sent by Count Hohenlohe, managed, by swimming for a few meters under water, to pass under the bridge and ascertain how much damage had been inflicted by the *Hope* [(41)]. The Hollanders stationed in Lillo then understood what a great opportunity to strike a decisive blow to the Spaniards they had let escape [(42)].

---

39 *Liber relationum*, f[os] 174-175; Farnese to the King, April 13, 1585 (Loc. cit.).

40 STRADA, *o. c.*, v. IV, pp. 63-64; C. CAMPANA, *Assedio d'Anversa*, p. 50.

41 E. VAN METEREN, *o. c.*, f° 238.

42 [Note 42 was skipped or overlooked in the original] Cf. MOTLEY, *o. c.*, v. I, pp. 200 sqq.

The Offensive of the Besieged and Giambelli's "Infernal Machines"

In the ignorance of what had happened, the Antwerpians were satisfied on the morning of April 5th to attempt an attack on the Spanish fort of Saint-Sebastian, located at the Melsele Lock (Melson Sluys), on the left bank of the Scheldt, opposite the Boerenschans [43]. Their aim was probably to make themselves masters of that position so as to follow the Scheldt master-dike to the north and to assail the fort of Saint-Mary and the estacade.

Educated from the experience of what had happened at Liefkenshoek, Farnese had taken his precautions. He had immediately sent a Spanish light cavalry company, which was stationed at the Beveren headquarters, to be succors for the Walloon garrison, which occupied the Saint-Sebastian fort. The position was first attacked by a flotilla consisting of a large three-masted ship equipped with heavy artillery and some other lighter vessels. The cannon fire from the great ship inflicted considerable damage to the fort: however, the enemy did not attempt to disembark. It was not until the evening that boats brought in Antwerpian soldiers, who strove to make themselves masters of the dike. The intervention of the cavalry dispatched by Farnese, however, forced the assailants to hurriedly return to their flotilla [44].

There arrived that same night the soldiers whom the Prince had sent in the direction of Bruges, and who had been ordered to return on forced marches, as well as 1,000 of Don Juan Manrique's infantrymen, all excellent soldiers. Finally, at Stabroek, appeared at the same time several cornets of light cavalry which the Commissioner General of that arm had brought from The Campine [45]. Farnese was very happy about this, but these weak reinforcements were insufficient to face the dangers which were threatening from all sides. "I do not have enough soldiers," he wrote to Philip II, "neither to defend me nor to attack. For want of men, we're not able to occupy all the positions which would be necessary to hold for the enterprise of Antwerp. What distresses me the most is to see the suffering of the poor Spanish soldiers, who are already so few here. If reinforcements are not sent to me, I have reason to fear much." [46]

---

43 *Ibid.* (to note 41?).

44 Farnese to the King, April 13, 1585 (Loc. cit.); The same to the same, April 10, 1585 (Loc. cit.); ALONSO VASQUEZ, *Los sucesos...*, loc. cit., pp. 27-28.

45 *Ibid.*

46 Letter of April 13, 1585 (Loc. cit.).

Since the disaster caused by Giambelli's machines, the Prince also expected the appearance of other diabolical devices, but his fears did not come to be realized. On two occasions, the Admiral of the fleet stationed in Lillo sent boats loaded with explosives against the bridge, but they had no effect. Farnese had organized a watchful vigil and patrolled the Scheldt with vedettes manned with soldiers. The latter, armed with long iron bars, had the task of intercepting these fire-ships as they passed and to impress upon their rudder a movement which directed them towards the banks of the river. Those incendiary machines which managed to get through were stopped by the pikes of the rafts arranged in front of the bridge and exploded without causing much damage [(47)]. This method obviously gave no further result: the enemy had to consider another plan to get rid of Farnese's bridge or to mitigate its effects.

It was then that they conceived the project of making themselves master of the Kouwenstein dike [(48)].

---

[47] Ibid.; *Liber relationum*, f° 176.

[48] *Liber relationum*, f° 176.

CHAPTER IV

THE BATTLE OF KOUWENSTEIN

It will be remembered that, not so long ago, the Prince of Orange had advised the piercing of the Blauwgaren dike so as to cause the waters of the Scheldt to penetrate into the region which extended to the north of Antwerp and thus immerse the Kouwenstein counter-dike in such a way that shallow draught vessels could easily pass over it and get to the city. With Farnese having installed himself on the Kouwenstein dike and having fortified it, the plan of the Prince of Orange had to be abandoned. However, after the failure of Giambelli's attempt, the Antwerpians imagined attacking the counter-dike, in concert with the fleets of Justinus van Nassau and Hohenlohe, to take control of it and pierce large openings in several locations, so as to give passage to Hollander and Zealander ships loaded with ammunition and victuals.

This project was soon known to Farnese, and he communicated it to Philip II [1]. He had been suspecting the existence of this plan for a long time. In fact, when the butchers of Antwerp had previously been so vehemently opposed to piercing the Blauwgaren dike, Hendrik Tseraarts, Heer van Kouwenstein, owner of the castle of that name which stood not far from the dike, had joined his authority with that of Marnix to follow the advice of the Prince of Orange.

[1] «Que es el que mas les deule por la comodidad que apoderándose del y cortandole, a que pare ce va dirigido su designio principal, ternian de meter la ribera por alli en su madre vieja de cuando pasaba por Brabante, y asi podrian ir por ella hasta Amberes los navios que quisiasen y quedar nuestra obra de la ribera infructuosa». (Farnese to the King, Beveren, May 6, 1585, in A. G. R., *Copies de Simancas*, v. 16, non-foliated); *Liber relationum*, f° 177.

Since then the butchers had pursued that lord with such a tenacious hatred that he was obliged to leave the city. He took refuge at the camp of the Prince of Parma [2]. He probably did not neglect to let Farnese know what Marnix's plans had been. Moreover, when Téligny had been taken prisoner during an expedition on the Scheldt, before surrendering he had thrown papers which he was carrying on him into the water. These documents were retrieved by the Spaniards, who found therein the explanation of the maneuver by which the counter-dike would be pierced [3].

The Prince of Parma was therefore sufficiently aware of the existence of this plan, but he did not know when the enemy would set about realizing it [4]. At the end of April, 1585, multiple clues came to reveal that the moment had arrived. "The rebels will make a last effort by land and water:" he wrote to the King on the date of April 29th, "by cutting parts of the dike, they have extended the flood, they make bright signals almost without ceasing, they concentrate their warships, on both the Antwerp side and the Lillo side, and small boats loaded with soldiers come and go in the flooded region. In the islands of Zealand, the enemy has recruited a large number of sappers. They are consolidating their cavalry and infantry. Their main effort will be against the dike of Stabroek (Kouwenstein)." [5]

However, the moment was tragic for the "royalists". The soldiers were exhausted from continuously being on alert, especially the Spaniards, upon whom the heaviest burden of the campaign fell. The Italians were only a small number. The Walloons, as they were accustomed to, deserted in small bands. The Germans had suffered a lot of casualties in terms of killed and wounded. Half of the cavalry was forced to fight on foot. Deserters fled to France, where they enlisted in the service of the Catholic League: the countryside over there was richer and a soldier there enjoyed more freedom than in Farnese's army. As a result, the latter kept harassing Philip II with requests for reinforcements and sending him letters whose tone were desperate. He had, however, received with demonstrations of joy the paymaster-general of the Spanish army, Juan de Lastur, who had ar-

---

[2] J. F. LE PETIT, *o. c.*, p. 503; GRIMESTON, *o. c.*, p. 866C-D.

[3] J. F. LE PETIT, *o. c.*, p. 503; GRIMESTON, *o. c.*, p. 866B.

[4] See the letter by J. V. Delft, well informed of what was happening in Antwerp, to Colonel Mondragón, Ekeren, March 13, 1585 (*Correspondance de Granvelle,* v. XII, p. 253).

[5] Farnese to the King, Beveren, April 29, 1585 (B. N. P., Spanish MS. 182, f° 402vo).

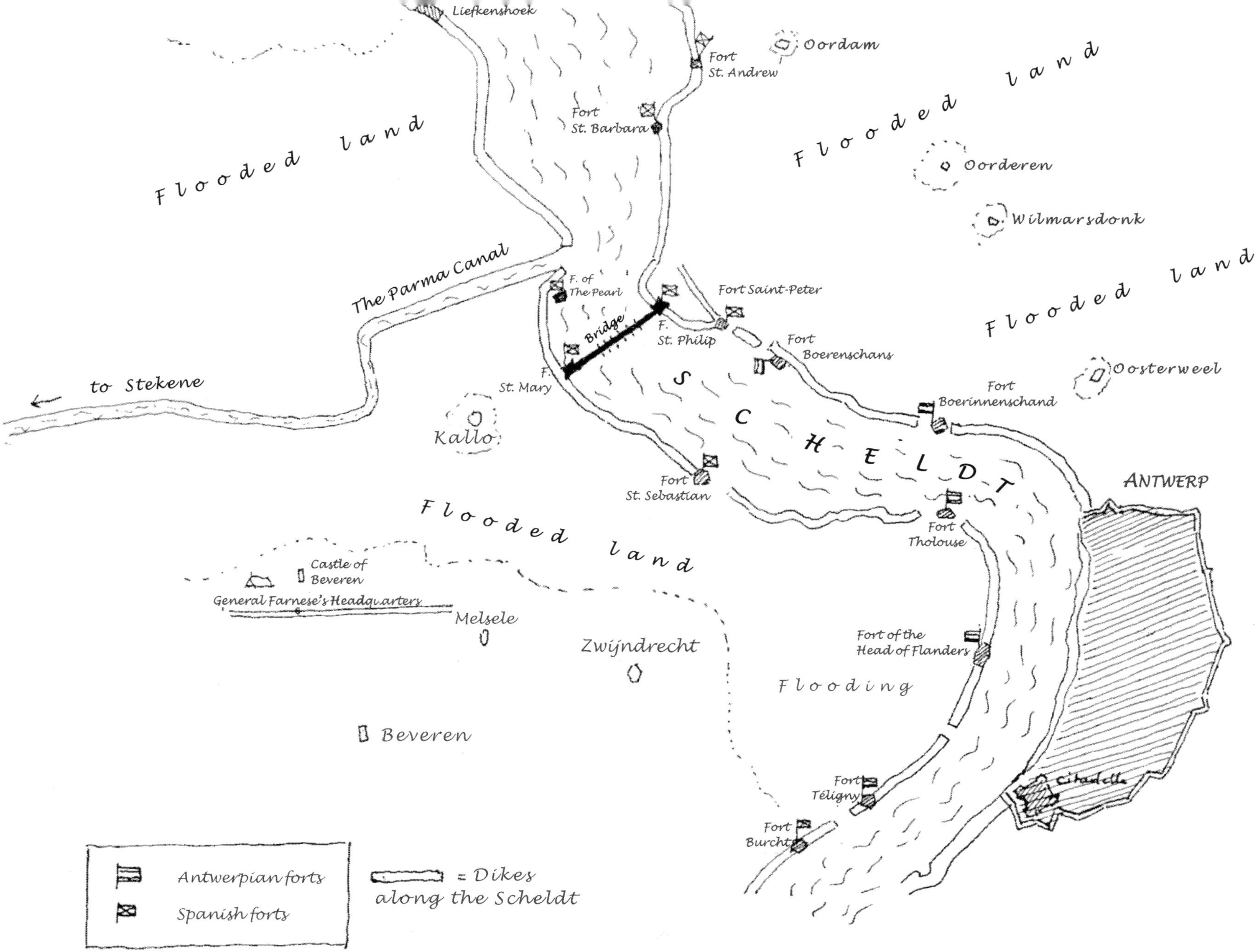
Liefkenshoek
Oordam
Fort St. Andrew
Fort St. Barbara
Flooded land
Flooded land
Oorderen
Wilmarsdonk
Flooded land
The Parma Canal
F. of The Pearl
Bridge
Fort Saint-Peter
F. St. Philip
Fort Boerenschans
F. St. Mary
to Stekene
Oosterweel
Fort Boerinnenschand
SCHELDT
Kallo
Fort St. Sebastian
ANTWERP
Fort Tholouse
Flooded land
Castle of Beveren
General Farnese's Headquarters
Melsele
Zwijndrecht
Fort of the Head of Flanders
Flooding
Beveren
Citadella
Fort Téligny
Fort Burcht
Antwerpian forts
Spanish forts
= Dikes along the Scheldt

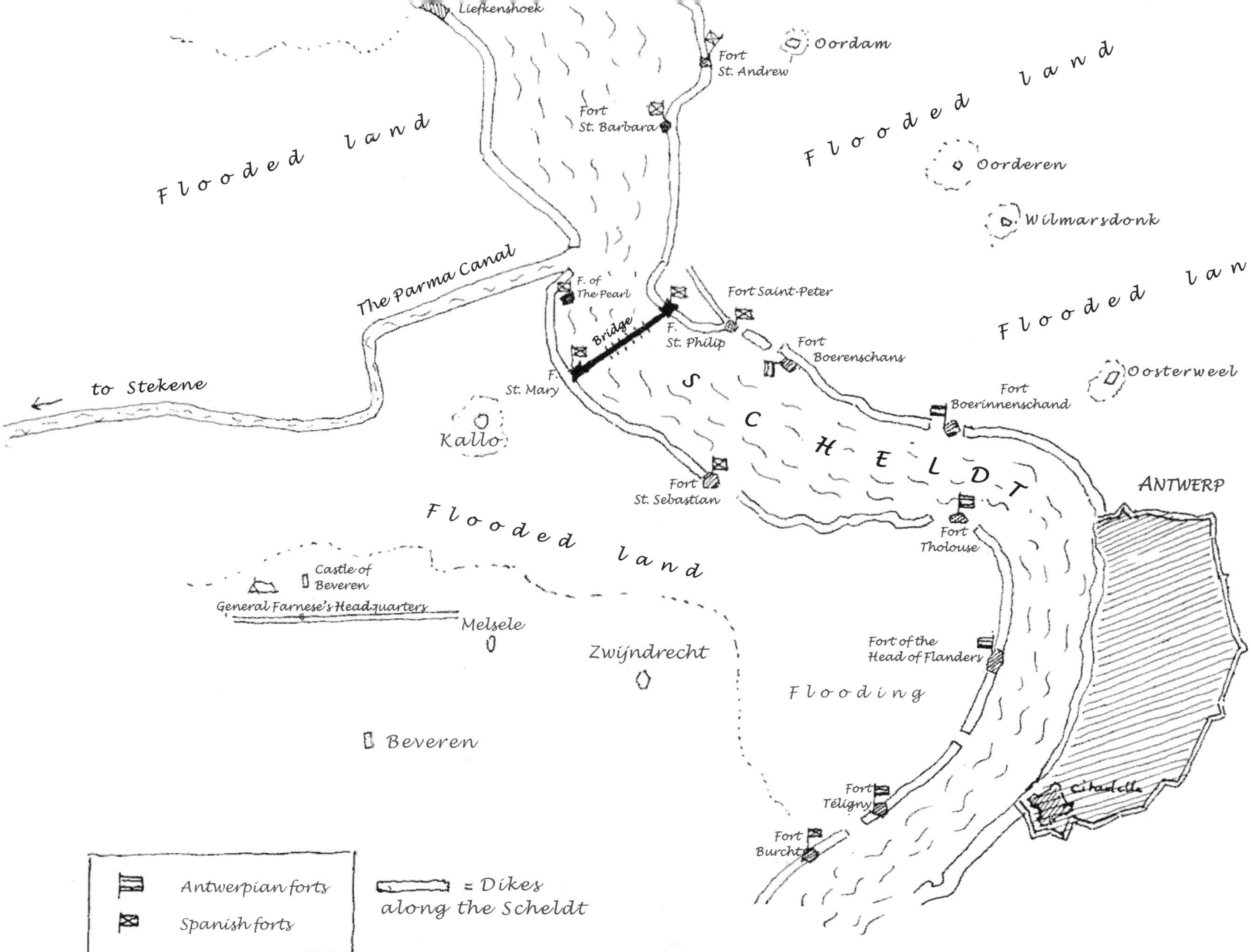
Liefkenshoek
Oordam
Fort
St. Andrew
Fort
St. Barbara
Flooded land
Flooded land
Oorderen
Wilmarsdonk
Flooded land
The Parma Canal
F. of
The Pearl
Fort Saint-Peter
Bridge
F.
St. Philip
Fort
Boerenschans
F.
St. Mary
to Stekene
Oosterweel
Fort
Boerinnenschand
SCHELDT
Kallo
Fort
St. Sebastian
ANTWERP
Fort
Tholouse
Flooded land
Castle of
Beveren
General Farnese's Headquarters
Melsele
Zwijndrecht
Fort of the
Head of Flanders
Flooding
Beveren
Fort
Téligny
Citadella
Fort
Burcht
Antwerpian forts
Spanish forts
= Dikes
along the Scheldt

rived bearing 200,000 ECU. But what did this sum represent, in the midst of the almost inextricable difficulties in which, with increasing urgency every day, the Prince of Parma was struggling? (6)

Concealing the anguish which had seized him from his officers and his men, Farnese had quickly made the necessary arrangements to deal with the great enemy attack which he foresaw (7). He had first replaced the officers who had perished during the explosion of Giambelli's machine: Alfonso Félix de Ávalos Aquino y Gonzaga, Marquis del Vasto, succeeded Richebourg as the chief commander of the cavalry, and the administration of the defense of the bridge and everything related thereto was entrusted to Karl von Mansfeld (8). Farnese further reinforced the Kouwenstein dike by adding three new entrenchments and, in anticipation of being able to deliver a battle there, widened it on both sides. He drove piles on the Lillo side and the Antwerp side, some distance from the dike, and joined them together with solid chains and wooden beams, so as to completely immobilize them. On these piles, he nailed deck planks, which formed a floor where soldiers could easily move about.

Leaving Karl von Mansfeld to guard the bridge over the Scheldt, the Prince of Parma quartered for some time in Stabroek, to there give the necessary instructions. Without taking any rest, the Prince was constantly traveling between Stabroek and Kallo, inspecting the defenses of the bridge over the Scheldt and those of the Kouwenstein dike, so as not to leave any chance of being surprised by the enemy (9). "There is not one of us who sleeps at night," he wrote to the King, "there is no officer nor soldier who is not perpetually mounting guard, and who does not constantly keep his weapon in his hand." (10)

* * *

However, in early May, Marnix and the leaders of Lillo's fleet had agreed to launch an attack against the dike. The Hollander-

---

[6] Farnese to the King, Beveren, May 6, 1585 (A. G. R., *Copies de Simancas*, v. 16, non-foliated).

[7] Farnese to his mother, Beveren, April 26, 1585, in A. F. N., *Carte farnesiane, Fiandra*, fasc. 1676.

[8] *Liber relationum*, f°s 44vo-44ro; STRADA, *o. c.*, v. IV, p. 66; A. VASQUEZ, *Los sucesos...*, loc. cit., p. 53. I believe van der Essen erroneously named him Giovanetto di Pescara, Marquis del Vasto. The latter was the Marquis of Pescara when he was a young man, his moniker being Giovanetto di Pescara, "little Pescara." That changed in 1571.

[9] *Liber relationum*, f°s 176vo-177ro; C. CAMPANA, *Assedio d'Anversa*, pp. 53-54.

[10] Beveren, May 6, 1585 (Loc. cit.).

Zealander fleet of 150 ships was divided into two parts. One, under the leadership of the Count of Hohenlohe, penetrated through a cut in the Scheldt dike, a little below Lillo, into the flooded countryside extending to the north of Kouwenstein. The other part of the fleet, commanded by Justinus van Nassau, was maneuvering in the Scheldt, pretending, sometimes heading towards the Flemish bank, sometimes towards the Brabantian bank, or navigating straight towards Farnese's bridge. Hohenlohe's men sometimes pointed their cannons at fort Holy Cross, sometimes towards the Kouwenstein dike, causing, in this manner, the defenders of these positions to be in a continual state of alertness. The enemy intended to thereby exhaust the Spaniards and induce them, as a result of fatigue, to relax their surveillance. Soon they believed to have achieved this goal: Farnese's soldiers were running with less readiness to their battle stations and were giving the impression of reacting more slowly to each renewed threat from the enemy [11].

Hohenlohe notified Marnix. The latter went to the fort called Thoulouse, located on the left bank of the Scheldt, north of the *Tête de Flandres*, there to prepare for the expedition. The signal for the Lillo ships to attack was to be given from the top of the tower of the Cathedral of Antwerp, by way of three successive rockets, which would be lit when Marnix had given the agreed beacon fire from the fort of Thoulouse. Those who had been in charge of the signals were momentarily absent: their replacements, lacking precise instructions, on the night of May 6th to 7th, mistook a bivouac fire on the bank of the river for the signal from Marnix and hastened to notify Lillo's fleet.

At once, Hohenlohe, who was but waiting for this moment, sent his ships off and, under cover of darkness, headed towards the Kouwenstein dike [12].

At the break of day, the enemy ships landed at a point on the dike between fort Saint-George and the fort of the Palisades. The Spanish sentinels, fatigued from long nights of vigil, had fallen asleep. The first group of Hohenlohe's soldiers who leaped onto the dike sur-

---

[11] STRADA, *o. c.*, v. IV, pp. 69-70.

[12] E. VAN METEREN, *o. c.*, f° 238vo. — « Il n'y a personne en Anvers qui puisse ignorer, que lors que cette notable faute se commit des trois signaux de feu, faicte à la tour de Nostre Dame, qui fust cause que ceux d'Hollande et de Zélande assaillirent la dicque de Couwensteyn, sans estre secondez de nous... ». MARNIX DE SAINTE-ALDEGONDE, *Brief récit de l'estat de la ville d'Anvers...*, loc. cit., p. 249.

prised them in their sleep and massacred them. At the sound of the clatter of arms, a group of Spaniards came out of the forts, but did not have time to attack: the captain and the sergeant were killed, and the rest of the troops fled behind the entrenchments. Hohenlohe's men had already occupied a portion of the dike, and other troops were preparing to leap from the ships, where they numbered more than 2,000, when the Spanish captains Ortiz and San Juan Verdugo, and Commander Gamboa came running with their men from the nearest forts. A savage melee ensued, while the artillery of the Spanish redoubts of Kouwenstein opened up on the enemy vessels without respite.

With the Spaniards having carried out an irresistible charge, the enemy eventually yielded and fled to the ships, leaving 40 killed. One hundred and fifty men drowned while trying to swim back to their ships. Three or four galliots loaded with soldiers were sunk by the artillery from the forts [(13)].

On the dike, the enemy abandoned numerous sandbags and wool filled sacks, and instruments used by pioneers and sappers, shovels and picks, in short, all the equipment intended to retrench hastily and to proceed with piercing the counter-dike [(14)].

The enterprise had failed: the Antwerpians, whose fleet Farnese had however watched be tidied up in good order and abundantly furnished with soldiers [(15)], had not budged, though not suspecting that Hohenlohe, deceived by the signals from the cathedral tower, had gone on the attack.

Though he had been able to remain doubtful until then, this time the Prince of Parma realized the exact intentions of the enemy: "Their plan was", he wrote to the King, "to pierce the narrow rampart of the counter-dike and to open a pathway to navigation, thus making our bridge on the Scheldt totally useless." [(16)] It was obvious that the enemy would repeat his attempt. So Farnese reinforced the

---

[13] Captain Asseliers writes from Antwerp to Walsingham on May 8 that the people of Hohenlohe had lost about 200 men (*Foreign Calendar, Elizabeth, August 1584-August 1585*, p. 438); Motley, *o. c.*, v. I, p. 209.

[14] Farnese to his father, Beveren, May 25, 1585, in A. F. N., *Carte farnesiane, Fiandra*, fasc. 1725; Farnese to the King, Beveren, May 23, 1585 (B. N. P., Spanish MS. 182, f° 403); The same to the same, May 25, 1585 (A. G. R., *Copies de Simancas*, v. 16, non-foliated. This letter is published in the *Correspondance de Granvelle*, v. XII, pp. 271 sqq.); *Liber relationum*, f° 177; Strada, *o. c.*, v. IV, p. 70; Captain James (?) to Walsingham, April 29 (?) 1585 (*Foreign Calendar, Elizabeth, August 1584-August 1585*, p. 439).

[15] Letters cited in the previous note.

[16] Letter of May 23, 1585, cited.

redoubts on the dike, equipped them with numerous artillery, and placed therein garrisons of hand-picked soldiers. He had established a series of closely-driven barrier-forming piles skirting the Kouwenstein dike, on the Antwerp side and on the Lillo side, in order to prevent large vessels from approaching it. The Prince also carefully noted all the early warning signs of a new assault: fires lit, signals exchanged between Hohenlohe's fleet and that of the Antwerpians, the ships of both squadrons arranged in order of battle, the departure of Marnix's soldiers, abandoning the redoubts and the forts, for a new destination, and preparations for new incendiary devices. All the officers of the Spanish army were of the opinion that they could expect a general attack on the counter-dike, going hand in hand with a new expedition of fire-ships against the bridge barring the Scheldt [(17)].

They didn't have to wait long. On Monday, May 20th, after midnight, taking advantage of the wind and the tide, the Antwerpians launched 17 flat-bottom vessels in the direction of the bridge, loaded with heavy materials and linked to each other with chains, with the goal of breaking and smashing the protective rafts and opening a pathway for vessels loaded with explosives. Farnese immediately sent out galliots and boats manned with soldiers armed with anchors and iron harpoons. At the same time, the fort of Saint-Sebastian opened fire on the enemy flotilla. Some of the *pleyten*, driven by the very violent current of the Scheldt, jostled or smashed the rafts and came to rest against the bridge, which they damaged in certain locations. Behind them appeared the "infernal machines." To avoid exposing his men to danger, the Prince of Parma quickly opened the center of the bridge, removing three of the boats that were anchored there. One of the "infernal machines" passed like an arrow through the opening thus practiced: harpooned by the Spanish sailors, it was pulled through the cut in the Kallo dike until it was in the flooded countryside, where they could leisurely examine the secret which it bore in its flanks. The other five machines ran aground on the Brabantian bank before arriving at the bridge and exploded there, without any damage [(18)].

---

[17] *Ibid.*; Letter of May 25, 1585, cited; *Relaçion del successo del domingo 26 de mayo y martes 28 de mayo 1585* (B. N. P., Spanish MS. 182, f°s 406 sqq.), This *Relaçion* is published, according to fasc. 1673 of the Farnesian Archives of Naples, in the *Correspondance de Granvelle*, v. XII, pp. 287-297.

[18] Letters of May 23 and 25, 1585, *cited.*

When dawn appeared, the enemy vessels were spotted on both sides of the Kouwenstein counter-dike, with the obvious intention of attacking, but everything was confined to a violent cannonade [(19)].

Finally, on May 25th, at four o'clock in the afternoon, a new convoy of 12 flat-bottom boats chained to each other made their way towards the bridge over the Scheldt: this time, since it was in broad daylight, they spotted them in time and managed to divert them toward the riverbank [(20)].

Farnese and his soldiers could not conceal the admiration they felt for the obstinacy of the enemy and the inventive genius of Giambelli: "Thus one can see", wrote the Prince to the King, "the obstinacy of these people, and the *brio* and courage, which they display by sending us all manner of accursed inventions. The old soldiers of my army do not remember having ever seen or heard mention of such a thing." [(21)]

Also, everyone was constantly on his guard: day and night, they remained ready for any eventuality and the Prince himself circulated everywhere, attentive to the slightest noise and heroically struggling against fatigue and sleep [(22)].

On the Kouwenstein dike, he had the parapets of forts and redoubts raised in such a way so that they could overpower the enemy ships attempting to land, and had trenches dug on both sides of these forts. As a result, the space which remained free for traffic was very small: Therefore, Farnese ordered the guards to station themselves within the forts themselves, in the redoubts, and in the trenches, and filled the spaces separating the *blockhaus* in such a way that sentinels advancing from the first fort could easily bring themselves to the aid of those of the second fort, and so on. Finally, Peter Ernst I von Mansfeld-Vorderort had been ordered to stand ready, with the greatest possible number of soldiers from all nations, in the district of Stabroek.

The defense and the occupation of the various forts were as follows. In that of Oordam was Captain Pedro de Solis, with two Spanish

---

[19] *Ibid.*; STRADA, *o. c.*, v. IV, pp. 72-75. See Strada's description of one of these boats, which was equipped with an "underwater sail" invented by a German, pupil of Giambelli. Cf. MOIR, *o. c.*, p. 345. The ship was so swift that Farnese didn't have time to open the bridge and "it was actually driven asunder."

[20] *Ibid.*

[21] Letter of May 23, 1585, *cited.*

[22] Letters of May 23 and 25, 1585, *cited.*

companies, one German, and one Walloon, and four pieces of artillery. Fort Holy Cross was occupied by Colonel Cristóbal de Mondragón y Mercado, with two Spanish companies, one German, and one Walloon, and five pieces of artillery. The *Maestre de campo* Camillo del Monte commanded the defense of the Saint-James redoubt and Kouwenstein Castle, and had four Italian companies, two German, and one Walloon. To that must be added a considerable troop of Walloons belonging to the garrison of Maastricht and five pieces of artillery. The fort of Saint-George was occupied by Captain Juan de Gamboa, who had under his command Iñiguez's Spanish *tercio*, two other companies of Spanish soldiers, one of Walloons, some German ensigns, and six pieces of artillery. At the fort of the Palisades were Captain Simon de Padilla and Antoine Grenet, Seigneur de Werp, expert in the art of artillery, with two companies of Spaniards, a company of Germans, one of Walloons, and five pieces of artillery.

At Stabroek, Peter Ernst von Mansfeld kept two Spanish companies with him, two Italian companies from the *tercio* of Mario Cardoino, under the command of Mario Capizucchi, two German companies, and two of Walloons. All together, these forces exceeded 2,000 men. Given the limited width of the counter-dike, the majority of these soldiers were kept on alert in their quarters, ready to intervene as soon as they saw the enemy approaching the estacades. In the forts and the redoubts themselves, Farnese did not leave any more men than was necessary to hold them, and to maneuver the artillery they were equipped with [(23)].

* * *

It was on Sunday, May 26th, that the great attack occurred [(24)]. This time the agreement between the fleet of Lillo and that of the

---

[23] *Relaçion del succeso...*, cited, loc. cit.

[24] To tell the attack of Kouwenstein, we used the *Relaçion del successo del domingo 26 de mayo,* already cited; the letter sent by Farnese to the King, dated May 26, 1585 (A. G. R., *Copies de Simancas*, v. 16); the *Liber relationum* by Rinaldi (f°s 177-180); a report which was in A. F. N., *Carte farnesiane*, *Fiandra*, fasc. 1695; the history by Alonso Vasquez, *Los sucesos...*, loc. cit., pp. 53-67; that of Cardinal Bentivoglio, who enjoys the memories of his brother Hipolito, present at the battle (*o. c.*, pp. 230-232); STRADA, *o. c.*, v. IV, p. 77-95; C. CAMPANA, *Assedio d'Anversa*, pp. 77 sqq.; E. VAN METEREN, *o. c.*, f°s 238vo-239; the *History* by MOTLEY, *o. c.*, v. I, pp. 209-227, which is inspired by some of Farnese's letters preserved at Simancas, and whose copies do not exist at the General Archives of the Kingdom of Brussels; MOIR, *o. c.*, pp. 349-359; finally, the testimonies of English officers who took part in the action, and of which we find an extensive analysis in *Foreign Calendar, Elizabeth, August 1584-August 1585*, pp. 477, 478, 479, 480.

Antwerpians was complete and they acted in perfect liaison for the duration of the battle. The two fleets combined accounted for just over 200 vessels, of which approximately 160 were large, containing experienced Hollander and Zealander soldiers in the fleets of Hohenlohe and Justinus van Nassau, with Englishmen and Scotsmen in the Antwerpian fleet. These ships were equipped with abundant artillery. The remainder of the two fleets consisted of large shallow draught vessels, loaded with all the materiel needed to pierce the dike and to fabricate entrenchments.

Two hours before dawn, Hohenlohe and Justinus van Nassau arrived first before the Kouwenstein dike. The Spanish sentinels suddenly discerned, in the black and opaque darkness of night, heading towards a point situated between the fort of the Palisades and the fort of Saint-George, four fire-ships, whose sinister glow illuminated the approach of a large fleet. The pitch with which they were coated fed large flames, and since the fire-ships were loaded with sulfur and powder, they exploded on touching the estacade which Farnese had established in front of the dike on the Lillo side. The arrival of these destructive devices threw the Spanish guards into a panic. Dreading some disaster comparable to that of the Scheldt bridge, these soldiers hurriedly withdrew into the entrenchments and the forts. Hohenlohe's men took advantage of the opportunity to disembark safely. A considerable number of pioneers and sappers leaped ashore from the ships between the fort of Saint-George and that of the Palisades, and unloaded a special item of equipage prepared in advance: sacks filled with dirt or stuffed with wool and wheelbarrows in order to quickly transport them where necessary, cork parapets bound with ropes, palisades made from fascines and tree trunks, footbridges, iron stakes, shovels, picks, mattocks, axes, pruning shears in order to destroy the fascines of the dike, and cut tree trunks equipped with wheels on each end and iron thistles in order to prevent the opponent's cavalry from approaching. Protected by their soldiers, Hohenlohe's pioneers quickly entrenched themselves and, with a feverish pace, began to demolish the dike and pierce it in several places.

Scarcely had they installed themselves, under the cover of the fire from their ships, which were continuously firing on the forts of Saint-George and the Palisades, when the naval army of Antwerp, under the command of Marnix and Admiral Jacobsen, appeared in turn, on the other side of the dike. Here, in fact, since the protective palisade could not be completed in time, the Antwerpians managed to pass six to eight of their large vessels through an opening, easily approaching the Kouwenstein dike, arranging them widthwise, and disembarking their men in the blink of an eye. Marnix was one of the first to leap onto the dike. On that side, however, Captain Corbessi's Walloon soldiers defended themselves vigorously against the assailants. Hohenlohe's soldiers were attacked, after the initial surprise had passed, by the Spaniards who came out of the Saint-George redoubts. A furious melee took place on the dike and ended with the momentary defeat of the Zealanders, who were driven back to their ships, leaving two flags in the hands of the enemy. But the advantage did not last long for Farnese's soldiers. The ships from Lillo, as well as those from Antwerp, were tall sided, fitted with wooden pavilions, upon which were stationed excellent marksmen, and their masts carried, at a certain height, a gallery from which the defenders of the Kouwenstein dike were continuously fired upon. The latter, almost uncovered on the dike, and not possessing an artillery capable of countering against that of the adversary, soon had so many dead and wounded that they were forced to withdraw to their entrenchments, abandoning to the enemy the ground stretching between the fort of Saint-George and that of the Palisades. The latter could have come into action and supported the efforts of the defenders, but its commanding officer did not carry out the orders given. Several Spanish and Italian captains had already fallen in this first engagement.

At that moment, some 1,500 men from the fleets of Hohenlohe and Marnix had managed to secure a foothold on the Kouwenstein dike and cut through it in nine different locations, both to cover themselves against attack from the garrisons of the forts and to deliver, if possible, passage to ships loaded with ammunition and victuals destined for Antwerp. While pioneers and sappers worked so hard to execute Marnix's plan, a veritable artillery duel was going on between the Zealander and Antwerpian ships, and the Spanish forts. Farnese's soldiers, demoralized by the rapid success of the assailants and by the terrible fire from the enemy ships, kept themselves held up in their redoubts and entrenchments and did not fight back. Captain Simon de Padilla, of the fort of the Palisades, disgusted by the spinelessness of his men, sallied forth himself with a handful of soldiers, but he fell mortally wounded when he reached the adversary's entrenchment. "Devoid of spirit and courage," said the witness Paolo Rinaldi [25], "ours do not know what attitude to adopt. The two redoubts of Saint-George and the Palisades were lacerated by the opposing artillery, which did not allow the captains and the King's soldiers to advance. The number of wounded Spanish and Italian soldiers was considerable."

The fort of Saint-George soon found itself in a critical situation: by way of piles which they had planted in the water, and which they had reinforced with soil filled sacks and fascines, the assailants had constructed a raised levee, whereon they placed the elite of the musketeers from the ship closest to the dike, under Colonel Morgan's command. At the same time, Colonel Balfour, with a Scottish company, and Seigneur de Haultain, Governor of Walcheren, with a troop of Zealanders, stormed the redoubt. In that dangerous moment, the Italian officer Camillo del Monte, stationed in Kouwenstein Castle and who was also in charge of the fort of Saint-James, came to the rescue with a troop of Italians and Walloons, and, although he was flanked by the fire from Hohenlohe's ships, managed, not without great losses, to repel the assailants from the fort of Saint-George.

Meanwhile, the pioneers, in the water up to their girdles, continued their difficult and hard work. The merchants who were in charge of the vessels loaded with food destined for Antwerp, excited at the idea of the profit they were going to make, continually pressured the workers, shouting at them that victory depended mainly on their hands.

Del Monte's soldiers, after driving the assailants out of the fort of Saint-George, now turned their efforts against the pioneers. Though the work of digging and piercing by the latter was mainly being done at the foot of the dike, a savage battle was raging on the water. Yet the soldiers responsible for protecting the pioneers defended themselves vigorously and, finally, an opening was pierced in the Kouwenstein dike, large enough to allow a *pleyten* type vessel, which was laden with food, to pass through.

Hohenlohe and Marnix leaped into that ship and cast thereon the bloodied body of the Italian captain Ferrante Spinola, who had fallen seriously wounded, which they promised to show the Antwerpians as proof of victory [26].

---

[25] *Liber relationum*, f° 177.

[26] The wounded captain died a few days later in the house of merchants from Genoa, who were his parents and who were established in Antwerp. (C. CAMPANA, *Assedio d'Anvena,* p. 58).

Amid the triumphal clamor of the pioneers and the soldiers, the ship, forcibly launched by the current through the breach, soon sailed through the flooded meadows of Oordam and headed towards Antwerp. Its arrival there provoked enthusiastic demonstrations: Hohenlohe and Marnix were triumphantly received, amid ringing bells and blazing bonfires. The poor Spinola, extracted from the ship, was carried through the streets, amid the cries of the populace.

From the fort of Lillo, where he stood during the action, the young son of William the Silent, Maurice of Nassau, addressed a letter to the States of Holland, announcing the taking and piercing of the Kouwenstein dike and urging the States to prepare corn and victuals in order to immediately send them to Antwerp [27].

In the meantime, the situation for the soldiers of the Royal Army was becoming more and more serious every moment. In several locations along the dike, the enemy had quickly organized redoubts and entrenchments, and any communication between the fort of Saint-George and that of the Palisades was now impossible. The fort of the Palisades was in great danger: its commander had been seriously wounded. That fort bore the name of the Palisades because, the dike being very narrow in this location, the Prince of Parma had built, protruding out and into the water, a kind of estacade covered with a floor to widen the redoubt and give it more importance. Now this part, which was continually bombarded by the enemy ships, had been reduced to pieces and its debris was dangling, lamentably, opening a breach through which the Zealanders could easily penetrate therein. Eventually, on the Kouwenstein dike itself, the number of Antwerpian and Zealander soldiers who had landed and become heavily entrenched had reached nearly three thousand.

In Stabroek, in his headquarters, Peter Ernest von Mansfeld had not been idle. He had quickly sent reinforcement troops to succor the fort of the Palisades, but these soldiers, frightened by the fire from the ships which were cannonading their flank, had not been able to advance and had lost a considerable number of their own. Mansfeld, who was an experienced old warrior and knew how to cope with difficult and dangerous situations, seems to have lost, in this moment, his confidence. Distraught, he gathered together his most senior officers and consulted them on what measures should be taken. Most of

[27] *Foreign Calendar, Elizabeth, August 1584-August 1585,* pp. 476-477.

them were hesitant and even though there were valorous Spanish and Italian leaders, they seemed to be lacking any decisiveness. All were of the opinion that any attempt during the day to regain the ground already lost would send the soldiers to a certain death. The night, they said, would be more favorable for a counteroffensive, because the enemy would be tired and would not guard as well. Besides, they opined, the Prince of Parma would not delay in arriving at the noise of battle: with his sure glance he would immediately see what measures were necessary and he would restore the situation.

Then rose the Italian captain Camillo Capizucchi. He pronounced himself energetically in favor of an immediate attack and offered to lead it at the head of his regiment. He was supported by his Sergeant-Major Piccolomini, the father of Duke Ottavio Piccolomini, who was to make himself famous in the Thirty Years' War.

Galvanized by the energetic language of these two men, Mansfeld agreed and ordered Capizucchi to choose 300 soldiers from among his Italian companies stationed in Stabroek. At the time when this troop was preparing to march to succor the fort of the Palisades, it was joined by a corps of Spanish soldiers, under the command of Don Juan del Águila, Colonel of the *tercio* of Pedro de Paz. Don Juan del Águila, encamped six or seven leagues from the Kouwenstein dike, near Stabroek, had heard the cannonade and, without wasting time, had set out towards the dike with some two hundred elite soldiers. Upon his arrival, a dispute for precedence immediately arose between him and Capizucchi. The Spanish soldiers were considered, in the army of the Netherlands, as the first and had always retained the prerogative to attack first, if they so demanded. On the other hand, the Italians having taken the initiative of the counter-attack, had no intentions of letting themselves be preceded by Spaniards.

Don Juan del Águila put an end to the discussion by proposing to Capizucchi that they go together to attack the enemy positions. At the moment when these valiant officers gave the signal to advance, they suddenly heard, from the other side of the Kouwenstein dike, at the end of the dike in the direction of the fort of Saint-George, cheers, acclamations, and the sound of a cannonade. The entire front, on that side, seemed to come alive in a burst of fury: Farnese had arrived at the scene of the action!

The Prince of Parma, at the moment when the attack was

launched, was at his headquarters in Beveren. After spending part of the night on the bridge over the Scheldt, as he was wont to do, he had gone to take some rest. The roar of the cannons woke him up. He hastily got dressed and left Beveren, convinced that the long-anticipated great attack had just begun [28]. He galloped at full speed up to Kallo, and there gathered together all available pikemen he could find. Soon he was on the bridge blocking the Scheldt. He was detained there for some time due to a diversion involving enemy ships, which pretended to recommence Giambelli's maneuver. When he realized that the real danger was not there, but rather over by the Kouwenstein dike, he left Count Karl von Mansfeld to defend the bridge, and quickly continued his race towards the counter-dike, a distance of three leagues from Beveren. He arrived there at last, accompanied by two hundred pikemen whom he had collected from everywhere along the way and a large number of noble "volunteers" belonging to all the nations which composed the army. As he approached, the news had become more and more distressing. As soon as he was on the dike, he immediately evaluated the gravity of the situation. Visiting the forts and the entrenchments on the side of Saint-George, he noticed the flagrant inferiority of his troops due to the insufficiency of artillery. The superiority of the adversary, whose ships were equipped with a rather considerable number of cannons, endangered all the Spanish entrenchments, which could only respond feebly to the enemy's fire.

Nevertheless, it was a question of, first and foremost, succoring the fort of Saint-George, which was in a critical situation, in spite of the efforts already made by Mondragón and Camillo del Monte. Farnese sent 50 Spanish pikemen and just as many Walloon musketeers to succor the fort and a large quantity of soil filled sacks to consolidate the defenses, both against the fire from the enemy ships and against that from the adversaries occupying the dike. He hastily sent a courier to the fort of Saint-Barbara and fort Holy Cross, with orders to bring as many pieces of artillery as could be spared. Then, while waiting for this reinforcement, he established himself with the Marquis del Vasto in the fort of Saint-James, and had the five pieces

---

[28] He was to have received, at that moment, a letter from Peter Ernest von Mansfeld, communicating to him the information from a prisoner, captured by the Spaniards, and announcing the imminent attack of the Kouwenstein dike. See this letter in the *Correspondance de Granvelle*, v. XII, pp. 276-277.

of heavy artillery that were there brought into action. Soon, considerable damage had been inflicted on the enemy's ships: there were a large number of wounded evacuated via small boats toward Antwerp and towards Zealand.

By this time, the battle had already lasted seven hours. Seeing the effect produced by the artillery fire, the Prince felt that the time had come to launch a counter-attack. Farnese, moreover, hoped that, over near Stabroek, Mansfeld, having learned of his arrival, had not remained idle. As the artillery fire from Kouwenstein Castle, from the Saint-James redoubt, and from the pieces coming from the forts of Holy Cross and Saint-Barbara had silenced the Antwerpian and Zealander ships positioned near that location by the dike, the Prince of Parma gathered around him most of the Spanish and Italian captains and *alférezs*, to inspire their courage. He was met with nothing but dejections and only heard pessimistic declarations. All of his officers affirmed that attacking now would be to face certain death and inevitable disaster. The Prince felt anger grow within him. Addressing the leaders in an irritated tone, filled with exaltation, he spoke to them in this language: "I beg you to take courage and hope, for we have righteousness with us. These people are rebellious not only to the King, but to God: we must defeat them! The Pope, the court of Rome, and the King anxiously await a good end to this enterprise. If we do not fight, our reputation will be finished; we will be treated as cowards! I want that you make the Antwerpians repent for their audacity and folly. I know you will do your duty. I want to be the first to assail the enemy with the pike which I hold in my hands. Those who do not follow me, I will hold them for enemies: to those who follow me, I promise benevolence, honors, and gifts. He who loves the service of God and the King follows me!" (29)

With these words, the Prince launched himself forward, rallying all his officers, eager to avenge the losses suffered and to redeem their lack of confidence and courage. The Spanish pikemen who Farnese had brought followed him, together with the Italian and Spanish volunteers of quality, such as Manriquez, the Counts of Bevilacqua and Sforza, the Marquis Hipolito Bentivoglio, brother of the famous cardinal who was Nuncio to Brussels at the beginning of the seven-

[29] We recount this scene according to Paolo Rinaldi, who was present, and who noted the smallest details (*Liber relationum*, f° 176vo).

teenth century. Led by the Prince, the troop, to which some musketeers had also joined, quickly regained the land which stretched between the fort of Saint-James and that of Saint-George. The assault wave occupied the entire width of the Kouwenstein dike and advanced, overwhelmingly, sweeping away the pioneers and the sappers, carrying the entrenchments erected by the enemy, crossing the canals formed in the dike by the cuts made therein, ascending, after being breast-high in water, the opposite slope, always pushing forward, so as to meet Mansfeld's troops who had unleashed an attack from the opposite side.

During this march forward, Farnese exposed himself to danger with his customary temerity. Sometimes, armed with a pike, he repulsed the enemy's soldiers who disembarked from their vessels onto the slippery bank of the dike in order to come to the rescue; sometimes, walking amidst his troop of Spanish pikemen and his volunteers, armed with a sword and buckler, he struck those opponents in the face who stood in his way and left them for dead or seriously wounded. Near him, Colonel Mondragón exerted himself with "so much valor, strength, and *brio*" that, in his report to the King, the Prince devoted to him a very special mention.

As Farnese and his men were thus gaining ground towards the center of the Kouwenstein dike, the soldiers of Capizucchi and Don Juan del Águila had begun the assault at the other end of the dike. After having kneeled down and prayed to God to grant them victory, Italians and Spaniards, integrated with some sixty German pikemen, launched forward and managed to drive out the enemy soldiers who were already surrounding the fort of the Palisades. The latter was immediately equipped with the artillery necessary to effectively defend itself. In this march to succor the fort, the musketeers had preceded and flanked the mass of pikemen, marching on either side of the dike to shoot at the enemy's boats which were trying to bring reinforcements. Once in possession of the fort of the Palisades, Capizucchi and Don Juan del Águila prepared to attack the enemy entrenchments which extended between them and the Prince of Parma's troop.

From that moment on, the battle was about to concentrate on the short space between the fort of Saint-George and that of the Palisades. On this dike, barely seventeen feet wide, nearly 5,000 men, pressed against each other, were going to confront each other in a fight to the death. The men of Hohenlohe and Marnix had sworn to

O
P
I
H
G
D
EL. DIQUE DE COUVESTEN.
A. Dique de Couvesten hauierto porlos dela Armada olandesa de Olak B. Armada de Olak quetraia Socorro á Amberes. C. fuerte que hicieron los de Olak D. S cruz.
E. S jorje ganado porlos énemigos. F. viene Alexandro farnese Conlos éspañoles. S A delante conespada y Rodela y Cobra el fuerte y echa los énemigos del Dique. G. Torralba.
H. Capisuci. I. lapalada K. naves de Amberes. L. naves de Nasao. M. Puente. N. naves defuegos para diverter. O. Amberes.
P. barcon enquepaso Olak el Dique a Amberes y les dio aentender que entraba el Socorro.
El Capⁿ Ingen. Lodoeme Dip.
R. d. Hooge. fecit.

THE BATTLE OF KOUWENSTEIN
Engraving by R. de Hooghe,
according to master engineer Ledesma.

vanquish or die, and in his letters to Philip II, Farnese reported that, in combat, "soldiers, citizens, and all — they were like mad bulldogs." It was, for the Spaniards, a matter of becoming masters of the great entrenchment which the enemy had erected on the central part of the Kouwenstein dike, by gathering together sandbags, wheelbarrows, tree trunks, fascines, and piles studded with iron spikes. Three times in a row, Farnese and his men on one side, Capizucchi and Águila on the other, tried to approach them, but were vigorously repelled. The dead and wounded were piling up in front of the entrenchments. On the adversary's side, the losses had also been very severe. Captain Heraugiere, who had brought 200 men into battle, had but 13 left around him.

A fourth assault was decided. At the moment where it was about to be launched, a sort of collective hallucination took hold of Don Juan del Águila's Spanish soldiers. They thought they saw an apparition in the air before them, the specter of their former *Maestre de campo*, Don Pedro de Paz, who had been killed at the siege of Dendermonde [(30)]. They affirmed, after the battle, that the specter, clad in his well-known armor, and using the gestures which had been habitual with him in life, had animated them in battle and led them to victory. Filled with exaltation, to the cheers of *España! España!*, the soldiers rallied once again to storm the great enemy entrenchment. Captain Bartholomew Torralva, climbing onto the back of one of his soldiers, was first to vault into the breastwork, but was immediately gunned down. Capizucchi, who followed him closely with some of his men, in turn charged forth. The defense weakened.

It was at this same moment that several of Lillo's ships weighed anchor and abandoned themselves to the current which led them toward Zealand. The battle had lasted longer than Marnix's and Hohenlohe's men had anticipated. It was time for the Scheldt to ebb, and this movement of the tide was also acting on the floods around Kouwenstein. Under the action of the current ebbing towards the sea, the Antwerpian ships became wedged against the dike, maneuvering being an absolute impossibility, while the ships of Justinus van Nassau, overwhelmed by artillery fire from the Spanish forts, took advantage of the ebb to move away and get out of range.

---

[30] It will be remembered that after the battle of Mons in 1914, several soldiers of the English army of Marshal French claimed to have seen Saint George, who encouraged them in the fight against the Germans.

This was what caused the debacle, all the more so since the pivotal entrenchment of the Kouwenstein dike, attacked on one side by Capizucchi and Águila, was undergoing, on the other side, a furious onslaught by the Prince of Parma himself. The enemy was stricken with panic. Caught in the middle of the firefight, and panicked at the sight of the preparations for the departure of their vessels, Hollanders and Zealanders tried to flee from all sides. The English captain James, who took part in the battle, sent details to Walsingham which were informative and picturesque. The English and the Scots in the pay of the Antwerpians had hitherto resisted, without weakening, the furious assaults of Farnese's soldiers. Seeing the ships moving away, they imagined it was to take a better position: "Our galleys...put off", wrote James, "to have more room to play on the enemy, The Hollanders and Zealanders seeing the enemy come on so hotly, and thinking our galleys would leave them, they abandoned their string. the Scots seeing them to retire left their string, the enemy pursued very hotly, the English men stood to repulse and are put mostly to the sword." [31] The English officer indicated, in a postscript, what seemed to him to be the principal cause of the rout: "We had cut the dike in three places," he said, "but we left it most shamefully for *want of commandment.*"

It is a fact that Marnix of Saint-Aldegonde and Hohenlohe, instead of remaining on the Kouwenstein dike to direct the battle, had sacrificed it to their vain satisfaction of going to Antwerp to announce that victory was won, and that at a time when this news was certainly premature. They bear a share of the responsibility in the disaster which descended upon their troops [32].

The men of Lillo's army, seeing their ships moving away from the dike, swam to join them. Many were drowned; others, pursued into the water by Farnese's soldiers, were massacred. The soldiers of the Antwerpian army tried to take refuge on board their ships, believing that they could better defend themselves. But access was prohibited by the Spaniards who, pursuing the routed enemy with sword

---

[31] "The small troup which I had... upon the dyke of Cowestayn did so sufficiently show what Englishmen can do... that the Spaniards and Italians... do daily make honourable mention of us", *Colonel Morgan to the Privy Council*, Antwerp, May 31, 1585 (*Foreign Calendar, Elizabeth, August 1584-August 1585*, p. 507).

[32] Marnix later tried to justify himself. Cf. TH. JUSTE, *Vie de Marnix de Sainte-Aldegonde*, pp. 144-145.

in hand, finished a large number of them on the banks of the dike. Then, since the vessels from Antwerp could not detach themselves from the latter, the Prince of Parma's soldiers climbed into them and killed all those whom they encountered therein.

Several personages of importance found their death in this panic. Admiral Haultain, Governor of Walcheren, who was one of the last to leave the Kouwenstein dike, missed a rope that was thrown from one of the ships, fell into the water and, dragged down by the weight of his armor, sank. The Antwerpian admiral Jacobsen also died in the adventure. Justinus van Nassau miraculously escaped death. Having rushed into the water, he alighted himself in the reeds and divested himself of his armor. He then swam to a boat, which conveyed him to Lillo. Of the approximately 4,000 soldiers the enemy engaged in this enterprise, roughly half perished [(33)], all old experienced soldiers, Scottish, English, and French. Of the ships from Antwerp, abandoned and stuck in the silt at low tide, the Spaniards captured 32, wherein they found 50 pieces of bronze and iron artillery. Twenty-one banners were captured. With regards to Farnese's soldiers, more than 600 men had died and an equal number of wounded were registered. Among the dead were four Italian captains and several Spanish captains and officers.

This was a terrible failure for the Antwerpians, which the hopes at the beginning made even worse. They had expended all the ingenuity and all the tenacity of which they were capable. Although, their foolish audacity was sincerely admired by the Prince of Parma's entourage, who knew heroism when they saw it, and Paolo Rinaldi echoed these sentiments when he wrote: "To tell the truth, the enemy had made there an enterprise worthy of valiant soldiers, the most courageous and most remarkable that was ever made in the Netherlands since the beginning of the revolution. They came completely resolved to do battle, facing our soldiers, our artillery, and our forts, without showing any fear. The meticulous and admirable preparations they made and their manner of fighting was the work of intelligent and very valiant soldiers, who showed evidence of a long experience of warfare." [(34)]

---

[33] The English captain Littelton, who took part in the action, estimates the losses suffered by the men of Hohenlohe and Marnix at about 1,400 (*Correspondance de Granvelle*, v. XII, pp. 280-281).

[34] *Liber relationum*, f°s 179-180.

CHAPTER IV

Alessandro Farnese, in making his report to the King, departed from his usual calm by writing: "Today, Sunday, June 26th, the Lord has been pleased to grant to your Majesty a great and most signal victory!" but he adds that the defeat of his troops "had only been stayed by a thread, because of the lack of manpower." [35]

When news of the disaster was made known in Antwerp, immense discouragement took hold of the population [36]. The arrival of the ship laden with supplies, where Marnix and Hohenlohe were found, had led to the belief that the Kouwenstein dike was pierced and that Farnese's plans had been defeated. Beacons and bonfires were lit, the bells of all the church steeples were merrily ringing, and cannons were fired to spread the good news. A banquet was organized at the Town Hall to celebrate Hohenlohe. The triumphant Calvinists were already making terrible threats against the Catholics. It was proposed to hang them or drown them in the Scheldt, and the most moderate spoke of expelling them as soon as the siege was lifted. At the banquet table, Hohenlohe, pampered and celebrated, drained huge goblets amid great bursts of laughter. Suddenly screams and howls rang out in the streets. The diners rushed out and saw a furious mob, who cried out that the "patriots" had just suffered a bloody defeat, and that boats filled with survivors were docking at Antwerp's wharf. Soon, men with faces tensed from pain and anger carried into the Banquet Hall the wounded, who were about to die. Hohenlohe scarcely had time to flee and hide: by way of land, he returned in secret to Bergen op Zoom [37].

However, the Prince of Parma, in the company of his officers, having given thanks to Providence in the little village-church of Stabroek, and after having had a service celebrating the memory of the dead, took, without delay, the necessary measures to rehabilitate the counter-dike. The thirteen openings practiced by the enemy pioneers were filled with earth, fascines, and, to go faster, the soldiers still exasperated with the losses suffered, heaped pell-mell thereunto the en-

---

[35] Farnese to the King, Beveren, May 26, 1585 (A. G. R., *Copies de Simancas*, v. 16, non-foliated). A victory bulletin was sent all over the place by the Prince of Parma, of which the text was published by GACHARD. *Documents concernant le siège d'Anvers...*, loc. cit., pp. 210-211.

[36] E. VAN METEREN, *o. c.*, f° 239; BENTIVOGLIO, *o. c.*, p. 233.

[37] Letter from Guillaume Ronck to François Le Vasseur, Secretary of State for Farnese, Brussels, June 2, 1585 (*Correspondance de Granvelle*, v. XII, p. 284); Cf. MOTLEY, *o. c.*, v. I, pp. 225-226.

emy corpses, for whom Kouwenstein was thus really a tomb [38]. The Prince of Parma reinforced the defenses by having a large fort built, capable of accommodating 1,000 soldiers. In front of the dike, he planted solid tree trunks in the water, upon which he threw a floor to widen the positions, and arranged on both sides a barrier whose elements were brought so close together that a small dingy could scarcely pass through [39].

In reality, these precautions were unnecessary. The bloody defeat just suffered by the Antwerpians put an end to any effective resistance from them.

* * *

Alessandro Farnese, as we know, not accustomed to resting on his laurels, was always ready to thoroughly exploit all the success he had gained.

He had noticed that, in their flight, the Antwerpian ships had withdrawn close to the flooded village of Oordam and there, had stood guard around an enormous ship, which had been stranded there for a few days. This ship — also an invention of Giambelli — was actually a floating battery, intended to attack the Spanish forts and the bridge over the Scheldt. It was provided with four masts, three of which were furnished with bullet-proof tops, and from whence musketeers put therein, could shoot from above into the inside of the enemy's forts. The ship's hull was surrounded with cork and other impenetrable materials in such a way to render it invulnerable. Openings were pierced into its flanks, whereby twenty large cannons could fire, not counting the medium and small pieces. This heavy machine, which exceeded the water level by only two feet, was made unsinkable through the use of pieces of cork and several empty barrels, wrapped in oakum and robust iron hoops. Five hundred musketeers filled the ship, both for offense and defense. It had been named *The End of the War*, and this name sufficiently indicated the hope upon which this new invention of Giambelli was based [40].

---

38 C. CAMPANA, *Assedio d'Anversa*, p. 62.

39 *Liber relationum*, f° 180; STRADA, *o. c.*, v. IV, p. 95.

40 Description from the *Relaçion del suceso*..., loc. cit.; J. F. LE PETIT, *o. c.*, v. II, p. 501; GRIMESTON, *o. c.*, p. 864B-C; STRADA, *o. c.*, p. 76. Preparations were already being made in November, 1584, for The End of the War, according to a letter from Captain John Morrys to Walsingham, Antwerp, November 23, 1584 (*Foreign Calendar, Elizabeth, August 1584-August 1585*, pp. 151-152). Cf. also C. CAMPANA, *Assedio d'Anversa*, pp. 54-56.

However, this hope was far from being realized. The *End of the War* first took part in the attack on the fort of Saint-Sebastian, but was severely damaged by Spanish artillery. It was reconditioned and they decided to take her to the Kouwenstein dike, in order to cannonade Farnese's forts. It was with great difficulty that the sailors sailing thereon were able to pass through an opening in the Scheldt dike near Austruweel (Oosterweel) and introduce her into the flooded meadows. The heavy machine approached the fort of Oordam, with the intention of attacking it, but she failed almost immediately, without it being possible to put her back in motion (41). The Spaniards, who had dreaded, in its sight, a new infernal invention, had since then nicknamed her *Carantamaula*, that is to say Bugaboo for scaring small children, and the Antwerpians, angry and furious at how she had cost them so much, called it *The Elephant*, *Noah's Ark* or the *Lost Money* (42). The Antwerpian ships, after two days of guarding near the great vessel, finally returned to Antwerp, leaving four galliots to protect it.

The Prince of Parma immediately resolved to make himself master of it, thus depriving the enemy of the means of using it again against the Kouwenstein dike. On Tuesday, May 28th, at four o'clock, he sent four galliots and six shallow draught rowboats, in the style like those which the enemy evolved in the flooded lands, through the cut in the Scheldt dike, near the fort of Saint-Peter. The Prince had soldiers embarked upon these ships, and he allowed Count Karl von Mansfeld and Count Arenberg to join the expedition. These two Lords had supplicated Farnese to do them this favor, because they had not been able to participate in the battle of Kouwenstein: Mansfeld had to guard the bridge and Arenberg had commanded the flotilla of warships protecting that bridge. Some of the galliots, followed by small boats, made a reconnaissance of the coveted ship. Immediately, the enemy ships which guarded it withdrew to Antwerp, pursued by Mansfeld and Arenberg, who tried to cut off their path and sent them a strong volley of harquebus and musket. One of the Antwerpian ships was already preparing to surrender, when an accident stopped the pursuit. On the galliot carrying the two Counts, the

---

41 *Ibid.* C. CAMPANA, *o. c.*, p. 54.

42 *Liber relationum*, f° 180vo; J. F. LE PETIT, *o. c.*, v. II, p. 501; GRIMESTON, *o. c.*, p. 877B; STRADA, *o. c.*, loc. cit.; ALONSO VASQUEZ, *Los sucesos...*, loc. cit., pp. 50-51; MOTLEY, *o. c.*, v. I, p. 228.

THE FLOATING BATTERY "END OF THE WAR"
Contemporary engraving extracted from Strada, *La guerre des Païs-Bas*, Ed. Brussels, 1727.

match-cord of an harquebusier set fire to a powder keg. An explosion followed. Since the ship was covered with a thick layer of pitch, it caught fire and soon all its occupants were engulfed by flames. Some were burned alive, others escaped by swimming. The face, neck, and hands of Karl von Mansfeld were affected, and Arenberg did not escape without injury. They found themselves forced to stop the pursuit and return to Kouwenstein on another galliot. However, Farnese's other ships continued the pursuit of the enemy and managed to take control of one of their boats. Arenberg, who was less wounded than Mansfeld, returned with reinforcements, then headed towards *The End of the War* and approached it. The great machine was completely empty: the Antwerpians had removed the artillery that was there and had taken the musketeers away which made up her crew. Immediately the Prince of Parma was brought to the captured vessel, quickly visited her, and, realizing that they could, by inspecting her, learn some secret, did not destroy her. The next day, *The End of the War* was towed by the Spaniards to the bridge over the Scheldt, where they could study its construction with all necessary leisure [(43)].

The ignominious end of this machine, which had cost them so much money and effort, came to further overwhelm the Antwerpians more deeply and gave them the impression that there was no way to defeat the Prince of Parma.

[43] *Relaçion del succeso...*, loc. cit.: Letter from Farnese to the King, June 6, 1585 (A. G. R., *Copies de Simancas*, v. 16); *Liber relationum*, f°s 180-181.

CHAPTER V

MARNIX ENTERS INTO NEGOTIATIONS

That wasn't all. One of the redoubts which the Antwerpians possessed on the right bank of the Scheldt, the *Boerenschans*, fell into the hands of the enemy. This was the only point on the river's master-dike from whence they could, through the cut which was made there in that dike, launch their fire-ships and other destructive engines in the direction of Farnese's bridge and try to destroy the latter [(1)]. The day after the defeat at the Kouwenstein dike, a good number of Scottish soldiers, who had escaped the massacre, had been placed as garrison in that fort. Since they had tossed their weapons during the flight, they were provided with harquebuses. But they pretended that they could not use them and surrendered as soon as the redoubt was attacked by the Spaniards [(2)].

From then on, a great discouragement seized the Antwerpians [(3)]. The "peiswillers" again propagated the idea that, in view of the situation, it was better to treat with the Prince of Parma [(4)]. The state of the provisions was starting to become critical. The "Munition Masters", charged with the supervision of the provisions, pointed out to the College of Magistrates that, since they were not equipped to face the threat of famine, it was necessary to expect disorders, main-

[1] « Ce qui nous osta tout à un coup et la commodité que nous avions d'endommager le pont de l'ennemi par nos enginz de feu... » MARNIX DE SAINTE-ALDEGONDE, *Brief récit de l'estat de la ville d'Anvers...*, loc. cit., p. 254.

[2] BOR, *o. c.*, 2nd part, f° 600.

[3] BOR, *o. c.*, loc. cit.; VAN METEREN, *o. c.*, f° 239.

[4] VAN METEREN, *o. c.*, f° 239.

ly on the part of the poor supported by public assistance. These revelations having made an impression, and in the face of the losses suffered, the magistrate expressed the opinion that, since they had waited for assistance in vain, it was important to get in touch with Farnese, in order to initiate the conclusion of an agreement. At first, Marnix strongly opposed this proposal, declaring that he wanted to wait until the very end, promoting the assistance of his confederates, recalling the promises and the representations made by the Count of Hohenlohe when he left Antwerp [(5)].

Moreover, had not the States of Holland, after having heard Hohenlohe's report on what had happened at Kouwenstein, sent a letter on the date of May 29th, 1585, to the Antwerpians encouraging them in their resistance and promising them that they would spare "neither their property nor their blood" in order to help them? They had requested Marnix to make known, by way of an encrypted letter, how long the Antwerpians believed they could still hold out, so that they could hasten to do what was necessary in order to succor them before the fatal date [(6)].

Nevertheless, most of the members of the magistrate of Antwerp, apart from three, who agreed with Marnix, insisted on starting negotiations with the Prince of Parma, declaring that they did not want to be made accountable to God for the loss of 80,000 souls. They pointed out to Aldegonde that he had to agree with the opinion of the majority and not be stubborn in his own opinion. In the meantime, restlessness had also taken hold of the guilds, who, during extraordinary meetings, decided to join the "peiswillers." On two or three occasions, Marnix went to these meetings, and through persuasion or threat, put an end to the tumult. But the guilds nevertheless presented a request to the magistrate, demanding that they be made aware of what means they thought could be made available in order to deliver the city and insisting that they should enter into negotiations with Farnese, so as to avoid the ruin of the citizenry. This attitude encouraged the mass of supporters for peace to resume the conventicles which had previously been forbidden [(7)].

---

[5] MARNIX DE SAINTE-ALDEGONDE, *Brief récit...*, cited, pp. 254-255. *Avvisi* from Antwerp, June 7, 1585: "although many of the principal men incline to an accord with the Prince of Parma, on the same conditions as those made at Brussels, yet M. d'Aldegonde with his followers will not consent." (*Foreign Calendar, Elizabeth, August 1584-August 1585*, p. 532.)

[6] BOR, *o. c.*, f° 601 (text of the letter).

[7] MARNIX DE SAINTE-ALDEGONDE, *o. c.*, loc. cit., p. 255.

The burgomaster, no longer seeing any means of escaping from this pressure, then proposed to carry out a new inventory into the provisions of grain, in order to take measures designed to make possible the continuation of resistance until the moment when they would come to the succor of Antwerp. But most of his colleagues opposed it, on the pretext that the previous inventory, made in March, had been carried out very conscientiously and that the proposed measure was intended only to seek delay and waste time.

However, they ended up accepting Marnix's proposition, but they added the reservation that, while conducting the inquiry, it would not be forbidden from probing, "by particular persons", into the Prince of Parma's intentions regarding a general agreement in which Holland and Zealand would be included. While instructions were drafted for the investigators responsible for checking the provisions of grain [(8)], Alderman Jacques Swerius was sent to Holland to publicize the city's tragic situation [(9)].

The investigation, carried out with care and great severity by the *Hooftmannen*, *Wijkmeesters*, colonels, and captains of Antwerp, revealed that, since March 27th, the supply of grain had declined at a disturbing rate. There were enough resources for a duration of no more than a month and a few days. The bread had become so scarce that it was momentarily necessary to bring it in from Burcht and Mechelen: The Hollander sailors in service of the fleet, faced with this shortage, preferred to return on foot to their homes rather than wait in Antwerp for the wages which were to be sent to them. Marnix even had to lodge soldiers on ships for a few days, in order to be able to increase the ration of the civilian population. The provisions of meat, cheese, butter, and salted fish were likewise as scarce and were sold at exorbitant prices. The beer also began to run out, to the point that even in wealthy families they drank only water, mixed with a little wine.

The financial distress was great, and despite all the authorizations given by the *Breeden Raedt*, it was no longer possible to obtain money from the burghers, who preferred to be imprisoned rather than to give what little that remained to them and which was necessary to help their families. Members of the magistrate and people of

---

[8] Text of the instructions in BOR, *o. c.*, f°s 601-602.

[9] MARNIX DE SAINTE-ALDEGONDE, *o. c.*, loc. cit., p. 256.

quality, however, lent sums of up to 16,000 florins [10].

In these circumstances, Marnix "being convinced in his conscience" that it was necessary to save the people and avoid disturbances and massacres, which could have provided the enemy with the means of entering the city, and without ceasing to maintain the hope of being succored in time, decided to enter into communication with the Prince of Parma [11].

Alessandro Farnese had previously tried to enter into direct communication with the burgomaster of Antwerp. In the previous March, after the surrender of Brussels, he had written a letter to Olivier van den Tympel. Suspecting that the latter would retire near Marnix after the reconciliation of the capital of Brabant, he had suggested to him to render "some remarkable service to His Majesty" by treating with Aldegonde for the reduction of Antwerp to the obedience of the King [12]. Whether van den Tympel did not see Marnix, or he refused to render the "service" requested, this test produced no result.

There is no doubt that, despite certain, quite honestly, very fragile appearances [13], Marnix did not decide to enter into relations with the Prince of Parma until the city's situation, the defeat at the Kouwenstein dike, and the change in public opinion which were the consequence thereof, had obliged him to take this step. He rightly judged that these negotiations should first be conducted without the knowledge of the general public and the *Breeden Raedt*, so as not to provoke panic and trigger irreparable damage. He only spoke to the Council Members and the city colonels, and all agreed that Marnix would first write a letter on his own behalf to Farnese, so that, in case of failure, the body of the city or the magistrate would not have

---

[10] MARNIX DE SAINTE-ALDEGONDE, *o. c.*, loc. cit., pp. 256-260.

[11] *Ibid.*, pp. 260-261. It should be noted that on May 31, Colonel Morgan, writing to Elizabeth's Privy Council in England, said: "As to the state of this town [Antwerp], I will only say that, except God miraculously assist them, and not receiving any present succour from Her Majesty [Elizabeth], they must needs come to their destruction and be reduced under the Spanish yoke" (*Foreign Calendar, Elizabeth, August 1584-August 1585*, p. 506).

[12] *Bulletins de la Commission royale d'histoire*, 3rd series, v. VIII, p. 418 (text of the letter); TH. JUSTE, *Vie de Marnix...*, pp. 148-149.

[13] We are thinking here of the very partial study by Kervyn de Lettenhove, published in the *Revue Générale* of 1883, under the title *Marnix. La capitulation d'Anvers*, and the pamphlet by P. M. ALBERDINGK THIJM, *De vroolijke historie van Philips van Marnix*. Kervyn's assertion that negotiations were already under way with Marnix *by the end of March 1585* is completely unfounded. The examination of Farnese's secret correspondence allows us to oppose a formal denial.

to bear the unfortunate consequences. Having been put in communication with a drummer of Farnese's army, the burgomaster handed him a letter for the latter. After paying tribute to the "singular prudence" which made Farnese "admirable in all his actions", Marnix explained how he had been dragged into the war against the King and how, once engaged in this struggle, he had been unable to withdraw, without abandoning the people "to extreme ruin". He confessed that he did not see a way to achieve "a general tranquility". The military preparations which, since the failure at the Kouwenstein dike, were being made on both sides, could, in his opinion, only bring about the ruin of all, and make the country prey for foreigners. He supplicated the Prince of Parma to allow him to treat with "those of Holland and Zealand" — allies that could not be abandoned — so that they would cease all preparations for war, and that together with Antwerp and Mechelen, and "other provinces and cities" they would return under the King's obedience. Marnix was determined to induce them, at least some of them if not all, if Farnese granted "good and reasonable" conditions of peace and pardons for the past. By allowing a certain amount of "freedom of religion", even if it was only provisional until "some General Council or Provincial Synod" would have decided in this matter, he would bring the hearts of the subjects back to their King and establish a firm and eternal peace. If, instead of showing his goodness and righteousness, the Prince of Parma pushed the rebels to the last extremity, then they would take God to witness that they were not responsible for the bloodshed and calamities of this war [(14)].

Thus, from the outset, the burgomaster linked the surrender of Antwerp to the reconciliation of the cities which still resisted, and especially of Holland and Zealand, and made a point of bringing them there by way of concessions in the matter of liberty of conscience. That showed great skill on his part. In this way, he did not give the air of wanting to conclude a separate peace with Farnese and break the oath that bound him to his Hollander and Zealander allies. On the other hand, by suggesting to the Prince that a concession in the matter of liberty of conscience would also bring about the pacification of Holland and Zealand, he urged his adversary to find a

---

[14] Text of the letter in A. LACROIX, *Œuvres de Philippe de Marnix de Sainte-Aldegonde, Ecrits politiques et historiques*, pp. 298-300; MOTLEY, *o. c.*, v. I, pp. 235-236.

conciliation formula which could decide the future. He was, of course, mistaken about the possibility of such a policy, and he was ignorant or could not understand the King's provisions in this respect; he was mistaken about the ascendency he could have exercised in Holland and Zealand. But we do not believe, as some have said [(15)], that Marnix wanted to "play a role" and that he abandoned the ideal for which he had fought all his life [(16)]. The circumstances were such, after all the victories won by Farnese in Flanders and Brabant, and after the failure of the attempt to destroy the bridge over the Scheldt and the capture of the Kouwenstein dike, that the burgomaster of Antwerp could only try one thing: to save what was still possible to save. Had not the only hope which had always guided him so far, the direct intervention by the King of France, gone up in smoke? From England, Marnix could not have reasonably expected any effective succors, as he very clearly showed in his written justification after the surrender of Antwerp [(17)]. Leicester's foolish and reckless undertaking in the northern provinces and his lamentable failure are there to give him reason.

Marnix had also been reproached for having confessed to Farnese, in this first letter which marked the beginning of contact with the latter, that "he had never been of the opinion that on no particular subject was it permissible to take up arms against his superiors in order to maintain religion." But we forget that after this theoretical assertion, Marnix immediately added that "since the States and governors of this country had begun this quarrel to defend the people, who, through sinister information, were oppressed without being able to be heard in court", he had taken the matter to heart and had persevered to the end. He therefore justified the fight against the sovereign by way of the decision which had been made by those whom he regarded as the appointed representatives of the population, in the hope that the latter would obtain "better attention and awareness of the cause."

---

[15] e.g. MOTLEY, *o. c.*, v. I, p. 236; KERVYN DE LETTENHOVE, *Marnix,* loc. cit., p. 13.

[16] TH. JUSTE, in his *Vie de Marnix* (pp. 235-236) wrote very aptly: « Depuis le fatal assassinat de Guillaume le Taciturne, Marnix désespérait, il est vrai, de l'avenir des Provinces-Unies. Il aurait donc voulu, pour conserver en corps d'Etat les dix-sept provinces, négocier, mais sur des bases honorables, un accommodement avec le Roi catholique ».

[17] *Brief récit...*, cited, loc. cit., pp. 274-275.

Marnix's letter did not reach Farnese [18]: at least that is what the former said later, and we know that this assertion is true [19].

In the face of Farnese's disturbing silence, the magistrate insisted with the burgomaster so that he would write the Prince again or that he bring the matter of negotiations before the *Breeden Raedt*. Marnix refused to do either. However, after having promised the magistrate and the colonels to keep this secret, he had drafted a letter to be addressed to President Richardot, who had negotiated the surrender of Ghent and that of Brussels. This letter, he did not write himself. He dictated it to a man named Jean van Damme, who made known to Richardot that he had secretly communicated with Marnix and that he had found him "quite inclined to peace", if Farnese wanted to grant good conditions of surrender [20].

This Jean van Damme had been burgomaster of Kortrijk during the years 1578-1579, at the time of the excesses of the sectarians. He was the brother-in-law of Calvinist minister Jean Taffin. Thrown into prison after the surrender of Ghent, he had let himself be released by the Prince of Parma by promising to go to Antwerp to observe what was happening and to "keep good correspondence" with the Spaniards [21]. When he arrived in Antwerp, he declared to Marnix that he wanted to remain faithful to Calvinism and offered his services.

Marnix had given him his confidence and had one day asked him to write a letter to Richardot in which, under the pretense of providing information on the plans of the Antwerpians, he had in reality tried to distort the true intentions of the besieged [22]. It is therefore not surprising that the burgomaster of Antwerp again relied on the services of this rather shady character in order to probe Farnese's dispositions.

On receipt of this missive, Richardot undoubtedly showed it to the Prince of Parma. The latter hesitated with regard to the attitude

---

18 « Mais comme depuis j'ay entendu, elle n'a oncque estée livrée ». MARNIX DE SAINTE-ALDEGONDE, *Brief récit...*, loc. cit., p. 261.

19 Here is the proof. On August 18, Farnese, telling the King how the negotiations commenced, wrote: « Trois ou quatre jours après, vindrent lettres d'Aldegonde audict Richardot... avecq copie d'une lettre qu'il disoit m'avoir escript trois ou quatre jours auparavant, *que toutefois je n'ay receu* » (GACHARD, *Documents concernant le siège d'Anvers*, loc. cit., p. 258).

20 MARNIX DE SAINTE-ALDEGONDE, *Brief récit...*, loc. cit., p. 261.

21 Farnese to the King, August 18, 1584 (GACHARD, *Documents concernant le siège d'Anvers...*, p. 257.

22 MARNIX DE SAINTE-ALDEGONDE, *Brief récit...*, loc. cit., p. 287; KERVYN DE LETTENHOVE, *Marnix*, loc. cit., p. 13.

he should adopt. The tone of the letter written by van Damme on Marnix's orders had favorably impressed him, but he wondered whether he should not see it as a trap. Did Marnix not intend, under the pretense of treating with Farnese, to calm the impatience of the "peiswillers" and stop the change of opinion which had just manifested itself so vigorously? After having thought it over and consulted with his advisers, the Prince authorized Richardot to answer (23).

On June 7th, the Councilor of State wrote to the burgomaster of Antwerp to propose an interview (24). The latter immediately declared himself ready to go to whatever place Farnese would indicate to him. He observed, however, that in his capacity as a "public person", whose absence would arouse suspicion, he intended to communicate the fact of the negotiations to the superintendents of the city, in order to obtain permission to go to the Spanish camp. But it was obvious, added Marnix, that his alliance with the other Confederate provinces would be immediately objected to, so that, in order to continue this negotiation, the treaty would have to be "comprehensive", that the city of Antwerp should not separate itself from the other provinces, because without them, there would be famine — their separate peace efforts stopping any provisioning — and at the same time the ruin of the city's commerce and that of the entire country. The general reconciliation of the remaining rebellious provinces was also to be the desire of the King and the Prince of Parma, which, "with some good and reasonable conditions" would not be too difficult to obtain. As soon as Marnix had the answer from Richardot, he would have "authorized people" appointed to start negotiations (25).

Very cautiously, Farnese abstained from answering in regards to the substance of the letter, that is to say, the proposal for a comprehensive peace in which Holland and Zealand would be included. He interpreted Marnix's letter in the sense that the burgomaster himself would not come to the rendezvous, but would send quite a large number of delegates from Antwerp. "Let them be as many as possible," he answered through Richardot, "but let us know, so that the necessary passports can be obtained." (26)

---

[23] Farnese to the King, August 18, 1584 (GACHARD, *Documents* cited, loc. cit., p. 258).

[24] We do not have Richardot's letter, but we know its contents from Marnix's letter of June 8, 1585. Cf. MOTLEY, *o. c.*, v. I, p. 236.

[25] Marnix to Richardot, Antwerp, June 8, 1585 (*Bulletins de la Commission Royale d'Histoire*, 3rd series, v. IX, pp. 329-332). Cf. MOTLEY, *o. c.*, v. I, pp. 236-237.

[26] Richardot to Marnix, June 11, 1585 (*Bulletins* cited, p. 332).

In reality, Marnix wanted to go alone to the rendezvous. On receipt of Richardot's first letter, marking his agreement to the opening of negotiations, several members of the magistrate had been of the opinion that they needed to consult with the *Breeden Raedt.* But Marnix, in order to "avoid the precipice" where one would fall in this case, offered to instead go to Beveren himself, to examine whether there was any hope of obtaining liberty of conscience and of coming to a general agreement. He would then have gone to the States-General to communicate what he had learned. But the magistrate felt that he could not go to Holland: the voyage to Farnese's camp, on the other hand, seemed to him desirable, but dangerous for the person of Marnix. The latter, convinced that he was not risking his life, but perhaps his reputation, declared that he would gladly devote "his life and honor to the salvation of the city." On this, the magistrate, thanking him, concluded that this trip was to be [(27)].

The burgomaster, writing to Richardot, pointed out to him that the substance of his letter had not been touched, that is, that there had been no mention of freedom of religion and general agreement, and that, in order to avoid the disadvantages of written negotiations, it was decided to go himself to see the Prince of Parma at Burcht, at Beveren, or whatever place he preferred. At the same time he requested the dispatch of the safe-conduct necessary to come and go freely [(28)].

To this letter, Richardot replied that if he had not spoken of the substance of the negotiation, it was because this issue was reserved for the interview they would have together. Since Marnix thought it best to come to terms with Farnese, the latter was ready to receive him, and very happy to see the confidence that the burgomaster of Antwerp had in his words. To reassure Marnix even more, Farnese had ordered Richardot to go to Antwerp and to become a hostage there while the burgomaster resided in Beveren [(29)]. On June 16th, Richardot would be in Burcht, receiving from the hand of Marnix his own safe-conduct and crossing the Scheldt to go and put himself in the custody of the Antwerpians. At the same time handing to Marnix the safe-conduct granted by Farnese [(30)]. Thus everything seemed very well set. The burgomaster of Antwerp, by acknowledging the

---

[27] MARNIX DE SAINTE-ALDEGONDE, *Brief récit...*, p. 262.
[28] Marnix to Richardot, June 14, 1585 (*Bulletins* cited, p. 333).
[29] Richardot to Marnix, Beveren, June 15, 1585 (*Ibid.*, p. 334).
[30] Marnix to Richardot, Antwerp, June 16, 1585 (*Ibid.*, p. 334).

receipt of this safe-conduct, remarked to Richardot that he ought not to be a hostage: how could one doubt the word of a Prince "who had been found in all his actions sincere and true?"

Farnese waited in vain for Marnix's visit. At the last moment, the latter made it known that he would gladly have gone to Burcht that day, June 16th, but that his travel was no longer possible, as the negotiations had been disclosed. As a result, the burgomaster had to communicate "with several people" and could not arrive until the following day [31].

The Prince of Parma was soon informed of the reasons for this change. Marnix's secret negotiations had been known, both through various reports and in documents, as a result of a visit made by Seigneur Theodore van de Werve to Farnese's camp at Beveren. Van de Werve had asked the burgomaster for a passport to leave the city, on the pretext that he had to take care of certain private affairs. Since he was to proceed to Stabroek and there could see Count Peter-Ernest von Mansfeld, Marnix, without expressly charging him with any mission, had authorized him to declare to the Count that, if there was any prospect of obtaining a sort of "peace of religion" for Antwerp, there would be some way of inducing Holland and Zealand, and all the rest of the Confederate provinces to reconcile with the King. Seigneur van de Werve had also travelled to Beveren, where he had spoken to Richardot. The latter, without going into any detail, had revealed that he and Marnix corresponded and that he had found the burgomaster "very desirous for public repose." [32]

On his return to Antwerp, van de Werve had mentioned these negotiations, in conversations he had had with people of the city.

The news spread and the *Breeden Raedt* assembled. They showed themselves very excited and indignant that these negotiations had been undertaken without the Council's knowledge. From that moment on, Marnix was the object of suspicion and was forced to postpone his visit to Farnese's camp for the time being. As was to be expected, the people of the *Breeden Raedt* established the rule that no separate peace could be concluded and decided to send delegates to Holland and Zealand to

---

[31] The passport drawn up for Richardot for this trip to Antwerp is in GACHARD, *Documents concernant le siège d'Anvers...*, loc. cit., p. 211. Cf. MOTLEY, *o. c.*, v. I, p. 239.

[32] Marnix to Richardot, Antwerp, June 16, 1585 (*Bulletins* cited, pp. 335 seq.); MARNIX DE SAINTE-ALDEGONDE, *Brief récit...*, loc. cit., pp. 262-263; Richardot to Marnix, June 17, 1585 (*Bulletins* cited, pp. 339 seq.).

hear the opinions of the Confederates [33], both in terms of the negotiation itself and in regards to what succors might be expected. These delegates, who were, for the captains and the *Wijkmeesters*, Jacques l'Hermite and Daniel van der Molen, and for the guilds, Pierre Panhuys and Bonaventure de Molenaer, swore an oath to return to Antwerp, as soon as their mission was over [34]. The instructions given to these delegates required them to give an accurate account of the origin and purpose of the negotiations and to represent the critical situation in which Antwerp found itself. The main thing they were to learn was, if the city could not be succored in time and if, on the other hand, the Confederates did not want a general peace agreement, how they should behave to avoid a catastrophe. It was anticipated, the delegates had to say, that as soon as the provisions were exhausted, the people would revolt and force the magistrate to treat with the enemy. In the meantime, it was urgent to succor the city, either by water or by land [35].

* * *

After the departure of these delegates, and pending the decision of the *Breeden Raedt*, in whose hands resided the affair of negotiations with Farnese, Marnix immediately set to work on prolonging Antwerp's resistance for as long as possible. "Extremely cheerful" for not having to occupy himself with peace negotiations at that time, he resolutely committed himself to the task of immediate and realistic goals [36]. The first measure that seemed to be imperative was to expel a large number of inhabitants, in order to reduce the quantity of mouths to feed. It appeared to the colonels and the captains that it would be appropriate to make 30,000 or 40,000 persons, "suspicious or useless in the war", leave. But that wasn't an easy thing to do. First of all, it was necessary to strengthen the authority of the colonels and captains, whose influence had diminished considerably [37], by putting at their

---

33 *Avvisi* from Antwerp, June 23, 1585, in *Foreign Calendar, Elizabeth, August 1584-August 1585*, p. 558.

34 BOR, *o. c.*, f° 603; MARNIX DE SAINTE-ALDEGONDE, *Brief récit*, loc. cit., p. 262; Marnix to Richardot, June 16 and 17, 1585 and Richardot to Marnix, June 17, 1585 (*Bulletins* cited, pp. 336-341); *Avvisi* from Fugger, Cologne, June 27, 1585 (KERVYN DE LETTENHOVE, *o. c.*, p. 16).

35 BOR, *o. c.*, f°s 603-604 (text of the instructions); *Bulletins de la Commission Royale d'Histoire*, 3rd series, v. XII, pp. 213-216.

36 *Brief récit...*, loc. cit., p. 262.

37 Note this appreciation by Gilpin, in a letter to Walsingham, May 1, 1585: "The magistrates [of Antwerp are] good and sound, but weak in martial affairs, and little respected. The colonels and captains are merchants, and unfit for such matters." (*Foreign Calendar, Elizabeth, August 1584-August 1585*, p. 451).

disposal ten or twelve new burgher companies, each of 150 men, levied at half-pay. The presence of these companies seemed all the more desirable as they could also reinforce the garrisons of the forts, where the burghers still refused to surrender. But when it came to execution, Marnix faced enormous difficulties. Money was found to pay for only three companies; moreover, the measure appeared suspicious to many; finally, the guilds threatened to oppose it by force (38). Then the expulsion of suspects and unnecessary mouths was attempted. But even with the help of the colonels and the captains of the city and with the support of the new burgher companies, it could not be carried out. They somehow managed to make 400 or 500 people leave, and yet the latter, barely brought out through one of the gates, were able to enter through another gate the next day. That was because the members of the guilds had custody of these gates and as they were opposed to the decision taken, they allowed all those who were expelled to reenter! In fact, everyone found a friend or an accomplice to protect him or to avoid the prescribed measures.

Marnix, faced with this anarchic situation, had to admit with bitterness "that all this went up in smoke." (39). Nevertheless, the captains insisted that a certain number of qualified burghers be expelled, particularly those suspected of wanting peace with the Spaniards. However, since they did not keep this subject a secret, the rumor spread throughout the city that they were going to hunt or massacre all the "papists." Right away, the people armed themselves and kept watch, in armor, at night, in their homes. Members of the guilds, a number of Lutherans, and even members of the city council followed suit. They were on the verge of a bloody battle (40). Finally, Marnix managed to calm all this unrest. It was nonetheless true that nothing could be done to prolong the resistance.

* * *

While these events were unfolding in Antwerp, the Prince of Parma wondered, in his camp at Beveren, whether the excuse in-

[38] *Avvisi* from Antwerp, June 23, 1585, in *Foreign Calendar, Elizabeth, August 1584-August 1585*, p. 558: "to the great displeasure of many, who would rather accept a good treaty than continue the miseries of this pestiferous war."

[39] *Brief récit...*, pp. 264-265.

[40] *Ibid.*, pp. 265-266.

voked by Marnix not to go to the rendezvous was not a sham [41]. He was not far from thinking that it was Marnix himself who had aroused the change in public opinion which, at that time, kept him in Antwerp [42]. The news which came to him about the activity of the Confederates and the measures which they seemed to be taking to succor Antwerp, was to confirm this idea. "Since the Kouwenstein affair," he wrote to Philip II, "the people of Holland and Zealand, and those of Antwerp are seeking reinforcements from all sides, in England and elsewhere; they are preparing new incendiary machines, and every day they are augmenting their fleet of warships stationed near Lillo. According to the information I have, they will also recommence the attack on the Scheldt bridge. Also, we live here arms in hand during the day and during the night." [43]

However, Marnix and Richardot continued to correspond, the burgomaster apologizing for being detained by the attitude of the *Breeden Raedt*, observing that "popular governments are full of a thousand hazards" and supplicating that he be allowed "to follow the impressions of the people down the path of reason." [44]

Richardot, for his part, reassured Marnix, letting him know that Farnese was "in no respects dissatisfied with him", that he harbored no indignation against the poor people of Antwerp, and that he was rather inclined to be sympathetic to "his infirmities" than to be offend by them. He pointed out that, undoubtedly, a comprehensive reconciliation of the remaining rebellious provinces would be very agreeable to the Prince of Parma, but that, though this reconciliation could not occur in a short period of time, it was not necessary to delay that of Antwerp, at the risk of letting this city perish: *Dum Roma consulitur, Saguntum perit* [45].

About ten days later, the tone of Richardot's letters changed completely. They became severe and threatening. The President did not hesitate to write: "And if you, Sir, concerning whom many of our

---

[41] Farnese to the King, June 20, 1585 (B. N. P., Spanish MS. 182, f° 410).

[42] This is what he confessed to Philip II in his letter of August 18, 1585 (GACHARD, *Documents concernant le siège d'Anvers,* p. 258). On the other hand, the Nuncio Bonomi wrote to Rome: «Il principe di Parma mi scrive con l'ultime sue che la prattica d'Aldegonda era poi riusita vana per li motivi del popolo *suscitati ad arte da lui* o *da altri, per usare delle sue stesse parole...*» (S. EHSES and A. MEISTER, *Die Kölner Nuntiatur,* 1st part; *Bonomi in* Köln, p. 105.

[43] Farnese to the King, June 30, 1585 (Loc. cit.).

[44] *Bulletins de la commission royale d'histoire*, 3rd series, v. IX, pp. 340-342.

[45] Antwerp, June 17, 1585 (*Bulletins* cited, pp. 339-340). "While Rome debates, Sagunto is in danger", Spanish proverb referring to Hannibal's Siege of Saguntum[Sagunto].

friends have at present a sinister opinion, — as if your object was to circumvent us..." (46) What had happened? It is difficult to know precisely. Richardot made allusions to "bravados and impertinent demonstrations", which some Antwerpians were to have made on June 29th and 30th, or shortly before. The historians of the siege of Antwerp do not refer to any particular fact which could explain these allusions of Richardot. We believe that it must have been skirmishes which had taken place around the city, south of the walled metropolis, during expeditions conducted by the Antwerpians to seek provisions.

What makes us believe that is, in the letter wherein Farnese sent to the King the account of the punitive expeditions he undertook, and of which we shall speak in a moment, he began that narrative with the following passage: "As the people of Antwerp were trying to resupply themselves with grain, I went to Borgerhout..." (47)

Indeed, likewise from the north side, no succors in food could come any longer, and as the threat of famine intensified, the Antwerpians sought provisions in the region situated to the south of the city, which the Prince of Parma, for want of manpower, did not keep very tightly blockaded. The Prince resolved to impede them on that side by cutting them off from communications with the neighboring region (48). At the end of June (49), in Stabroek, after having assembled a force of cavalry and infantry of about 1,100 men, to which had joined as many peasants, he marched on the suburb of Borgerhout, where the mercenary troops in the pay of the Antwerpians were lodged. The defenses were quickly swept away and the enemy was pursued to the gates of the city (50). The castles and fortified houses along the approaches to Borgerhout were occupied, and vegetables and fruits were seized, in order to prevent the Antwerpians from dining on them. Going then on to Deurne, the Prince of Parma sum-

46 *Ibid.*, p. 343.

47 Farnese to the King, Beveren, July 30, 1585 (B. N. P., Spanish MS. 182, f° 410vo). This interpretation is also shared by STRADA, *o. c.*, v. IV, p. 100.

48 This measure was suggested to him in a letter from Antwerp, written on June 24, 1585, by a supporter of peace or a spy: « Le vray remède pour rompre leurs malicieux desseings et abbréger cest affaire, c'est de s'emparer des maisons de Mercxem, Deurne et, Berchem, et lever quelques petits forts ou trenciz là où que lesdites maisons pouriont estre trop esloignées l'une de l'aultre, et par là de tout serrer de près ceste ville... et avecq ce leur fouldroit rendre infructueulx lesdicts graines au Buytenschanse » (GACHARD, *Documents concernant le siège d'Anvers*, loc. cit., p. 217).

49 According to BOR, *o. c.*, f° 605.

50 C. CAMPANA, *Assedio d'Anversa*, p. 63.

moned the garrison of Sterckshof Castle to surrender. At the ninth cannon shot, the captain and the French soldiers who occupied it ceased their resistance. From there, they marched on Berchem, where it was necessary to put the artillery into position in order to force the occupants to capitulate. After capturing the castles of Stralen, Cantecroix, and *Lantaarnhof*, the Spaniards went to besiege a fort located near St. Bernard's Abbey, Hemiksem, in Bornem, called fort Saint-Margaret. After two days of bombardment, this redoubt surrendered. In this way, by putting a garrison in all the positions he had just captured, Farnese, in a single stroke, cut the last lines of communications from the Antwerpians to Bergen op Zoom, Lillo, and Mechelen. But he was not satisfied with just closing the net around the city: he ordered his soldiers to reap the standing grain and wheat, and to collect all agricultural produce, in order to prevent the besieged from sourcing food from this area [(51)].

This time, several of Antwerp's defenders, who hitherto had felt that nothing was impossible, completely lost their courage, slipping away little by little, and abandoned the city [(52)]. However, in order to save what little wheat remained in the vicinity of Antwerp, which Farnese's soldiers had not yet destroyed or reaped, it had been decided to organize an expedition at night to harvest it. The leadership of this enterprise was entrusted to the Colonels, and mainly to Balthasar de Moucheron. But when they wanted to leave Antwerp through the Red Gate, the guards of the latter opposed them: a violent altercation occurred, during which Moucheron was nearly killed. Marnix hastened to intervene, but in the morning the quarrel resumed [(53)].

The arrival of the *Alderman* or Syndic for the Hanseatic merchants of Antwerp, Daniel Gleser, had to have been looked upon, in that moment, as a harbinger of the end by the populous. Coming from Germany to the camp of the Prince of Parma, he had obtained permission from the latter to go to the besieged city to take the necessary measures to safeguard the letters, privileges, and important papers of that "nation", which were at the Hanseatic House [(54)].

---

[51] Farnese to the King, July 30, 1585 (*Loc. cit.*); *Liber relationum*, f° 181; MARNIX DE SAINTE-ALDEGONDE, *Brief récit...*, *loc. cit.*, p. 270; J. F. LE PETIT, *o. c.*, v. II, p. 517; BOR, *o. c.*, 2nd part, f° 605; STRADA, *o. c.*, v. IV, pp. 100-101; GRIMESTON, *o. c.*, pp. 881E-882A.

[52] *Brief récit...*, loc. cit., p. 270.

[53] *Brief récit...*, pp. 270-271.

[54] BOR, *o. c.*, 2nd part, f° 605.

Meanwhile, the *Peiswillers* had gathered secretly in the house of the Knight of Schoonhoven, a member of the magistrate. The latter, convinced that Marnix was putting on an act, denounced him, as well as his supporters, as responsible for the disasters which were going to befall the city [(55)]. Immediately, this multitude took up arms and went to the house of the burgomaster: there, vociferous demands were made for peace and the end of this "long misery", and the dissolution of the recently formed burgher companies. No sooner had Marnix calmed these rabble-rousers, when they went to the Red Gate and occupied the guard-house there. The burgomaster ran there and finally, half by threats, half by persuasion, got them to lay down their arms and go home. About an hour later, the rioters were back on the streets. This time they were prevented from seizing the Red Gate and the magistrate apprehended one of the principal leaders. Immediately, the crowd assembled and, forcibly, released the prisoner, without the authorities being able to oppose it [(56)].

However, for their part, the supporters of defense would not disarm until the very end. On Sunday, June 30, the Calvinist preachers had spoken with such violence and conviction that on leaving the Council, many people roamed the streets of the city shouting that they did not want peace, but war [(57)]. Thus the spirits were deeply divided and no one could say how this tragedy was going to end.

* * *

What efforts, meanwhile, were being done outside to succor the beleaguered city? The States-General of the United Provinces, having learned that Marnix had already been in contact with Farnese and that in Antwerp the supporters of peace were becoming more and more agitated, sent the *Greffier* of the Council of State, Calvard, to revive their courage and to promise succors. Calvard brought a letter from the States of Holland, claiming that everything was ready to try to deliver the city by way of the Scheldt, and that they would take advantage of the weather and the favorable wind. In the meantime, the States had taken the decision to raise a force of cavalry and in-

[55] This detail is provided by Paolo Rinaldi in his *Liber relationum*, f°s 183ro-183vo and it is confirmed in part by the *Avvisi* from Cologne, of June 20, published in *Foreign Calendar, Elizabeth, August 1584-August 1585*, p. 535.

[56] *Brie, récit...*, loc. cit., p. 271; *Liber relationum*, loc. cit.

[57] KERVYN DE LETTENHOVE, *o. c.*, p. 17.

fantry sufficient to try to lift the blockade on the ground, as long as they were assured that the city would still defend itself for three months [(58)]. It is not certain whether this letter was delivered by the *Greffier* Calvard [(59)]. But what is beyond doubt is that the latter promised a succor of 7,000 cavalrymen and 12,000 infantrymen. In this regard, Marnix later wrote in his *Brief récit*: "If ever before I had had the slightest hope that we would be succored by water, I lost it entirely." [(60)] Marnix knew that the expedition by way of the Scheldt, in order to be done at night, depended on the concordance of the wind and the tide — something that only happened two or three days a month and could just as well happen only once in an entire year. However, by day, the expedition was too hazardous for the Confederates to put the fleet, whose existence was so important to them, into the adventure [(61)]. Moreover, the burgomaster was aware, as a result of letters received from Hohenlohe, that the only way in which the Hollanders were thinking, at that moment, to help the city was provisioning by way of sacks of grain, which they proposed to transport on horseback to Ekeren, where the Antwerpians should be able to take delivery [(62)]. Marnix resolved to solicit a frank and personal opinion on the situation from the envoy of the States-General. After hearing the burgomaster's doubts about the possibility of succoring the city in a timely manner, and after having become acquainted with the actual situation of the defense and the provisions still available, Calvard had to admit that the Antwerpians would be right to continue the negotiations already begun, before an inevitable catastrophe would occur [(63)].

The States-General had not only sent the *Greffier* Calvard to Antwerp, in order to stop the negotiations with Farnese, but at the

[58] BOR, *o. c.*, 2nd part, f° 606.

[59] *Ibid.*

[60] Loc. cit., p. 272.

[61] *Brief récit...*, pp. 206-207. Let us not forget to mention here that at this very moment the leaders of the Zealand navy had drawn up and delivered to Admiral Justinus van Nassau a declaration, the Scheldt now had so many dry and dangerous passages, and that the summer nights were so tranquil and short that there was no success to be expected from an attempt to succor the city by water (MOTLEY, *o. c.*, v. I, p. 233). Hence reconciled in the letter written by P. d'Inioso to Davison, The Hague, on July 9: "I am told privately that our men despair of breaking the bridge on the Scheldt by the boats prepared for the purpose, but set a good face upon it, in order not to dishearten the people" (*Foreign Calendar, Elizabeth, August 1584-August 1585*, p. 569).

[62] *Brief récit...*, p. 267.

[63] *Ibid.*, p. 272; BOR, *o. c.*, 2nd part, f° 606.

same time they had solicited succors from Elizabeth of England [64]. Here was how they came to implore English support.

As long as the States-General had been able to maintain the hope that King Henry III of France would accept the sovereignty of their country, they had listened only very distractingly to the suggestions that came to them from England.

They were convinced that English aid was offered only in the interest of the English themselves. What they did not want at any price was to put into the hands of Elizabeth some of their ports, as sureties for the sums that the Queen would spend to help them. Undoubtedly, a number of influential men were supporters of English protection, and the States' agent in England, Joachim Ortel, had made proposals in London on their behalf, but all this lacked official support and character [65].

However, after much discussion, Elizabeth's Privy Council had come to the conclusion that, all in all, it was better to succor the rebels than to let Philip II crush them completely. To this end, it was decided to send a "prudent agent" to the Netherlands, in the person of William Davison, who would study the situation on the spot and who, in case the negotiations between the States-General and France did not succeed, could offer succors and discuss conditions. Davison, after having presented his credentials at The Hague, conducted himself with infinite discretion, avoiding entering into any specific conversation on the subject of English aid, in order to avoid the reproach of interfering with the efforts of the States to win the support of Henry III [66].

By the end of February, 1585, it had become clear that the King of France would refuse to officially intervene in the Netherlands, let alone accept its sovereignty. Davison was then instructed by Elizabeth to suggest to the States-General — but only as if it were from himself — that the Queen could perhaps take them under her protection, if they offered her serious guarantees. When Henry III's refusal became clear, Elizabeth went one step further. She offered her protection, provided that Flushing, Enkhuizen, and Brielle were put into her hands. Since it was feared, at that moment, that the States, des-

---

[64] Bor, *o. c.*, 2nd part, f° 607. Cf. E. Spencer Beesly, *Queen Elizabeth*, pp. 162-164; Mandell Creighton, *Queen Elizabeth*, pp. 216-220.

[65] *Foreign Calendar, Elizabeth, August 1584-August 1585*, pp. V-VI.

[66] *Ibid.*, pp. X-XII.

pairing of being abandoned by the King of France, should throw themselves into the arms of Spain, this offer was to be made openly. The contact was facilitated by the fact that, at that precise moment — April 1585 — the delegation from the States-General had returned from France with a negative answer from Henry III: at once, the news was brought to the attention of the English agent Gilpin and the desire was expressed to conclude a treaty with Elizabeth [(67)].

These affairs, however, did not advance quickly: as soon as the news coming from Antwerp had improved, Elizabeth changed her offers; on the other hand, the departure of the Hollander delegates who were to go to London was repeatedly postponed from one week to the next [(68)].

The main point of the discussions was this: would the Queen take on the sovereignty or simply protect the United Provinces? According to the English agents in the Netherlands, the vast majority of the people wanted sovereignty; Elizabeth, on the contrary, did not want to go beyond protection. But it seems that the States-General had little desire for English sovereignty: if they offered it to Elizabeth, it was because they could not offer her less than what they had presented to Henry III. In reality, they only wanted the protection and assistance of the Queen of England [(69)].

Twice delayed by storms, the delegation of the States-General did not arrive in London until early July. Including Jan van Oldenbarnevelt, Pensionary of Rotterdam; Joos van Menin, Pensionary of Dort; civil lawyer Jacob Valck of Zealand; and Doctor Paulus Buys, heer van Zevenhoven, they met with the English negotiators, among whom Walsingham was the dominant figure [(70)].

On July 10th, Elizabeth sent a hand-written letter to the magistrate of Antwerp, telling him that, having been notified by the delegates of the United Provinces in what terms Antwerp was reduced to by the closure of the Scheldt, and how the magistrate had been obliged to enter into negotiations with the Prince of Parma, she had forthwith given orders to send succors and that she made every promise to save them [(71)].

---

[67] *Foreign Calendar, Elizabeth, August 1584-August 1585*, pp. XV-XVIII.

[68] *Ibid.*, pp. XVIII-XIX.

[69] R. Fruin, *Mottley's geschiedenis der vereenigde Nederlanden*, loc. cit., pp. 122-130.

[70] *Foreign Calendar, Elizabeth, August 1584-August 1585*, pp. XIX-XXI; W. Oldys, *The Harleian Miscellany*, v. III, p. 139; Motley, *o. c.*, v. I, pp. 310-317.

[71] Gachard, *Analictes belgiques*, 1st cahier, p. 21. Cf. also J. H. Kernkamp, *De handel op den vijand*, I, 1572-1588, pp. 161-165.

It was too late: Marnix of Saint-Aldegonde and the delegates of the city were, at that moment, already at the camp of Alessandro Farnese in Beveren.

* * *

It is certain that Marnix did not attach great importance to Elizabeth's promises of succor. Some, outraged at seeing him enter into communications with the Prince of Parma, even went so far as to spread the rumor that the burgomaster seemed to fear a treaty with the Queen of England, that he wanted to hasten the negotiations with Farnese before that treaty was concluded, and that he had said he preferred to be Spanish than English [72]. Of course, these are calumnies from those who wanted to resist at all costs, but, nevertheless, they show how well the burgomaster's reluctance to enter into relations with the English was known.

However, it is not right to conclude that Marnix, in order to avoid calling upon England or receiving succors from her, would have preferred to betray the cause of the revolt and would rather come to an agreement with the Spaniards. Knowing what the status was in the city, he was coldly considering the situation. The public provisions, which the magistrate had distributed with such prudence and solicitude, were exhausted and they could only feed the population with resources from the homes of private individuals [73]. The conundrum; the city would starve before the arrival of Hollander succors or English succors [74]. Given the presence of a "peace party", growing evermore demanding, what would happen if it became necessary to announce to the population that food would soon be exhausted?

At that moment, the Prince of Parma declared himself still ready "to receive and benignly listen to those whom they would like to send to him" [75], but would it be the same if they persisted on pro-

---

[72] Kervyn de Lettenhove, *Marnix...*, loc. cit., p. 28.

[73] *Brief récit...*, pp. 268-269. "Others write that the guilds [of Antwerp] had been assembled; and having consulted upon the state of the town and the means for supporting the people, found that the rich could maintain themselves, but that for the poor there remained only about five hundred *razieres* of corn, wherefore it was resolved to send thirty chosen men to represent this to the magistrates and let them understand that they ought to seek an agreement with the Prince of Parma." *Jacques Rossel to Walsingham, Middelburg*, July 13, 1585 (*Foreign Calendar, Elizabeth, August 1584-August 1585*, p. 579).

[74] A letter written from Antwerp to Farnese on June 24 also outlines the situation and adds, regarding the available provisions of food: « ce que les mieulx advisez n'estiment suffire que pour six semaines de temps au plus » (Gachard, *Documents concernant le siège d'Anvers...*, loc, cit., p. 217).

[75] Richardot to Marnix, July 1st, 1585 (*Bulletins de la Commission royale d'histoire*, 3rd se-

longing their resistance? Could one not hope — at least Marnix believed — to obtain a kind of peace for religion, which would tolerate the exercise of the Calvinist religion alongside the Catholic religion?

These were the reasons which caused Marnix to no longer postpone the decision. "That is why", he wrote later in his defense, "I conclude in my mind, that it would be my burden of conscience and eternal reproach, since I had exposed this citizenry, for whom I was responsible, to such a clear danger of falling into the greatest misery and desolation which had never been seen in the world without a shadow of serious succors." (76) He took the advice of the members of the magistrate who unanimously agreed with him. Thereupon, he assembled the *Breeden Raedt*, where, for almost three weeks, this was discussed without being able to reach a firm conclusion, and where supporters of peace and supporters of resistance also showed obstinacy and vehemence. Some, leery of Marnix, did not want him to go to Farnese's camp alone. He would let himself be won over, they claimed, by money and would conclude an agreement according to the desires of the Prince of Parma. It seemed more prudent to them to send a dozen burghers to Beveren. To which the supporters of the resistance replied that, since they had made war jointly with the Hollanders, peace could not be concluded without the express consent of the latter (77).

At the meeting of the *Breeden Raedt*, which was held on July 4th, Marnix, speaking on behalf of the magistrate, explained the reasons militated in favor of continuing negotiations with Farnese. He felt that they should no longer await the consent of the Confederates, but send some commissioners to the Beveren camp, to which the magistrate would join. After hearing the speech from the city leader, the *Breeden Raedt* was adjourned on July 6th. Immediately, Marnix hastened to inform Richardot, expressing the hope that soon the Antwerpian delegates would be at the camp of Beveren. He still insisted on the need to grant "some liberty for our religion" if they wanted to remove all defiance and lay the groundwork for a real peace (78).

However, the burgomaster felt himself the object of the calumnies from those who did not want to negotiate, and who cast suspi-

---

ries, v. IX, p. 344.

76 *Brief récit...*, p. 268.

77 KERVYN DE LETTENHOVE, *Marnix*, loc. cit., p. 23.

78 *Bulletins de la Commission royale d'histoire*, 3rd series, v. IX, p. 345.

cion on the motives which made him act. He tried to justify himself in a plenary assembly of the colonels and captains, the magistrate, the *Hooftmannen*, *Wijkmeesters*, and deans of the trades and the guilds. He gave a brief description of what he had done for the defense of Antwerp and ended by declaring that if they had no confidence in him, he would beg them to remove him from office. In the face of this formal notice, the Assembly unanimously declared that there was no other way to save the city than to enter into negotiations with the Prince of Parma and that, if the Confederates really intended to succor Antwerp, they would have time while the negotiations were ongoing [(79)].

Also when, on July 6th, the *Breeden Raedt* met to take a final resolution, all of its members agreed to continue the negotiations. The commissioners proposed by the magistrate were approved; they were Marnix himself; Willem van Merode, Heer van Duffel; Alderman Jan van Schoonhoven; and Adrien (André) Hessels [(80)]. Immediately the burgomaster of Antwerp informed Richardot and begged him to give him the necessary passports to go to Beveren [(81)].

---

79 *Brief récit*..., p. 269.

80 Marnix to Richardot, July 7, 1585 (*Bulletins* cited, p. 347); *Brief récit*..., p. 269.

81 Marnix to Richardot, July 8 and 9, 1585 (*Bulletins* cited, p. 348). Commission pour les commissaires, dated July 8, in GACHARD, *Documents concernant le siège d'Anvers*, pp. 227-228.

CHAPTER VI

THE ANTWERPIAN NEGOTIATORS IN THE PRINCE OF PARMA'S CAMP

It was on July 9th, at about three o'clock in the afternoon, at the rising tide, that the commissioners crossed the Scheldt and landed at Burcht. From there they were taken to the Spanish headquarters, where the Prince received them and treated them generously.

At that time, Farnese suffered from a high fever, which was determined to be the result of a military expedition he had undertaken during the previous days.

While the *Breeden Raedt* of Antwerp was still debating, the Prince had gone with a group of soldiers to Borgerhout, where there was a well-fortified castle, surrounded by water, and occupied by a strong garrison. Farnese had it bombarded and then gave the order to storm it. To encourage his men, he had entered the water himself and, with the bottom of the fosse being swampy, he sank therein up to his waist. He wore his wet clothes all night and the next day until the conquered position had been fully organized. When he returned to Beveren, he was shivering with fever (1).

It is certainly an extraordinary coincidence that, once again, he was going to engage in very important negotiations at a time when illness threatened to diminish his intellectual energy: it will be remembered that it was the same during the siege of Maastricht when he had to lead the decisive negotiations for the reconciliation of the Walloon provinces. But, accustomed to dominating the body, he kept

[1] *Liber relationum*, f° 184vo.

all his mental lucidity to deal with the serious questions which were going to arise [2]. This was the first time he had seen Marnix of Saint-Aldegonde in his presence and, as Th. Juste very rightly remarked, "was witness, in the Walloon provinces, of so many ambitious and greedy pretensions, of so many failures and interested palinodes", he must have esteemed the fierce Calvinist, who had sacrificed repose and fortune to defend the cause which was dear to his heart [3]. For his part, Marnix felt, without a doubt, happy to converse with the man whose military genius he sincerely admired and even more his clemency and sense of justice. Did he not reply later to his detractors, who reproached him for saying good things about Farnese: "Only barbarians speak equally ill of virtue and vice, because of the people they hate. As for His Highness, I think I have said nothing in public, other than what everyone sees: namely that one can judge his sincere clemency and the affection which he bore toward this country, because, having been able to hold several cities on this side in his power, either by force or by famine, he preferred to preserve them, giving them reasonable capitulation, even to the indignation of almost all his soldiers... All those who, having served the States, now follow his party, can by their example testify that he is in no way vindictive and that for the sake of everyone he would not want to have failed his word." [4]

When the delegates from Antwerp found themselves in Farnese's presence, Marnix took the floor on their behalf and, in front of the Councilors of State and of War, the Colonels, *Maestres de campo*, and the people of the Prince's Court, spoke in French for half an hour, with an eloquence and elegance that impressed all those present [5]. He recommended Antwerp and its population to the Prince's clemency.

Farnese, responding in Italian, took up the speech of the burgomaster of Antwerp point by point. After speaking in his capacity as a servant of the King, he declared that he would also say a few words as a private man, driven by the affectionate inclination he had towards all the people of the Netherlands. "If you want war," he said, "the

---

[2] «Diziendole [to Marnix] lo que Dios me inspiro a nuestro proposito y mejor que me permitio la flaqueza y travajo de la terçiana,» *Farnese to the King, July 30, 1585* (B. N. P., Spanish MS. 182, f° 410vo).

[3] TH. JUSTE, *Vie de Marnix*, p. 167. — Letter from Paolo Rinaldi to J. B. Pico, Beveren, July 13, 1585, in A. F. P., *Carteggio farnesiano, 1584-1589*, fasc. 2.

[4] *Brief récit...*, p. 289.

[5] Paolo Rinaldi, present at the speech, says: «Fece un horatione... molto dotta, elegante et con buon hordine distesa» (*Liber relationum*, f° 183vo).

King will make it, for you, more bitter and more terrible than you desire, and you will be completely annihilated. Think of the great forces he has at his disposal, which always end up having the upper hand, thanks to the gold from India. Don't listen to the demon who embraces you, but listen to me. What is needed is a general reconciliation, to put an end to the atrocious evils that come with war. I tell you this because I have compassion for all these innocent people, who bear no responsibility whatsoever. I have no personal interest in this, I am driven solely by my affection for this country. On the other hand, I can lose my life, which I intend to use honorably for the service of God, the King, and what is to come." [(6)]

After the Antwerpian commissioners thanked the Prince, the latter retired and had a long private conference with Marnix, in which the burgomaster of Antwerp made known the instructions he had been given [(7)]. The latter instructed him to ask first that no peace be imposed without including Holland and Zealand. Otherwise, all traffic and all trade would cease, via the interruption of navigation on the Scheldt, which would be to the great detriment of not only the reconciled provinces, but also of Spain, Portugal, Italy, and other countries as well. How could the population of Antwerp feed themselves without trade from the north? As most of the affluent people have taken refuge in Holland and Zealand with their property, the city would be completely emptied of its wealth. It was therefore necessary to authorize a general agreement and gradually bring the other provinces to join it.

The second point suggested by the instructions was the establishment of the *Religions-vrede* for the city of Antwerp and its inhabitants, with the assurance that the other provinces could also enjoy it. It was also hoped that all the misdeeds of the revolt would be wiped clean and that the Prince would ratify the Acts put together by the States of Brabant and the magistrate of Antwerp. No reconstruction of the citadel to lodge a foreign garrison; that was the fourth point. With the concession of these four points, the commissioners were authorized to assure Alessandro Farnese that the city of Antwerp would return under the King's obedience.

While these points were being discussed, and after a report on their mission by the commissioners, a large number of plenipoten-

---

[6] Summary of the speech noted by Paolo Rinaldi (*Liber relationum*, f° 184).

[7] Text in GACHARD, *o. c.*, loc. cit., pp. 228-230.

tiaries would be sent to "fulfill the above-mentioned promises" and to resolve the difficulties which might arise, without waiting for the advice of those of Holland and Zealand.

According to the report which Farnese sent to the King about the conference at Beveren, Marnix, in his remarks, "was weary of the war and very eager to work toward the conclusion of a good peace." But there was no lack of emphasis on freedom of religion, strongly affirming that this was the true and only way to bring the entire country under the obedience of His Majesty [(8)].

That was the central and most difficult point of negotiation. The conception of the *Religions-vrede* ran directly contrary to the designs of the King, and Alessandro Farnese knew it well. Nevertheless, before the delegates from Antwerp had gone to the camp of Beveren [(9)], he had written to Philip II to consult with him about a mixed form of religious agreement, which had been applied during the reconciliation of Bruges. The Prince had submitted the idea that perhaps the heretics could be allowed to reside in Antwerp, provided that they did not create a scandal, that is to say, to be content to practice their religion amongst themselves, at home, without any outward demonstrations, and that this tolerance might not be limited in time, nor could a date be fixed for which they would have to choose between the Catholic religion and exile. Thus, they could stay in the city, as long as there is an appearance of bringing them back to religion and making them feel better [(10)].

Not only had Farnese written to Philip II, but he had taken advantage of a visit to Beveren by the Apostolic Nuncio, Giovanni Francesco Bonomi, residing in Cologne, and who was also responsible for the affairs of the Netherlands. The latter had arrived on June 7th at the Spanish camp to deal with the case of the theologian Michael

---

[8] Farnese to the King, August 18, 1585 (GACHARD, *o. c.*, loc. cit., p. 259).

[9] This is apparent from what is written on this subject by STRADA, *o. c.*, v. IV, p. 109.

[10] We do not have this letter of Farnese, but Strada summarizes the content (*o. c.*, v. IV, p. 109). We can very well imagine what it contained when we saw the answer given by the King, with the usual delay, on August 17, the very day of the capitulation of Antwerp. Philip II writes: «Porque a este proposito accordais la reducion de Brugas y lo que entonces escrivistes, digo que me acuerdo bien dello y como tuvistis paresceres de nombres graves de sciencia y consciencia para concluir aquel concierto por menos mal y por templarse la clausula que tolera *sin limitacion de tiempo* los que non se reduzesen á nuestra santa fee católica con obligarlos a vivir sin mal ejemplo ni escandalo, mas con todo sintiera yo mucho per esta tolerancia sin limite à no esperar que por esta prohibición del mal ejemplo y escándalo se habia de poder entrar á poner con el tiempo el remedio cuando el estado de las cosas diese a ello lugar...» (A. G. R., *Copies de Simancas*, v. 16, non-foliated),

Baius and his theories, about which Rome was concerned. The Prince of Parma had taken the opportunity to ask the Nuncio for his opinion on the policy to be followed towards the heretics in the cities which would surrender to the King of Spain. That was the moment when Marnix had entered into relations with him and there can be no doubt that by raising the problem before a representative of the Holy See, Farnese was thinking of the future capitulation of Antwerp. He explained to Bonomi that Ghent had already surrendered on the condition that the heretics should leave after two years and to withdraw, with their property, to another country; that, on the other hand, Bruges had capitulated with permission, for the reformed, to be tolerated in the city for an unlimited time; it had been understood, however, that one day, at a time which the Prince and the King would deem good, they would be driven out, if they did not convert. By thus allowing them to remain in the city, it was expressly understood that they would not practice their worship and their outward acts would not cause any outrage to Catholics. The Prince added that a more severe policy, which is the immediate expulsion of all heretics, was commonly disapproved by all those who knew the Netherlands. It seemed to him that this tolerance, if extended for some time, induced the rebels to render themselves more readily, did not depopulate the country, did not increase the enemy's strength, and provided many the opportunity to acknowledge their error and return to Catholicism. He pointed out that tolerating the presence of the reformers, even without time limits, would not preclude, when judged expedient, the cities from being purged of their presence. It was enough to install a good Catholic magistrate, for the latter could, at any moment, demand the expulsion of the heretics, without exposing himself to the reproach of not observing the word given in the concluded agreement. Aside from that, why be encumbered by scruples toward those who did not keep their word to God and their legitimate sovereign? It was this request to expel the heretics which the magistrate of Bruges would have already done, if the Prince had wanted to consent to it and if there was no fear of provoking a change of mind.

Farnese informed the Nuncio, through the Spanish ambassador to Rome, that he had made the Holy See aware of what he had done hitherto in this domain and that he had learned that his policy had not displeased the Pope.

The Antwerpian Negotiators in the Prince of Parma's Camp

Unfortunately, the Apostolic Nuncio could not give the Prince a sufficiently categorical answer. He merely said that he would never dare, without the Pope's command, speak openly of this matter, and that he urged Farnese, in every case, never to concede anything to the heretics. He added, however, that as a private man, he thought it best that any slowness and delay in reconciliation should be avoided since, the sooner the country returned to the King's obedience, the sooner it will came back to the obedience of the Holy Church [(11)].

Following this conversation, the Nuncio asked for the opinion of the Cardinal Secretary of State, the Pope, and the Holy Office in this matter [(12)].

Rome did not answer in due time. As for Philip II, he did not make his opinion known until August 17th, the very day that Antwerp capitulated! So that now, having no precise indication of the sovereign's thought on this point, Farnese could only respond to Marnix by removing all hope of *Religions-vrede*, and telling him that this system, "dividing the cities and provinces into sections and factions, would not allow them to maintain peace, neither between themselves, nor with God, nor with the princes, who are God's ministers." [(13)]

On July 12th — the fourth day of their presence in Beveren — the Antwerpian commissioners were provided with the conditions to which the Prince of Parma consented to negotiate [(14)]. Farnese, in this document, began with his astonishment at the fact that the delegates from Antwerp had no power to conclude an agreement and pointed out that he could have considered their mission as solely for the purpose of probing his intentions [(15)]. However, in order to show that he did not withdraw from anything when it involved the welfare of the people of the Netherlands, he declared himself ready to receive them under the safeguard and protection of the King, to use gentleness and clemency toward them, and, pardoning the past excesses, to treat them henceforth as good and loyal subjects, if they submitted

---

[11] Letter from Nuncio Bonomi to Cardinal Secretary of State Rusticucci, Ghent, June 13, 1585, in S. EHSES and A. MEISTER. *Die Kölner Nuntiatur*, 1st part: *Bonomi in Köln*, pp. 91-92.

[12] *Ibid.*

[13] STRADA, *o. c.*, v. IV, p. 111. ...« Insistant toutesfois [Marnix] sur ceste liberté de religion..., *au contraire de quoy* je luy ay fait les remonstrances que j'ay jugé convenir. » Farnese to the King, August 18, 1584 (Loc. cit.); C. L. S. V., *De ortu et progressu Calvinianae retormationis in Belqio*, pp. 126-127.

[14] GACHARD, *Documents concernant le siège d'Anvers*, loc. cit., pp. 234-235 (text of the response).

[15] In fact, it was so, as is clear from all the above.

to the following conditions. They had to endeavor to induce Holland, Zealand, and the other remaining rebellious provinces to reconcile with the King. However, the submission of Antwerp would not be delayed for that reason. The separate treaty with that city could initiate the much desired general negotiation. They would not insist on obtaining, on the point of religion [16], "anything new" — that is, the *Religions-vrede* — and they would submit to the King and His Highness concerning the custody and security of the city.

One can imagine the disillusionment of the commissioners and especially that of Marnix, seeing that on the four points of their instruction, it was the adversary who dictated his conditions. The burgomaster had to be particularly upset when he was denied the *Religions-vrede*, which he had put forward to persuade his fellow citizens to enter into relations with Farnese. All the delegates, however, had been greatly impressed by the good reception they had received and by the Prince of Parma's affable manners.

The latter had no illusions about the commissioners' minds: he foresaw that they would persist in "their extravagances" and that they would again seek liberty of conscience and the exemption of any garrison. "I will try to make them hear reason," he wrote to Philip II, "otherwise we shall continue the siege until the end." [17]

* * *

It was already dark on July 13th when the delegation returned to Antwerp. Therefore, it was not until the next morning that the commissioners were able to report on their mission to the magistrate. The same report was made to the colonels, captains, and deans of the guilds. On Sunday, July 14th, it was the *Breeden Raedt*'s turn to be made aware of what had happened in Beveren. During his presentation, Marnix did not forget to make known what had been said between him and the Prince of Parma during the private conference with him and to highlight Farnese's "mood and inclination" [18].

The burgomaster's eulogy of Farnese [*] provoked astonishment and anger among several members of the *Breeden Raedt* of which let-

---

16 «La riposta è che nel perdono non ci sarà difficoltà... *che della religione, non c'era che trattare...*». Richardot to the Nuncio Bonomi, Beveren, July 14, 1585, in EHSES and A. MEISTER, *Die Kölner Nuntiatur*, 1st part: *Bonomi in Köln*, p. 107.

17 Letter of July 30, 1585 (B. N. P., Spanish MS. 182, fº 410vº).

18 Marnix to Richardot, July 15, 1585 (*Bulletins de la commission royale d'histoire*, 3rd series, v. IX, p. 349),

* MOTLEY, *o. c.*, v. I, pp. 248-249.

ters sent from Antwerp by supporters of the resistance sufficiently testify [19]. He was violently slandered by some who claimed that he mocked the warnings which were being sent from outside, that he deciphered the letters received from England, Holland, and Zealand as he pleased, and that he withheld them and concealed them to let the Confederates' preparations for succors be ignored [20]. The Calvinist preachers, above all, had greatly condemned him: some had gone to see him and had bitterly censured him, but he justified himself or attempted to do so [21].

It is certain that after his return from Beveren, Marnix was no longer thinking of defending Antwerp: he had made up his mind in favor of capitulation, and he was trying to convince everyone that it was the only possible means of salvation. He was willing to accept Farnese's proposals, but not without making a final effort to obtain the *Religions-vrede*, the garrison exemption, and the non-reconstruction of the citadel.

The letter he wrote on this subject to Richardot on July 15th is typical in this respect and deserves its essential parts reproduced, in order to make it possible to accurately evaluate the burgomaster's feelings at this moment.

"I can assure you", he said, "that our want of appearance, of religion, and the rest of the other points of our charge made our negotiation (as I had predicted) extremely difficult, and did little to alter their hearts, even of the Catholics, so that, instead of continuing to manifest the joy provoked by our return, the people are struck down with sadness, foreseeing the ruin and desolation of the city by the deprivation of the said religion (Calvinist) and because they fear that soldiers will be introduced or that the citadel will be restored, two things lethal to a great commercial city.

"I have represented to them the kindness and clemency of His Highness, assuring them that all the relief He may give them while retaining His Majesty's reputation, will be given to them and that, if

[19] "M. de St. Aldegonde, who hath a singular good opinion of the said Prince, other than his own writings will testify". Steven Le Sieur to Walsingham, Antwerp, July 16, 1585, o.s. (*Foreign Calendar, Elizabeth, August 1584-August 1585*, p. 604); — "If they persuade themselves of the contrary, and he [Marnix] is esteemed other than the most brazen-faced traitor that treason has ever produced, they deceive themselves..." Letter from Antwerp to the Sieur de Marquette, Governor of Berges [op-Zoom], Antwerp, July 27, 1585 (*Ibid.*, p. 605).

[20] Letter from Antwerp, cited in the previous note.

[21] *Ibid.*

there is another way to establish the security of the city, He would not expect to charge them with a garrison. This makes them persist in the desire for peace that animates them, and I hope to soon bring them to a good end by this treaty."

Marnix still insisted on the idea that if Farnese had been more condescending from the point of view of religion, by taking under his protection both the Calvinist religion and the Catholic religion, he would have won the heart of the Antwerpians from that day and soon after, those of the inhabitants of the other provinces. "The clemency and magnanimousness of the great monarchs is not about getting what they could demand from the people so much as to grant them, freely and spontaneously, that which, by reason and equity, they are humbly entreated to concede. The more I consider the mood of this people, the more I confirm myself in this opinion," added Marnix, "that the advice I gave will be, resulting from experience, found salutary."

"If you think", he said again to Richardot, "that this city, by chance, will find itself like some others which, by the banishment of a certain number of persons, will be content to abandon the profession of the reformed faith [Calvinism], I can assure you, honest man's faith, that either I can not see anything or that you are greatly mistaken. You will see, with time, that the exile of this religion will soon be accompanied by a depopulation, and a sorrowful ruin and desolation of such a flourishing city. But this will be as it pleases God." [22]

During the discussions which followed, several members of the *Breeden Raedt* were of the opinion that it was better to defend themselves to the bitter end than to conclude a separate treaty with such meagre conditions [23]. Outside events which were happening at that moment would quickly change that mindset.

* * *

In fact, the city of Mechelen was about to surrender. While the Marquis del Vasto was patrolling the areas surrounding Antwerp with his cavalry, ravaging the fields, the gardens, the orchards, and the wheat that was still standing, Farnese had ordered Don Ambrosio Landriano to do the same in the region of Mechelen. When these ravages had been accomplished and the means of provisioning themselves had been considerably diminished for the inhabitants of that

---

[22] *Bulletins de la Commission royale d'histoire*, 3rd series, v. IX, pp. 349-352. Cf. MOTLEY, *o. c.*, v. I, pp. 245-246.

[23] *Brief récit...*, p. 270.

city, the Prince of Parma sent Baron de Licques, the Marquis de Renty, and La Motte, with a good number of troops and artillery to make themselves masters of the fort of *Blockhuys*.

The Marquis de Renty not only took the fort in question, but also captured that of Nekkerspoel and other important positions around the city. He made trenches and barred the roads, and soon made the place completely isolated [(24)].

Soon, Charles de Liévin, Seigneur de Famars, who commanded Mechelen, asked to enter into negotiations. At first, the Prince of Parma was of the opinion of being very harsh on the garrison, which had committed many excesses and had more than once mutinied to the great damage of the burghers. But Marnix, aware of this fact, intervened and obtained rather light conditions of surrender [(25)]. On July 19th, the city and the garrison of Mechelen surrendered [(26)] on the following conditions: the soldiers would come out with arms and baggage, the match-cord for their harquebuses extinguished, and leaving their banners in the hands of the Spaniards. They had to promise not to serve in the Confederate armies for a duration of six months. The burghers who did not wish to live as good Catholics could leave with their property or sell them within seven months. The rest of the inhabitants surrendered to mercy and received a general pardon. The destroyed churches were to be restored, and the divine worship reestablished. The Archbishop of Mechelen, Joannes Hauchin, could safely retake possession of his seat [(27)].

Jean van der Burcht, President of the Grand Council of Mechelen, soon reinstalled this important body and took care to renew the magistrate. As the number of Catholics was considerable — most, however, were poor — Farnese was content to send a garrison of 200 Walloons into the city under the command of M. de Provė [(28)].

Not without pride, the Prince of Parma could write to the King that, at the moment, except Antwerp and Bergen op Zoom, all the fortified cities of Brabant were in his power [(29)].

---

[24] Farnese to the King, July 30, 1585 (Loc. cit.); The same to the same, August 18, 1585 (Loc. cit.); *Liber relationum*, f° 184vo; STRADA, *o. c.*, v. IV, pp. 102-103.

[25] Marnix to Richardot, July 16, 1585 and Richardot to Marnix, July 17, 1585 (*Bulletins de la Commission royale d'histoire*, 3rd series, v. IX, pp. 352-354).

[26] Farnese to his father, Beveren, July 30, 1585, in A. F. N., *Carte farnesiane, Fiandra,* fasc. 1725.

[27] Farnese to the King, July 30, 1585 (*Loc. cit.*); STRADA, *o. c.*, v. IV, p. 103.

[28] Farnese to the King, July 30, 1585 (*Loc. cit.*).

[29] *Ibid.*

The capture of Mechelen came to cast dismay among the Antwerpians [30]. Henceforth they remained alone, without any neighboring towns being able to send them any succors. Thus, the letter which Richardot had sent to Marnix on July 16th must have taken on a very particular significance in the eyes of the latter and the supporters of peace. The State Counselor said, "The events, as you say, are in the hands of God: the latter will turn stones into bread, even though we do not deserve it. Let us try only to avoid this wretched bloodshed; the rest will be remedied little by little, since the King and the Prince who govern us have such good insides that they desire nothing more than the repose of this poor people." [31]

On July 23rd, the magistrate and the other superintendents of the city of Antwerp decided to continue the negotiations with Alessandro Farnese.

Commissioners were appointed with the approval of the Magistrate, the City Council, the *Breeden Raedt*, the colonels, the deans of the guilds, and the captains. They numbered twenty-one and included the three delegates who had already travelled to Beveren, as well as Marnix. They were provided with extensive instructions which would allow them to negotiate the reconciliation of Antwerp with the King, on conditions that were clearly worded in the document which was remitted to them. If disputes were raised on important points, they would have to return to Antwerp to reconnect with their constituents and listen to the latter's opinions [32]. According to Marnix, this restriction on the powers of the delegates had been devised to gain time, in the event that the Confederates made a last ditch effort to lift the siege [33].

At the moment when the instructions for the commissioners were being prepared, a petition was given to the magistrate from the representatives of the foreign merchants who continued to reside in Antwerp during the siege. This fact suddenly illuminates a situation which, at first glance is surprising, but which is very well understood in the sixteenth century, where, in the midst of political and religious wars, commercial operations continued to be carried out in a more or

---

[30] *Brier récit...*, p. 270; *Liber relationum*, f° 185.

[31] *Bulletins* cited, 3rd series, v. XII, p. 236.

[32] Text from the commission of delegates, dated July 23, 1585, in GACHARD, *Documents* cited, loc. cit., pp. 238-240.

[33] *Brief récit...*, p. 273: « Affin de veoir encor, si cependant on attenteroit quelque chose pour nostre secours ».

less normal fashion. The request was signed by the consuls of the Portuguese nation [34], the consul of the nation of Lombardy, that of the nation of Florence, that of the nation of Genoa, a merchant from Lucca, three Spaniards, eight Germans, and a Flemish merchant, who appears to be one Cornelius de Hartoge.

These merchants begged the magistrate to insert into the treaty of reconciliation clauses concerning their security "something inseparable from the welfare of this city." They asked to be included in the treaty, irrespective of their nationality, quality, or condition, and regardless of the time where they came to reside in Antwerp. In the capitulation, they also begged for consideration of the foreign merchants who, during the troubles, had withdrawn to a neutral country or to Holland and Zealand, provided that they returned to settle in Antwerp within six months from the date of the conclusion of the agreement with the Prince of Parma.

Since the signatories of the petition and other merchants in the city had sent goods and merchandise to Holland and Zealand, and there was a fear that the Confederates would seize these goods and merchandise when Antwerp surrenders to the Spaniards, they demanded that the Prince of Parma, in this case, not conclude, in the future, any agreement with the Confederates without requiring the payment and restitution of the seized property. Otherwise, merchants owning property in Holland would be obliged, in order not to see them confiscated, to relocate their domiciles and their commerce elsewhere, to the great detriment of the city of Antwerp [35].

Thus arose, in all its acuity, the problem which the surrender of the commercial metropolis would bring about, which would transform the former Hollander and Zealander Confederates into enemies and make them adopt immediate retaliatory measures against those whom they would consider as "traitors to the common cause."

It was on the evening of July 24th that the Antwerpian delegates, led by Marnix, arrived at Farnese's headquarters in Beveren [36]. The

---

[34] What is meant by "nation" was the grouping of foreign merchants belonging to the same country who resided in Antwerp to trade there. Cf. A. GORIS, *Etude sur les colonies marchandes méridionales... à Anvers*, pp. 32 sqq.

[35] Text of the request in GACHARD, *Documents* cited, loc. cit., pp. 218-221.

[36] All that we can say about the conference of Beveren, we know only from a single document, the letter written by Farnese himself to a minister of the King, dated August 25, 1585. This crucial piece has been published in the *Documentos inéditos para la Historia de España*, v. LXXV, 1880, pp. 321-326, according to the MS. Cc. 58 from the National Library of Madrid.

Prince reserved a generous hospitality for them and impressed them with great kindness in order to create the atmosphere necessary for the delicate maneuvers he was about to undertake. To characterize the latter, he himself speaks of *suavidad* and *blandura*, the latter word designating gentleness not free from firmness and which so often appears under the pen of the skillful politician when he reported his efforts to win the Walloon provinces in 1579.

The Prince first received all the delegates together in a public and solemn audience, during which Marnix once more pronounced a well-constructed circumstantial harangue to declare his intentions. Farnese, knowing that this was not a working session, answered it with the first words that came to his mind. The Antwerpian delegates then presented their letter of credence (37) and the document containing their proposals regarding the agreement (38).

Left alone, the Prince of Parma quickly examined these proposals and, noting that all the points were essential, passed the document for study to three eminent jurists; Richardot, member of the Council of State and Privy Council; Guillaume de Joigny, Seigneur de Pamele, leader and President of Privy Council; and Jean van der Burcht, president of the Grand Council of Mechelen. The latter, after having studied the document, made a report to Farnese, who retained the essential parts of it, so as not to get lost in vain discussions, to focus only on important issues, and thus complete the negotiations as soon as possible.

Many of the points proposed by the Antwerpians were otherwise reasonable or even such that the Prince had not expected them from them. They promised to return to the King's obedience by renouncing "all ties, treaties, and confederations concluded during these troubles"; they proposed the complete forgetfulness of the past, as of the date of April 15th, 1566, no crime being reserved; they agreed to the return of all ecclesiastical colleges, monasteries, and chapters, and of all ecclesiastical persons who had stayed in Antwerp, but they asked to confirm the sale of ecclesiastical property done during the period of the Calvinist regime, declaring themselves willing to compensate the owners up to the amount which had been withdrawn from the sale. They also asked for the ratification of the measures taken, and the concessions made, by Archduke Mathias and the

We found a copy in B. N. P., Spanish MS. 182, f°s 413ro-413vo.

[37] See this letter in GACHARD, *Documents* cited, loc. cit., p. 255.

[38] GACHARD, *Documents* cited, loc. cit., pp. 241-254.

Council of State residing with his person. Acting on the petition from the foreign merchants, they expressed the desire to see these merchants included in the treaty and protected against any measure of confiscation of the goods and merchandise they had sent to Holland and Zealand. They also called for, with regard to Antwerp and the country of Brabant, the implementation of the Pacification of Ghent and the departure of foreign soldiers out of Brabant, as soon as the situation permitted. Finally, they asked for the men of war in the service of Antwerp and the States of Brabant or retained at their disposal by the Commission of the States-General the permission to withdraw freely with their arms, baggage, ensigns, and drums in Holland and Zealand to wherever they wished.

What made the negotiation more delicate was the maintenance of the points already mentioned by Marnix during the first contact: no garrison, no restoration of the citadel, and liberty of conscience.

In order to demand the latter, they relied on the argument formerly used by the magistrate of Antwerp to obtain the exemption from the *placarts* of Charles V [39]: "Because the city of Antwerp is a main commercial city, founded solely on traffic and trade of all kinds of people, belonging to various nations and also professing various religions, which cannot be excluded without depopulating the city and driving trade to other provinces, to the chagrin of His Majesty and all his countries in general." They demanded that anyone, of any religion or nation, could freely remain there, without being harassed or sought for "religion" [40].

The three jurists commissioned by Farnese discussed all the points with Marnix and with the other delegates, with Farnese taking part in these interviews, sometimes speaking with two or three of the Antwerpian commissioners, sometimes with all of them together.

In the general assemblies, he endeavored, without going into the technical detail of the issues, to give them an accurate view of the reality and the situation in which they were reduced. He urged them to put themselves resolutely in the hands of the King, confident in his benevolence and clemency, who would pardon them and readily grant them forgiveness of the past. He endeavored above all to convince them of the impossibility of satisfying them with regard to lib-

---

[39] A. GORLS, *Les colonies marchandes...*, pp. 22-23.

[40] See the text of the commissioners' instructions for the technical details of other unimportant issues in GACHARD, *Documents* cited, loc. cit.

erty of conscience, the garrison, and the restoration of the citadel. He was also trying to broaden the issue so far as to provide a means of attracting Holland and Zealand to reconciliation.

Everyone was desirous of this general reconciliation, wrote Farnese in his letter of August 25th. They understood it, since thus the Confederates would not be future enemies ready to destroy Antwerp's commercial prosperity.

The delegates listened to Farnese without becoming exasperated, except when it came to the topic of liberty of conscience. However, they quickly realized that on that point there would be nothing to obtain, the Prince of Parma being bound by the instructions of his sovereign.

They then outlined an offensive regarding the other two issues close to their hearts: the garrison and the restoration of the citadel. It was Marnix who devoted himself to it with all the persuasive eloquence which he was capable of, returning incessantly to the charge [41], showing that in a commercial city like Antwerp, one could not introduce a garrison without committing an irreparable mistake. Catholics and Calvinists, unanimously, remembered the bloodshed during the *Spanish Fury* and were ready to go into exile if they were again exposed to the same danger.

To this argument, Farnese replied that it would suffice to change the magistrate, the colonels, the captains, and the officials, to disarm those who were malicious, and to occupy the fort of the *Tête de Flandres*, which, from the left bank, dominated a large part of the city and the port itself.

Marnix hastened to point out that these means were impracticable. Disarmament was made impossible by the large arms trade which was done in the shops of Antwerp: the occupation of the *Tête de Flandres* would give nothing, since, if one day the royal army was far away, engaged in some enterprise, a *coup de main* could easily be attempted. As a conclusion of his discourse, the burgomaster said that a garrison and a citadel would be out of the question, for they would not tolerate it.

Faced with this obstinacy, the Prince of Parma took another tone: he made it clear to Marnix that he could not yield on this point. "Perhaps," he said, "once Zealand is pacified, we could re-

---

[41] «Con largas platicas y persuasiones». *Letter from Farnese,* already cited.

nounce this security measure, but in the meantime it will be necessary to use this means and, without these conditions, agreement and peace would be out of the question."

Burgomaster Marnix did not admit to being defeated yet. He requested permission to appear, with two or three of the commissioners from Antwerp, before the members of the Councils of State and of War. Farnese immediately discerned the reasons for this request: to try to convince the others where he had not succeeded in making the Prince yield, or else, to be able to assert on his return to Antwerp that he had neglected no means of bringing the adversary to pity.

The Prince of Parma gave him permission. In this assembly, Marnix resumed his argument, which was equally eloquent. When he was finished, Farnese discussed it with his advisors and asked them for their opinion. It was then discovered that during his presentation, the burgomaster had suggested that Farnese could easily make his entrance into the city with an infantry and cavalry force sufficient to guard his person, as long as these soldiers were not Spaniards or Italians, but Germans or Walloons, nations considered "pleasant." This could be, in short, the "garrison" of which the Prince had demonstrated as absolutely necessary, but without that abhorred name being uttered.

Farnese then eventually conceded, from the religious point of view, the following: keeping the exclusive predominance of the Catholic religion, he allowed those who did not want to profess it to remain in the city for three years, provided that they did not cause a scandal; After these three years, if they persisted in not converting, they would have to leave and settle elsewhere. The city would pay a sum of 400,000 florins in recognition of the benefit it received from Farnese and to help support the soldiers of the royal army. The Prince would enter the city with the number of soldiers he deemed fit for his safety [42]. He told himself that, once the Calvinist magistrate was replaced by a Catholic magistrate and as circumstances allowed, not only could the soldiers introduced into Antwerp probably remain there, but they would furthermore be allowed to restore the citadel.

Such were the proposals on which he closed, and which were transmitted to the Antwerpian commissioners as definitive. It is interesting to note in what form some of them were written on the paper which was handed over to Marnix: and especially Article XXII, which

[42] The cited letter from Farnese says: «para asegurarme del pueblo».

speaks of the garrison: "His Highness... resolves to enter thereto (Antwerp) and put therein his guard of ( ) [43] infantry and two companies of horse, billeted to the slightest inconvenience of the burghers that can be done; promising His Highness that, if those of Holland and Zealand reconcile and return under His Majesty's obedience, the said city will be burdened neither with castle (citadel) nor with garrison. And in case that is not, as it would remain the boundary line, resolved then, with the participation and advowing of those of the magistrate..., on ways for to assure against the forces and guiles of the enemy." [44]

As it was worded, this article actually left the question open and safeguarded for the Prince of Parma every possibility of securing Antwerp as he saw fit.

After a final interview with the burgomaster and most of the commissioners, Farnese let them leave. He had a lively debate with Marnix about the interpretation of the word "scandal" as it applied to the way of life of reformers who could still reside in the city for the span of three years. The burgomaster of Antwerp, believing that, from the interpretations given to the word "scandal" following the Pacification of Ghent, a clearly pejorative meaning eventually being attributed to that term, drew the Prince's attention to this point and quoted some facts which the supporters of a strict interpretation of "scandal" would like clarified. "Thus, for example," he said, "if they did no reverence to the priests carrying the sacrament through the streets." Farnese hastened to reply: "Well, with regard to this last point, it would be a manifest scandal." Then, sharply interpellating Marnix: "Could you not do as that Roman peasant, who, passing before an *Ecce homo* [*], having made a reverence, then, he bethought himself that [Pontius] Pilate might attribute this honor unto himself? Wherefore returning and putting off his hat again, and said: 'It is to the Christ, not to the Pilate.' Do so, Monsieur de Saint Aldegonde, and think that the honor which you do unto the sacrament, you do it unto God." [45]

The Antwerpian delegation returned to the city on August 9th: however, some of the delegates remained at the Beveren camp to maintain contact and discuss some technical points with the jurists. On seeing Marnix and his colleagues leave, the Prince of Parma no-

---

[43] The figure was not indicated.

[44] GACHARD, *Documents* cités, loc. cit., pp. 268-269.

* Latin for "Behold the Man" is a phrase uttered by Pontius Pilate at the trial of Christ. The scene has been widely depicted in Christian art.

[45] J. F. LE PETIT, *La grande chronique...*, v. II, p. 519; GRIMESTON, *o. c.*, pp. 883E-884B.

ticed that they were worried about encountering a strong opposition among their constituents regarding the entry of soldiers into Antwerp, but it seemed to him, however, that the delegates were very determined not to spare their efforts to have this article admitted [46].

On the return of the commissioners, the *Breeden Raedt* was assembled: a reading was given of the various articles of capitulation, amid the interruptions and protests from supporters in favor of excessive resistance, who counted on the succors from England and who insisted that they wait for the latter.

Some articles were accepted, others rejected, especially those which dealt with the exclusive maintenance of the Catholic religion and the entry of soldiers [47]. The opposition was fortified by the arrival of an envoy from the States-General, Everwijn, who demanded to be able to communicate with all the superintendents of the city and who, on the pretext of preparing immediate succors, professed, with threats, that it was necessary to delay the conclusion of an agreement [48]. Marnix, outraged, pointed out that during the delegates' stay at the Beveren camp, a northwesterly wind, favorable to an enterprise by the fleet, had blown for eight to ten days, and yet never, however, during that time, had a single ship ever pretended to move [49]. A letter from Elizabeth, promising succors, had, no doubt, arrived in Antwerp [50], but the burgomaster persisted in having no confidence in the help that could come from there. It was even written at that time from Middelburg to Walsingham that a French soldier from the Mechelen garrison having travelled to Antwerp and having seen the burgomaster, the latter had said that "if one hair of his beard was inclined to the party of Her Majesty [Elizabeth], he would tear it out and burn it." [51]

While this was being discussed at the *Breeden Raedt* on Sunday, August 11th, artillery fire suddenly shook the entire city; from the

[46] «Poco seguros de que en ello no habia de arrostrar debajo de ningun titulo á rescibir gente de guerra dentro, pero muy resolutos de hacer su ultimo esfuerzo en ello.» Letter of August 25 from Farnese, cited.

[47] J. F. LE PETIT, *o. c.*, p. 518; GRIMESTON, *o. c.*, p. 883D.

[48] *Brief récit...*, p. 273.

[49] *Brief récit...*, p. 273.

[50] "From Antwerp, by way of Middelburg, we have divers news. It is said that the enemy has intercepted one of the letters from the Queen and that the other had arrived there, they [of Antwerp] having made a signal by fire on the tower of Notre-Dame" William de Maulde to Davison, Lécluse, August 7, 1585 (*Foreign Calendar, Elizabeth, August 1584-August 1585,* p. 633).

[51] *Foreign Calendar, Elizabeth, August 1584-August 1585,* p. 644.

Spanish forts on the dikes and the bridge over the Scheldt. Immediately everyone had only one thought: the Hollanders and the Zealanders or the English are there! They're fighting on the river! [52] Already some of the people took up arms; those who did not approve of capitulation aroused others to the resistance; the commissioners of the treaty were surrounded, and more time was demanded for deliberation, until there was some news and this furious cannonade explained [53]. On the tower of the cathedral, on the dikes of the Scheldt, and on the roofs of the houses, anxious faces looked towards Farnese's bridge, trying to unravel the mystery. Alas! Soon news brought by eyewitnesses put an end to this immense hope which had just arisen: the Spanish soldiers fired these cannon shots to celebrate the Prince of Parma, who was receiving, at that moment, from the hands of Peter Ernst von Mansfeld, the Insignia of the Order of the Golden Fleece [54].

The Prince had already known for some time that Philip II, to reward him for his magnificent efforts at the siege of Antwerp, had appointed him Knight of that Order. But he had postponed the ceremony of the reception of the insignia until the day when he would be sure of victory. That day had arrived and the time was indeed well chosen to impress the Antwerpians and quench their last hesitations about signing the capitulation. On August 11th, the Prince left his headquarters at Beveren, riding a magnificent Puglian horse, caparisoned with white velvet and pearls. The Prince's suit sparkled with fire from the rubies and the diamonds that adorned it. Farnese arrived in the midst of his troops, who formed a line from the Kallo dike to the bridge. He advanced slowly, elegantly, and powerful at the same time, looking with joy and pride at the bronzed faces of his men, who had accomplished extraordinary feats, under conditions hitherto unknown. In front of him, cavalrymen made sounds as though it were the Feast of Trumpets [*], and harquebusiers and musketeers preceded them. Each movement of the Prince's horse waved a crest of multicolored feathers, and it wore, enshrined in the embroidered harness which covered its forehead, a jewel of great value. When Farnese arrived at the bridge, the cannons from the ships,

[52] *Liber relationum*, fº 185.
[53] STRADA, *o. c.*, v. IV, pp. 114-115.
[54] *Ibid.*, p. 115.
* Leviticus 23:23–25 and Numbers 29:1–6.

the estacade, the forts, the redoubts of the Kouwenstein counter-dike, and even the furthest positions fired all together. The discharge of these 250 artillery pieces caused a deafening din, further augmented by the salvos of harquebuses, tired by soldiers from all nations stationed along the dikes of the Scheldt. After a quarter of an hour, silence was restored and the Prince crossed the bridge, on foot, to the fort of Saint-Philip. The latter had been richly decorated with festoons, flowers, and tree branches. Farnese was received there by Peter Ernst von Mansfeld, to whom was incumbent the honor of investing him with the Chain of the Order of the Golden Fleece, in his capacity as *Maestre de campo* General and the oldest Knight of the Order in the Netherlands [55]. It was in the fort's chapel, after a High Mass celebrated by Louis de Berlaymont, Archbishop of Cambrai, that the necklace was bestowed, while muskets, harquebuses, and cannons were again sounded.

With the same pageantry like that which had greeted him on his arrival, the Prince went back across the bridge and returned to the camp of Beveren, where a sumptuous banquet was offered to the great military leaders, the noblemen, and those members of his Court who were present at the ceremony. A tournament of cavalrymen and infantrymen, in full dress, concluded the festivities [56].

This time the disillusionment of the besieged was such that they no longer thought of resistance and they had only one notion: to capitulate as soon as possible. However, the presence of Everwijn and his continued requirement to halt negotiations in the face of the Confederate's promise of succors forced the members of the *Breeden Raedt* to continue their discussions. Proponents and opponents of peace clashed with each other again when shouting and vociferations were heard in front of the town hall, where the session was taking place. A few members of the *Breeden Raedt* approached the window and saw in the street a troop of furious and menacing people who cried out: *Peace! Peace! We will have peace!* Faced with this unmistakable sign of a popular riot, the last opponents of the council ad-

---

[55] A. F. N., *Diplomi farnesiani*, I, *Pergamene*: Act of Peter Ernst von Mansfeld, on behalf of Philip II, exempting Alessandro Farnese, from observing certain statutes of the Order of the Golden Fleece.

[56] *Liber relationum*, f°s 185ro-186vo; RENON DE FRANCE, *Histoire des troubles des Pays-Bas*, v. III, pp. 122-124; *Relation du siège et de la prise d'Anvers*, in *Correspondance de Granvelle*, v. XII, pp. 349-350; STRADA, *o. c.*, v. IV, pp. 115-117; A. CARNERO, *Historia de las guerras civiles,* p. 201.

mitted defeat. The window was opened and the demonstrators were informed that it had been decided to sign the treaty with Farnese [57].

Immediately, a wild delight seized the crowd. They spread through the streets of the city tearing down the arms of the Duke of Anjou from public buildings, which had remained attached thereto since 1583, and replaced them with the escutcheon of the King of Spain [58].

---

[57] *Brief récit...*, p. 273; Le Sieur to Walsingham, August 3, 1585 o.s. (*Foreign Calendar, Elizabeth, August 1584-August 1585*, p. 649); MOTLEY, *o. c.*, v. I, pp. 252-253.

[58] J. F. LE PETIT, *o. c.*, v. II, p. 518; GRIMESTON, *o. c.*, p. 883E; STRADA, *o. c.*, v. IV, p. 117; MOTLEY, *o. c.*, v. I, p. 253.

CHAPTER VII

THE CAPITULATION OF ANTWERP

This time the die was cast: Antwerp went to Alessandro Farnese. However, the commissioners who were going back to Beveren had to make one final effort to try to obtain concessions from the victor on the points which they had already put forward in the first interview [1]. When they arrived at the camp, they once again explained the need to grant more liberty of conscience to a city of great commerce such as Antwerp, where merchants of all religions resided, than what the project of capitulation allowed. They asked if it would be at least permissible to practice the reformed religion in their houses, behind closed doors, to perform baptisms and marriages as Calvinists, and to be able to bury their dead in accordance with the rites of their religion, in the respective parishes. They also supplicated that the articles of the capitulation of Bruges be applied to them, allowing those who would not cause scandal to be able to remain in the city for an unlimited time, by way of conducting themselves toward the rest as good and faithful subjects of the King. They also tried to persuade Farnese that he should bring into the city as few soldiers as possible, because of the presence of the merchants "who at times have already had occasion to doubt the neighborliness of the soldiers" and that they could easily ensure the security of Antwerp without introducing a garrison therein.

The Prince of Parma did not refuse to discuss all these points

[1] Remonstrance of the delegates from Antwerp to the Prince of Parma, s. d., in GACHARD, *Documents...*, loc. cit., pp. 274-281.

one last time [(2)], but he had to be adamant about that of religious freedom. Moreover, on the same day that the Treaty was signed, on August 17th, the King had written a letter addressed to his Governor-General in which he was formally opposed to letting Calvinists reside in the city, even without causing scandal, for an unlimited time. So that, if the Prince had yielded to the commissioners' solicitations, he would have found himself disavowed by his master and obliged, not without great peril, to put everything in question.

It was therefore on August 17th, 1585, that the capitulation was signed at Beveren, on the following conditions [(3)]: The burghers of Antwerp would return under the obedience of the King, as Duke of Brabant and Marquis of the Holy Roman Empire, "their Sovereign and rightful Lord, and natural Prince." They renounced all leagues and confederations made during the troubles. Farnese granted them, on the other hand, general and perpetual forgetfulness of the past "whose memory shall remain extinguished and assuaged, like things which have not happened." Those banished from the other cities which have already reconciled, who had taken refuge in Antwerp, could continue to reside there or leave with their movable property, according to their preference, provided that they no longer take part in the struggle against the King. Non-Catholics could continue to live in the city, without being sought or disturbed "for their consciences" or being forced into taking a new oath of religion, provided they live peacefully and without scandal. After four years, if they did not want to return to the Catholic religion, they would have to leave, but they could withdraw freely, in the full enjoyment of their property, which they would be allowed to sell or dispose of, or to have administered, after their departure, by those persons whom they would engage for this task. Ecclesiastical bodies and ecclesiastical persons would have their confiscated property reinstated

[2] «Despues de haber pretendido que se les concediese nuevas pretentiones, *sobre que hubo demandas y respuestas*, se vino á concluir...» Letter of August 25 from Farnese, cited.

[3] Text of the capitulation in GACHARD, *Documents...*, loc. cit., pp. 285-298; BOR, *o. c.*, 2nd part, fos 610-613. It was signed by Philips of Marnix; Alderman Jan van Schoonhoven; Alderman Mathieu van Lannoy; Cornelis Pruenen; former Alderman Philippe de Landtmeter; *wijkmeester* Hans de Weert; dean of clothiers Aerdt Boudewijns; former dean of mercers Guillaume van Schooten; Balthasar de Moucheron, colonel of the city; Herman van Dadenborch, dean of the new guild of crossbowmen; Jan Garin, captain of the city, Willem van Merode, Heer van Duffel, Master Adrien Hessels, Master Louis Meganc (Loys Meganeck); Adrien Bardoul, *hoofdman* of the *poorterie*; Gillls Santin, *wijkmeester*, Jean Godin, former colonel of the city; Jan Radermacker, colonel; Hendrik van Erp, dean of the former guild of archers; Dierick van Os, captain of the city.

and could still claim them, "except what is applied to the fortifications of cities, streets, marches, and other public uses"; in the latter case, commissioners would be appointed to agree on the sum which would compensate the proprietors.

Farnese promised the merchants and the inhabitants of Antwerp, whose goods or merchandise would be confiscated by "those of Holland and Zealand", as a result of the eventual continuation of the war, to ensure that, on the day when he would negotiate with the latter, these burghers and merchants would be paid for what was rightfully owed to them. The ancient privileges, both general and private, of which Antwerp enjoyed before the troubles, would be fully maintained.

The ruined or demolished churches had to be restored, at the lowest cost to the city. All the prisoners on both sides were to be released, except Téligny "whom His Highness could not touch", but for whose deliverance, the Prince promised to take the necessary steps. The Antwerpians had to put all their artillery, ammunition, and warships into the hands of the victor. Farnese would enter the city and install a guard of 2,000 infantry and two cavalry cornets, which would be housed "at the least inconvenience to the burghers." In this regard, the Prince promised that if those of Holland and Zealand reconciled with the King, the city would not be burdened with a garrison and should not endure the presence of a citadel. Otherwise, "becoming a boundary line", it should be secured against the forces and cunning of the enemy. With regard to the departure of foreign troops out of Brabant, Farnese contented himself with declaring that he did not "keep them to plunder the subjects, but to fight and recover the King's Patrimony." Finally, in order to defray the expenses that the siege had incurred, the city should remit the sum of 400,000 florins, the payment of which would be required only under reasonable terms and to the utmost convenience of the debtors.

The last article of the Treaty of capitulation imposed on Marnix of Saint Aldegonde was the oath not to bear arms against the King for the span of one year.

In the face of the remarkable moderation of the demands of the Prince of Parma, Motley himself could not help but pay homage to his clemency: "It redounds", he wrote, "to the eternal honor of Alessandro Farnese — when the fate of Naarden and Haarlem and Maastricht, in the days of Alva, and of Antwerp itself in the horrible *Spanish fury*, is remembered — that there were no scenes of violence and outrage in the populous and wealthy city, which was at length at his mercy after having defied him so long." [4]

Having arrived at the end of his long and difficult enterprise, the Prince of Parma offered the good news to the King as a precious gift: "I render to God", he wrote, "infinite graces for the great and singular mercy which he has shown towards me by guiding me with his divine hand, and by allowing me to have completed in a happy way this enterprise full of fatigues and risks; in this victory, His Majesty will enjoy such great bliss worthy of his greatness!" [5]

In fact, Philip II seldom engaged in outward manifestations of his joy, as he did when he received the news of the capitulation of Antwerp. The oldest of the courtiers assured that his contentment was no less great than when he learned of the victory at Saint-Quentin (1557), that of Lepanto, or that of Terceira Island (1583). The letter from the Prince of Parma announcing the surrender of Antwerp came to him in the middle of the night. After having feverishly continued reading it through to the end, he could not stay in bed. He got up and ran to the bedroom of his dearly beloved daughter, Isabella Clara Eugenia. He knocked on the door and shouted: *Antwerp is ours!* Then he hurried back to his apartments [6].

* * *

He had already given proof of his satisfaction by conferring onto the Prince of Parma the Collar of the Order of the Golden Fleece. He went further: he returned to the Farnese family the Citadel of Piacenza [7].

In the previous volumes of this work, we explained the importance that the recovery of this fortress represented for the Farnesian dynasty; how tenaciously the dukes had demanded it; what sacrifices Margaret of Parma had imposed upon herself, in vain, to bend the King on this point. Since 1555, though they were never discouraged in their efforts, Philip II had not wanted to render a pledge

[4] *History of the United Netherlands*, v. I, pp. 253-254.

[5] *Documentos inéditos...*, v. LXXV, p. 326.

[6] STRADA, *o. c.*, v. IV, p. 125; MOTLEY, *o. c.*, v. I, p. 263.

[7] For the state of negotiations since February 1584, Cf P. FEA, *La vertenza per la restitutione del castello di Piacenza...*, loc. cit., pp. 169 sqq.; *Liber relationum*, f° 185.

of loyalty to these rambunctious Italian princes. It was on September 2nd, 1584, that the King made known to Farnese, by way of an encrypted letter, that he was returning the citadel to him [8]. But the fulfillment of this promise was still awaited, the sovereign complicating the issue with important reservations. It was in April, 1585, that the King's provisions changed markedly [9] and that Granvelle, who had been interested in this issue with particular enthusiasm and devotion, had been able to make Alessandro Farnese see a favorable outcome. On the 29th of that month, the Prince wrote to his parents, from the camp of Beveren: "The affair of the citadel is on the right track: God be praised!" Finally, on July 10th, a month before the fall of Antwerp, the King consented to withdraw his troops who occupied the castle and to give the investiture of the fortress to Alessandro Farnese himself [10]. On July 15th, Ottavio Farnese, with joy, notified Margaret of Parma in Aquila [11], and she transmitted the good news to Cardinal Granvelle [12].

As P. Fea said, thanks to Alessandro, "after thirty long years, the Dukes of Parma and Piacenza finally had the satisfaction, desired for so long, of coming back into possession of the boulevard of the second city of their States; but, as Margaret of Parma had foreseen, neither of them, neither herself nor Ottavio, enjoyed it for long, since both died the following year (1586)." [13]

* * *

Marnix and the Antwerpian delegates returned home, accompanied by Richardot and President van der Burcht, who had the task of immediately dealing with administrative and political affairs in the recovered city [14], and, above all, to confirm the Articles of Surrender and solemnly publish them. These two magistrates were accompanied

---

[8] A. F. N., *Carte farnesiane*, fasc. 258, original.

[9] Paolo Rinaldi to J. B. Pico, Beveren, April 29, 1585, in A. F. P., *Carteggio farnesiane*, 1584-1589, 2nd fasc. Rinaldi exults at the news of the return of Count Torelli, sent by Ottavio Farnese and Alessandro to Madrid, and who brings the good news that the King will restore the citadel.

[10] A. GARNERO, *Historia de tas guerras civiles...*, p. 194; FEA, *Alessandro Farnese*, p. 500.

[11] A. CAUCHIE and L. VAN DER ESSEN, *Inventaire des Archives farnésiennes de Naples*, p. 164.

[12] *Correspondance de Granvelle*, v. XII, p. 82. Cf. NERINA FOLLINI, *Alessandro Farnese*, pp. 54-55.

[13] P. FEA, *La vertenza...*, p. 183.

[14] Letter of August 25 by Farnese, loc. cit.

by Diego Escobar, Sergeant Major of the Mondragón regiment, and engineer Barocci, director of fortresses and war machines [(15)], who were to thoroughly examine the city and take measures for the personal safety of the Prince of Parma during his stay in Antwerp.

On August 20th, the agreement between Antwerp and Farnese was solemnly published, on a platform erected in front of the town hall. In the presence of the Prince of Parma's delegates, the magistrate, the superintendents of the city, and the herald sent by Farnese, wearing his surcoat emblazoned with the Spanish coat of arms, cried out three times: *Long live the King!* amidst the cheers of the assembled crowd [(16)]. The assistants then went to the church of Notre-Dame, which was once again blessed by the bishop of Antwerp; the pulpits, from whence the voice of reformed pastors had resounded under the Calvinists, were beaten with rods and toppled. Then the arches of the temple resonated with the tones of *Te Deum laudamus.* They then returned to the town hall, where a banquet took place [(17)].

While the magistrate and the nations were making preparations to receive the victor, who would soon make his entrance, the burghers of Antwerp came out of the city to go and examine the Spanish forts and especially the famous bridge, which had been the principal cause of their surrender. Some, saying that these works were doomed to disappear, even hastened to draw its design and to sketch its appearance. Others pushed on to the Kouwenstein dike, where traces of the last engagements were still visible and where they still saw, not without shivering, in some inaccessible places, the putrefying corpses of those who had so valiantly fought for the deliverance of Antwerp [(18)].

Before entering the city, the Prince of Parma brought out from the fort of the *Tête de Flandres*, and from Téligny's fort, as well as from the urban agglomeration, all the enemy soldiers, to whom he granted

---

15 STRADA, *o. c.*, v. IV, p. 117.

16 J. F. LE PETIT, *o. c.*, v. V, pp. 519; GRIMESTON, *o. c.*, pp. 884C. In the Flemish poetry of circumstance, published August 20, 1585, it says:

Doen den pays wert ghepublieert
Ende alle ons quaet ghepardonneert,
Riep menich goet borgher, ick Mordent niet nooy :
Vive le Rooy! Vive le Rooy!

(A. ERENS, *Literarische archivalia voor Antwerpen*, in *Bijdragen tot de Geschiedenis*, 1933, v. XXIV, p. 278).

17 J. F. LE PETIT, *o. c.*, loc. cit.; GRIMESTON, *o. c.*, p. 884D; A. CARNERO, *Historia de las guerras civiles...*, p. 200.

18 STRADA, *o. c.*, v. IV, pp. 117-118.

particularly lenient conditions of capitulation: they were able to withdraw freely, with guidons, cornets, deployed ensigns, horses, weapons and ammunition, and lighted harquebus match-cords, but not sounding trumpets or fifes, and drums silent. Boats were placed at their disposal to convey them to Lillo, from whence they had to reach Bergen op Zoom (19).

Farnese then ordered the Catholic army to meet in Stabroek, where it was placed under the command of the Marquis del Vasto; Count Peter Ernest von Mansfeld having withdrawn, once the siege had ended, to his Government of Luxembourg, there to treat an illness from which he suffered. The Prince choose from among his troops 2,000 German and Walloon infantrymen, and two cavalry companies, one of lancers and one of mounted harquebusiers, whom he sent to Berchem to wait for him there. Meanwhile, the Commissioner of the Cavalry, Basta, had to scout, with 300 cavalrymen, starting from Borgerhout, and carefully reconnaissance all the places where the Prince should pass (20).

On the morning of August 27th, the victor left his headquarters in Beveren with his court and, after crossing the Scheldt, headed for Berchem. Arriving there, he sent a detachment of his infantry ahead, under the command of Baron de Licques, in order to put them in various places of the city as body guards, so that, in case of danger, these detachments could easily lend a hand.

With these preparations completed, the triumphant cortege began. In the lead came the remainder of the infantrymen, from which, in accordance with the treaty of capitulation, Spaniards and Italians were excluded. There were only German and Walloon veterans. The Prince was surrounded by an imposing procession of Lords, among whom were the Duke of Aarschot; the Prince of Chimay; the Count of Egmont — who had just returned from the enemy's prisons in exchange for La Noue (*) —; the Marquis de Renty; Marc de Rye, Marquis de Varembon; the Counts of Arenberg and Karl von Mansfeld; and the Baron de Hautepenne. Always in favor of not antagonizing the people, the Prince, at this moment, had only allowed this country's nobility near him. Behind this group of Lords, advanced the cavalry of his personal guard, composed of three companies commanded respectively by Nicolò Cesis, Count of Gombola, Pietro Francesco Nicelli, Count of Montechino, and

---

[19] GACHARD, *Documents* cited, pp. 298-300.
[20] STRADA, *o. c.*, v. IV, pp. 118-119.
* GRIMESTON, *o. c.*, p. 883B.

Léon Lazare Haller, old servant of the Farnese household.

To the accolades of the crowd, which grew larger as he approached the city, the Prince arrived in front of the Saint-Georges gate (*). At that moment he must have felt pride, for it was through that gate where Charles V, his grandfather, had once made his entrance.

From the magistrate's group, which awaited him in a posture of the most complete submission, a young girl stood out, representing the "Maid of Antwerp", in accordance with tradition, and surrounded by other young girls belonging to the aristocratic families of the city. She stepped forward towards the victor, bowed to him and offered him the key to the city. Farnese accepted this key and immediately fastened it ostensibly to his collar near his Order of the Golden Fleece, which shone around his neck and on his chest. He then entered Antwerp (21).

Therein he was greeted by an enthusiastic crowd, from whom demonstrations of joy and loyalty flowed freely (22), and who had prepared, for the victor, a welcome worthy of him. At each intersection, so to speak, he was stopped by representations done in his honor, by poets, comedians, and others, in the Latin language, in French, and in Flemish. There were even compliments in Spanish and Italian, probably on the part of foreign nation merchants, who had competed zealously and to whom these festivities cost several thousand florins (23). Everywhere, triumphal arches, cartouches, and columns adorned with flowers and inscriptions recalled the victories of the Prince, comparing him to Alexander the Great, to Caesar, and to Scipio the African. Ancient trophies showed verses where he was called Mars or Hercules. On the public square called the *Meire* was a gigantic column with the portraits and attributes of Alexander of Macedonia and Alexander of Rome, which was dedicated to him by the Genoese merchants, as the inscription read:

---

* As (erroneously?) named by STRADA, *o. c.*, v. IV, p. 119. MOTLEY, *o. c.*, v. I, p. 258 calls it the Keyser Gate. On plate I, it's item 20, Porta Kipdorpia, aka Kipdorppoort.

21 Farnese to his parents, Antwerp, September 1st, 1585, in A. F. N., *Carte farnesiane, Fiandra*, fasc. 1661; *Liber relationum*, f° 186; STRADA, *o. c.*, v. IV, pp. 119-120; Cf. GRIMESTON, *o. c.*, p. 884E; MOTLEY, *loc. cit.*

22 Farnese to the King, Antwerp, September 30, 1585, in French (A. G. R., *Copies de Simancas*, v. 16, non-foliated); «Puedo aségurar á V. M. que el concurso del pueblo fué tanto y el contento y negocie que dura por tres dias con fuegos y otras exteriores de alegria y con tanta paz y sosiego...» Farnese to the King, September 30, 1585 (A. G. R., *Copies de Simancas*, v. 16).

23 BOR, *o. c.,* 2nd part, f° 606. Cf. MOTLEY, *o. c.*, v. I, p. 258.

Invicto Principi
Alexandro Farnesio
Philippi II Maximi
Hispanorum Regis
Catholici apud Belgas Prefecto
Genuenses dd. [24]

But the welcome that must have struck the Prince of Parma the most and particularly pleased him was the one inscribed on the Croonenburg Gate, which said:

Fauste omne
Alexander
Fortitudo *Temperantia* [25]

The cortege finally entered into the cathedral, where they sang the *Te Deum* of giving thanks and where the Prince declared that he owed his victory to the Virgin "because, having done this enterprise through her inspiration, having happily completed it through her help, he revered his patroness in her seat and on her throne, and saw her restored by the arms of the Catholic army, after she had been driven out by the efforts of sacrilege." [26]

This crowd that cheered Alessandro Farnese was composed, it hardly needs to be said, largely of Catholics, [27] and people who were happy to see the anguishes of this long siege come to an end.

But there were also inhabitants in Antwerp who did not hasten toward the passage of the victor and who, with a heavy heart, were preparing to go into exile, not wanting to witness the defeat of the ideals for which they had suffered and fought. On August 20th, the last public preaching of the Reformers took place in Antwerp. The Calvinist pastors had urged the people to remain faithful to the religion that the treaty of capitulation forbade, not to return to the "popery", and, rather than to give in to the temptation to deny their ideals, to exile themselves and "leave this Babylon." A considerable

---

24 A. ERENS, *Literarische archivalia*, loc. cit., p. 279. See in this article, the text of the other inscriptions, almost all in Flemish, and expressive.

25 A. ERENS, *o. c.*, loc. cit., p. 281.

26 STRADA, *o. c.*, v. IV, p. 121. The Virgin was, and still is, the patron saint of the city of Antwerp.

27 « Et fust son entrée en icelle le 27 d'Aougst de l'an susdit, au grand contentement et joye du peuple et consolation des bons, fidèles et affligez catholiques, qui dès lors commençaient à reprendre nouveau courage de penser un chascun à ses àffaires » JEHAN LHERMITE, *Le Passetemps*, v. I, pp. 8-9.

number of people left the city and sought refuge in Holland or Zealand, in Germany, in England, and in other countries still [(28)].

It was for their benefit that the poet Jerome van der Voort composed his Flemish lament: *Farewell of the Protestant exiles in their home town.*:

> 't Is tijt te vluchten uut uwer waranden,
> O Antverpia, stellende in God tvertrouwen,
> Die de zijne spijst, troost, bewaart in all landen.
> Hoewel tscheijden bedroeft maect mans en vrouwen,
> Och! tgheven der handen sal ick langhe onthouwen,
> D'omhelsen, 't douwen, nau connen spreken;
> Hoe de ghelaten vrienden oock bleven staen schouwen
> Met grooter rouwen, totdat sij d'ooch zijn ontweken.
> Wat isser menich weenende na huis ghestreken,
> So haest als d'woort ghesproken was met eere :
> *Adieu, adieu, zijt ons leydtsman, Heere.* [(29)]

Nearly 800 heretical families took the path of exile before the Prince of Parma made his victorious entry [(30)].

* * *

While Farnese took possession of Antwerp with his German and Walloon troops, the Spanish and Italian soldiers, who had not been able to take part in these rejoicings, because of the commitment made by their leader in the treaty of capitulation, organized a festival for themselves, grandiose in its simplicity, on the bridge barring the Scheldt and in the redoubts and the entrenchments established on the dikes. They adorned the bridge with a great number of triumphal arches, made from tree branches, greenery, and flowers, and to which they attached cartouches covered with naive or literary inscriptions in Latin, French, Flemish, Italian, and Spanish, according to the talent and knowledge of those who prepared them. These inscriptions pompously celebrated the victory and the merits of the Prince of Parma. The boats supporting the bridge and the parapets of the latter were

[28] BOR, *o. c.*, 2nd part, fº 622.

[29] P. FREDERICO, *Het Nederlandsch proza in de zestiendeeuwsche pamfletten...*, p. 397.

[30] *Avvisi* from Antwerp, August 14, 1585 (Vatican Archives, *Nunziatura di Colonia*, v. IV, fº 98). — «Questa resa d'Anversa fa uscire gran squadra di mala gente fuori di quella città et delle vicine». *The Cardinal Secretary of State to the Nuncio Bonomi*, Rome, September 14, 1585. (S. EHSRS and A. MEISTER, *Die Kölner Nuntiatur*, 1st part: *Bonomi in Köln*, p. 142.)

adorned with gladiolas and sedges, and on the bridge even the soldiers were attired in verdurous garments of foliage and flower-work [*].

For three days, cannons and firearms continued to thunder in celebration, and the sound of drums, fifes, and trumpets was heard to harmonize in an impromptu concert, whilst the musicians of the royal Chapel of Brussels, in the middle of the bridge, played well-known tunes.

Having learned that his troops had organized these festivities, Farnese, always ready to share with his soldiers and to take part in their joy as well as their suffering, decided to mingle with their merry band and repaired himself to the bridge. Wishing to show that he enjoyed their festivities and that he approved of their initiative, he imagined offering in that same place a sumptuous banquet for the ladies of the nobility, whom he promptly invited by way of messengers sent to all parts. The Prince's guests arrived from Bruges, Ghent, Ypres, Brussels, Dendermonde, Leuven, Mechelen, Lier, and still other cities. Soon more than 800 ladies were gathered on the bridge and the estacade where immense tables, richly adorned with choice dishes, were erected. At this impromptu banquet, which went on for three days, the most illustrious lords of the country and the most famous leaders of the army were served at the table: Karl von Mansfeld, the Duke of Aarschot, the Marquis d'Havré, the Marquis de Varembon, Seigneur de Capres, the Prince of Chimay, the Marquis de Renty, Baron de Hautepenne, Mondragón, the Marquis del Vasto, and many more. Spaniards, Italians, and Flemings rivaled each other in gallantry, and Alessandro Farnese, accompanied by the gentlemen of his household, passed from one table to the next, lavishing on all the expressions of his attention and doing his best to make joy and gaiety prevail. Alonso Vasquez, who attended this banquet, noticed that there was no shortage of toasts "in the custom of the Netherlands", given by the ladies and their cavalier servants in honor of the Pope, the King of Spain, and the Prince of Parma. Eventually the tables were removed and on the flower-strewn bridge, making it soft as a carpet, they immediately organized a series of dances, which ended this celebration of Victory [31].

Meanwhile, not far from there, near the fort of Lillo, the sailors

---

* MOTLEY, *o. c.*, v. I, p. 259.

31 A. VASQUEZ, *Los sucesos...*, loc. cit., pp. 94-96; Karl von Mansfeld to Margaret of Parma, Antwerp, September 8, 1585, in A. F. N., *Carte farnesiane, Fiandra*, fasc. 1638; A. SALCEDO RUIZ, *El coronel Cristóbal de Mondragón*, pp. 160-164.

of the Hollander-Zealander fleet listened, impassively, to the echoes of these rejoicings and more than one must have had a bitter smile, thinking of "reprisals." This festival may have seemed to them to be the last which celebrated the grandeur of Antwerp. The Hollander ships, moored in Lillo [32], had already begun the relentless guard, which would close the river "on the side of the Lords of the States-General" and would reduce the great port, for a term of more than two centuries, to the mercy of the former Confederates, who became "the enemy."

* * *

While the victors were thus indulging without a second thought in the intoxication of their triumph, Marnix of Saint-Aldegonde went sorrowfully to the Sas van Ghent. He had felt the waves of hatred rising and the cries of wrath reverberate around him, because the reformers esteemed that he had betrayed them. On August 11th, Jaques Rossel had already written to Walsingham, from Middelburg, that "every one is so well instructed of his actions in the matter that it is believed he will rather remain with the enemy than return to a place where many have sworn his death." [33]

As it was at the time of the surrender of Maastricht, and at the time of the capitulation of Tournai, a victim was needed for the fury of the populous: this victim was Marnix. He alone was made responsible for the fall of Antwerp, whereas one should have wondered if by initiating the negotiations with Farnese, in agreement with the magistrate, he had not avoided a terrible catastrophe and spared the commercial metropolis of the Netherlands a second "Spanish Fury."

As he wrote to Walsingham, as soon as he arrived at the Sas, begging him to take up, in England, the defense of his reputation against his critics: "As long as the city could hold, I held it, in the midst of a thousand difficulties, works, and dangers to my life. Without any other leader, without authority, without means neither of money nor of food, and without succors, I spared myself neither day nor night in everything that a faithful governor or burgomaster and a vigilant captain of war (of which however never before have I wanted to make a profession) must or can do. When we were reduced to such

[32] On the consequences of the fact that Lillo remained in the hands of the Hollanders, see A. SALCEDO RUIZ, *El coronel Cristóbal de Mondragón*, pp. 158-159.

[33] *Foreign Calendar, Elizabeth, August 1584-August 1585*, p. 643.

an extremity that it was humanly impossible to further maintain it without exposing the burghers to slaughter, either between themselves or on the part of the enemy, I have, with all legitimate means, yielding to the time, the need, and the will of God (and even to the will of the magistrate and the healthiest part of the inhabitants), conducted affairs, by the grace of God, so that this city can boast of having been reduced to a greater and extreme need in all things than any other city has ever known before, and yet having obtained better conditions and a more favorable treaty than any other." [(34)]

What Marnix said here was true. Reference was made to a letter from Farnese, written to the Court on August 25th, saying that, at the time of its surrender, Antwerp still had food for four months, maybe even for eight if she had expelled all the useless mouths out of its walls [(35)]. But P. Fea had already done justice to this assertion by the Prince, showing that the latter had every interest in making Madrid believe that the resistance could have been even longer, in order to justify having granted such good conditions to the Antwerpians. The same author also rightly observed that Farnese did not enter Antwerp until August 27th and that on the 25th he could not yet realize for himself the scarcity which reigned there. Until he had resided in the city himself, he could only repeat the assertions of the besieged themselves, who had every interest in making all believe that food was far from exhausted, so as to obtain more favorable capitulation clauses [(36)]. When they went to Beveren for the first time, did Marnix and the three commissioners who accompanied him not bring their supper with them, in order to give the Prince the impression that victuals were not wanting? [(37)] We know from Van Meteren that three days after the capitulation, it was no longer possible to obtain bread against any sum of money and that this sudden famine provoked the threat of riot on the part of the crowd, as well as on the part of the sailors from the Antwerpian fleet and the soldiers who still occupied the forts, to the point that Farnese had to ask the treaty commissioners to bring in bread from the outside [(38)]. These findings were confirmed by the Nuncio of Cologne, Bonomi, who, on Au-

[34] *Foreign Calendar, Elizabeth, August 1584-August 1585*, p. 661.

[35] *Documentos inéditos...*, loc. cit. Van der Essen erroneously had August 5.

[36] P. Fea, *o. c.*, pp. 234-235.

[37] This fact is reported by A. Garnero, *Historia de las guerras civiles...*, p. 196.

[38] *O. c.*, f° 240vo.

gust 15th, wrote to Cardinal Secretary of State "that the lack of food was very much felt and the poor people suffered to the extreme" (39).

On the other hand, if, on August 12th, a treaty was concluded in London with Elizabeth in which she took the Netherlands under her protection and promised the immediate dispatch of succors (40), it must be observed, in Marnix's defense, that this aid could not have changed greatly the situation at that time. Undoubtedly, before the conclusion of this treaty, Elizabeth had decided to send to the succors of Antwerp 2,000 soldiers under the command of Norris, but their transport was going at a slow pace and they could not arrive in time. In fact, on August 1st, Georges de Montmorency, seigneur de Croisilles, informed Farnese from Bruges that he had learned, from interrogating prisoners captured by his men, that no Englishman had yet arrived in Ostend, nor at Lécluse, and that in Zealand they had only just landed about 600 English, "devoid of order." (41) Six hundred others, under the command of Colonel Norris, were to follow. But the latter did not land in Zealand until August 16th, i.e. the day before the Treaty of Surrender was signed, and they were certainly not ready to immediately enter into action (42). On the other hand, the Confederate fleet, as we have seen, did not move at the moment when favorable circumstances may have permitted an attack on the bridge; this explains the very interesting passage in a letter from Rossel to Walsingham, where the English agent says: "For my part I hold that all that has passed as to this succor and the fleet and all our enterprises have been stratagems. I have never been able to understand, therefore, how such practices should be carried on with the knowledge of her Majesty or of yourself, for I know the town could have been succored." (43)

We are convinced that Marnix of Saint-Aldegonde did not betray the cause for which he had worked all his life (44). He had the courage

---

39 S. EHSES and A. MEISTER, *Die Kölner Nuntiatur*, 1st part: *Bonomi in Köln*, p. 125.

40 On the events of this long negotiation, it is necessary to read MOTLEY, *o. c.*, v. I, pp. 286-332.

41 *Correspondance de Granvelle*, v. XII, pp. 333-334.

42 Colonel Norris to the Privy Council, Middelburg, August 21, 1585 o.s. (*Foreign Calendar, Elizabeth, August 1584-August 1585*, p. 669). I suspect van der Essen got some dates wrong. The letter states they *embarked* from England on Aug. 16/26, which is nine days after the treaty was signed.

43 *Foreign Calendar, Elizabeth, August 1584-August 1585*, p. 660.

44 See Motley's special appendix (pp. 264-284) on Marnix's attitude at the end of chapter V, volume one of his *History of the United Netherlands.* That is also the conclusion of the excellent

to face reality, and to act with composure, at the expense of his popularity, as a statesman aware of his responsibility [45].

This was, in any case, the judgment of the Huguenot, La Noue, whose testimony could hardly be suspected: "I have always known him", he wrote, "to be a zealous friend of his religion and his country, and I will bear him this testimony in his favor that his hands and his heart remained pure. Had it been otherwise, I must have known it... It is not to be imputed as blame to Saint Aldegonde that he lost Antwerp, for he surrendered when it could not be saved. What I now say is drawn from me by the compassion I feel when persons of merit suffer without cause at the hands of their fellow citizens. In these terrible tempests, as it is a duty rigorously to punish the betrayers of their country, even so it is an obligation upon us to honor good patriots, and to support them in venial errors, that we may all encourage each other to do the right." [46]

* * *

In Alessandro Farnese's career, the capture of Antwerp constitutes the zenith of his glory [47]. By placing the great city, which had for so long been the center of the revolt, under the obedience of the King of Spain, he successfully completed the conquest of the southern provinces of the Netherlands, and took away from the rebels the principal point of support which they still held there. As of the fall of Antwerp, a strong line of military positions separated the southern Netherlands from the north: the great commercial metropolis, as the Prince himself foresaw, has "become the boundary" for the States-General of the United Provinces. Under the protection of this boundary, Catholicism retains its exceptional position and exclusive preponderance in the south. On the other hand, behind the line, from its great rivers, running from east to west, the North will defend both

treatise devoted to Marnix by M. H. VAN DER LINDEN in the *Biographie nationale*, loc. cit. We could not get hold of Mr. ULRICH's dissertation. *Sind die Zweifel, welche man bezüglich der Ehrenhaftigkeit des Philipp von Marnix... hegt, begründet?* Erfurt, 1890.

[45] What is noteworthy in this regard is the letter he wrote on October 24, 1585, to M. de Meetkercke, in which he explains why negotiating with the enemy is often a means of preventing a greater evil. This letter is published by KERVYN DE LETTENHOVE, *Documents inédits relatifs à l'histoire du XVIe siècle*, pp. 278-288.

[46] GROEN VAN PRINSTERER, *Archives ou Correspondance de la maison d'Orange-Nassau*, v. I, pp. 79-80. Translation from MOTLEY, *o. c.*, v. I, p. 283,

[47] P. FEA, *Alessandro Farnese*, pp. 235 sqq.

the position of Calvinism and its independence [48].

Thanks to Alessandro Farnese, on August 17th, 1585, all conditions were fulfilled for the birth of the "Catholic Netherlands", predecessor of what is later called Belgium. This fateful date marks the de facto division of the seventeen Provinces of Charles V into a Catholic bloc, again subject to the King of Spain, and a bloc wherein Calvinism will be preponderant, a republic which will henceforth, free from all ties, be moving towards its new destinies.

From this point of view, the title of *conditor Belgii* (the founder of Belgium), which Juste Lipse gave to the Duke of Burgundy, Philip the Good, returns with infinitely more reason to Alessandro Farnese, the victor of Antwerp.

---

[48] P. GEYL, *The revolt of the Netherlands*, pp. 178-179.

BIBLIOGRAPHIC LIST OF THE MAIN WORKS CONSULTED

F. BARADO. — *Sitio de Amberes 1584-1585. Antecedentes y relación critica con el principio y fin que tuvo la dominación española en los Estados Bajos*, Madrid, 1891.

G. BENTIVOGLIO. — *The Compleat History of the Warrs of Flanders*, trans. by the Right Honourable Henry, Earl of Monmouth. London, 1654.

P. BOR. — *Oorsprongk, begin en vervolgh der Nederlandsche oorlogen.* 2nd part. Amsterdam, 1679.

J. Brouwer. — *Kronieken van Spaansche soldaten uit het begin van den Tachtigjarigen Oorlog.* Zutphen, 1933.

Calendar of Letters and State Papers Relating to English Affairs, Preserved Principally in the Archives of Simancas, v. III, 1580-1586 [*Spanish Calendar, 1580-1586*], London, 1896.

Calendar of State Papers, Foreign: Elizabeth, v. 18, July 1583-July 1584 [*Foreign Calendar, Elizabeth, July 1583-July 1584*], London, 1914.

Calendar of State Papers, Foreign: Elizabeth, v. 19, August 1584-August 1585 [*Foreign Calendar, Elizabeth, August 1584-August 1585*], London, 1916.

C. CAMPANA. — *Assedio e reacquisto d'Anversa fatto dal sereniss. Alessandro Farnese, prencipe di Parma*, Venice, 1595.

C. CAMPANA. — *Della guerra di Fiandra*, Venice, 1602.

ANT. CARNERO. — *Historia de las guerras civiles que ha avido en los estados de Flandes (1559-1609).* Brussels, 1625.

A. CAUCHIE and L. VAN DER ESSEN. — *Inventaire des archives farnésiennes de Naples au point de vue de l'histoire des Pays-Bas catholiques* (*Commission royale d'histoire*, in-8°), Brussels, 1911.

Bibliography

C. L. S. V. V. — *De ortu et progressu Calvinianae reformationis in Belgio.* Cologne, 1673.

Colección de Documentos inéditos para la Historia de España, v. LXXV. Madrid, 1880.

P. Colins. — *Histoire des choses les plus mémorables advenues en l'Europe depuis l'an onze cens XXX jusques à nostre siècle.* Tournai, 1643.

Correspondance du cardinal de Granvelle (1565-1586), v. XI-XII, ed. Ch. Piot. (*Commission royale d'histoire*, in-4°). Brussels, 1894-1896.

Mandell Creighton. — *Queen Elizabeth.* London, 1933.

S. Ehses and A. Meister. — *Die Kölner Nuntiatur.* 1e Hälfte : *Bonomi in Köln, Santonio in der Schweiz. Die Strasburger Wirren* (*Nuntiaturberichte aus Deutschland nebst ergänzenden Aktenstücken 1585* [1584-1590]). Paderborn, 1895.

P. Fea. — *Alessandro Farnese, duca di Parma, Narrazione storica e militare.* Rome. 1886.

P. Fea. — «La vertenza per la restituzione del castello di Piacenza al duca Ottavio Farnese specialmente nel carteggio del cardinale Granvella», in the *Archivio storico per le provincie parmensi*, v. XXII, 1922, p. 111 seq.

Nerina Follini. — *Alessandro Farnese, III° Duca di Parma e Piacenza 1545-1592.* Profilo. Bobbio, 1932.

P. Frederico. — „Het Nederlandsch prosa in de zestiendeeuwsche pamfletten", in the *Mémoires de l'Académie royale de Belgique*, class of letters, in-8°. Brussels, 1907.

V. Fris. — *Histoire de Gand.* Bruxelles, 1930.

R. Fruin. — *De Tachtigjarige oorlog, Verzamelde opstellen*, The Hague, 1909.

Gachard. — *Analectes belgiques.* 1st notebook. Brussels, 1830.

Gachard. — « Documents concernant le siège d'Anvers par le prince de Parme et la réconciliation de cette ville par Philippe II », in the *Bulletins de la Commission royale d'histoire*, 3rd series, v. XII, pp. 189 sqq.

Gachard. — *Les Bibliothèques de Madrid et de l'Escurial.* (*Commission royale d'histoire*, in-4°.) Brussels, 1875.

P. GEYL. — *The revolt of the Netherlands 1555-1609.* London, 1932.

A. GORIS. — *Etude sur les colonies marchandes méridionales (Portugais, Espagnols, Italiens) à Anvers, de 1488 à 1667. Contribution à l'histoire des débuts du capitalisme moderne.* Leuven, 1925.

E. GRIMESTON. — *A Generall Historie of the Netherlands*, London, 1608.

GROEN VAN PRINSTERER. — *Archives ou correspondance inédite de la maison d'Orange-Nassau*, 1st series, v. I. Leiden, 1839.

E. GUYU Y MARTI. — *El año militar español*, v. III. Barcelona, 1890. (Siege of Antwerp, pp. 710-719.)

H. HAUSER. — « La prépondérance espagnole (1559-1660) ». (*Peuples et civilisations. Histoire générale*, published under the direction of L. Halphen. and Ph. Sagnac). Paris, 1933.

TH. JUSTE. — *Vie de Marnix de Sainte-Aldegonde.* Brussels, 1858.

J. H. KERNKAMP. — *De handel op den vijand 1572-1609.* v. I. 1572-1588. Utrecht, s. d. [1931].

KERVYN DE LETTENHOVE. — *Documents inédits sur l'histoire du XVIe siècle.* Brussels, 1883.

KERVYN DE LETTENHOVE. — *Les Hugenots et les Gueux.* v. VI. Bruges, 1885.

KERVYN DE LETTENHOVE. — « Marnix et la capitulation d'Anvers ». Excerpt from the *Revue générale.* Brussels, 1883.

A. LACROIX. — *Œuvres de Philippe de Marnix de Sainte-Aldegonde. Ecrits politiques et historiques.* Brussels, 1854.

Le Passetemps de Jehan Lhermite, ed. E. Ouverleaux and J. Petit, v. II (Antwerpian Bibliophiles). Antwerp, 1800.

J. F. LE PETIT. — *La chronique ancienne et moderne de Hollande, Zélande, West-Frise, Utrecht, Frise, Overyssel et Groeningen, jusqu'à la fin de l'an 1600.* v. II. Dordrecht, 1601.

E. MARCKS. — *Königin Elisabeth von England und ihre Zeit.* Leipzig, 1897.

Mémoires sur le marquis de Varembon, ed. J. Borgnet (*Mémoires relatifs à l'histoire de Belgique*). Brussels, 1873.

G. MOIR. — "The Siege of Antwerp", in *The Historical Works of Frederick Schiller*, v. II, Edinburgh, 1828.

MONTPLEINCHAMP. — *L'histoire d'Alexandre Farnèze, duc de Parme et de Plaisance, gouverneur de la Belgique.* Amsterdam, 1692.

J. LOTHROP MOTLEY. — *History of the United Netherlands: from the death of William the Silent to the twelve years' truce—1609.* v. I. New York, 1888.

W. MURDIN. — *A Collection of State Papers Relating to Affairs in the Reign of Queen Elizabeth, from the year 1571-1596.* London, 1759.

W. OLDYS. — *The Harleian Miscellany: A Collection of Scarce, Curious, and Entertaining Pamphlets and Tracts, as Well in Manuscript as in Print, Selected From the Library of Edward Harley, Second Earl of Oxford,* v. III, London, 1811.

F. PRIMS. — *Antverpiensia 1933.* Anvers, 1933.

RENON DE FRANCE. — *Histoire des causes de la désunion, révoltes et altérations des Pays-Bas,* ed. *Ch. Piot.* (*Commission royale d'Histoire,* in-4°.) v. I-III. Brussels, 1886-1891.

D. ANGEL SALCEDO RUIZ. — *El coronel Cristóbal de Mondragón.* Madrid, 1905.

E. SPENCER BEESLY. — *Queen Elizabeth (Twelve English Statesmen),* London, 1900.

F. STRADA. — *Histoire de la guerre des Païs-Bas,* trans. by *P. Du Ryer,* v. III, Brussels, 1727.

Viscount CH. TERLINDEN. — « Le siège d'Anvers par Alexandre Farnèse (1584-1585) », excerpt from the *Revue Générale,* March-April 1915.

P. M. ALBERDINGK THYM. — *De vroolijke historie van Ph. van Marnix, heer van Ste-Aldegonde en zijn vrienden. Eene zedenschets,* Louvain, 1876.

L. VAN DER ESSEN. — « Inventaire analytique d'un recueil de lettres inédites échangées par Alexandre Farnèse avec des membres de la famille Capizucchi (1572-1692) », in the *Bulletins de la Commission. royale d'histoire,* v. XCV, 1931, pp. 73-93.

L. VAN DER ESSEN. — *Les Archives farnésiennes de Parme au point de vue de l'histoire des Pays-Bas catholiques* (*Commission royale d'histoire,* in-8°). Brussels, 1913.

H. VAN DER LINDEN. — *Marnix* (*Philippe de*), in the *Biographie nationale de Belgique,* v. XIII, 1894-1895, col. 800-844.

E. VAN METEREN. — *Historie der Nederlandscher ende haerder naburen oorlogen ende geschiedenissen tot den jare MVI^c XII.* S. I., 1614.

J. VAN VLOTEN. — *Nederlandsohe gcschiedsangen.* v. II. 1572-1609. Amsterdam, 1864.

A. VAZQUEZ. — «Los sucesos de Flandes y Francia en tiempo de Alejandro Farnesio», in the *Colección de documentes inéditos para la Historia de España.* Madrid, v. LXXII-LXXIII. Madrid, 1879.

Printed in Great Britain
by Amazon

35771155R00110